1/07

Argentina

Argentina

What Went Wrong

COLIN M. MACLACHLAN

Foreword by Douglas Brinkley

PRAEGER

Westport, Connecticut
London

Library of Congress Cataloging-in-Publication Data

MacLachlan, Colin M.
  Argentina : what went wrong / Colin M. MacLachlan; foreword by Douglas Brinkley.
    p.   cm.
  Includes bibliographical references and index.
  ISBN 0–275–99076–1
  1. Argentina—History—1810–   I. Title.
  F2843.M33 2006
  982—dc22   2005036832

British Library Cataloguing in Publication Data is available.

Library of Congress Catalog Card Number: 2005036832
ISBN: 0–275–99076–1

First published in 2006

Praeger Publishers, 88 Post Road West, Westport, CT 06881
An imprint of Greenwood Publishing Group, Inc.
www.praeger.com

Printed in the United States of America

The paper used in this book complies with the
Permanent Paper Standard issued by the National
Information Standards Organization (Z39.48–1984).

10 9 8 7 6 5 4 3 2 1

Contents

Foreword

Over the years I've developed a rare good habit of reading the great Argentine writer Jorge Luis Borges for relaxation. Too often, as a historian my mind gets rutted in footnotes and facts. Borges' fiction dealt with swirling spirits, midnight trances, and existential moments. To me his elegant prose was always an escape from reality. Paradoxically, however, in a real Borgesian twist, his fiction got me extremely interested in his home country. So it's with great interest and joy that I got to read Colin MacLachlan's title, a gripping historical survey, full of analytical savvy and apercus.

Argentina—at one time believed to be a new-world cornucopia—went from a grand illusion to a basket case within a tumultuous century. What happened to prosperity, cultural refinement, and an educated population, those socio-economic elements the rest of the world thought guaranteed greatness? When Borges was born in 1899 the whole world danced to the Tango and admired the distant South Atlantic republic's conquest of civilization. Its history appeared to mirror developments in the United States. Both countries relied on immigrants to supply the labor to build a nation. Italians, Eastern Europeans, British, Spaniards, and others arrived in large numbers in New York City *and* Buenos Aires. Indeed, some immigrant families had relatives in both countries. Fertile land and a ready market in Europe for meat and cereals brought boom-times to both the United States and Argentina. There was, however, a downside, best described as chronic dependency. The surplus wealth of Europe flowed into both economies. At a casual glance, Argentina seemingly evolved in the same ambitious fashion as the United States. The growth of a middle class, a national effort to create a literate educated population, the transformative impact of technology, modernization of gender roles, the invention of culture and urbanization—these were all realities of modern Argentina. It was a country brimming with intellectuals. Many of them lived or traveled in the United States, like Domingo Faustino Sarmiento, a close friend of American educator Horace Mann. Cecilia Grierson, the first Argentine-trained female medical doctor and active in the movement for women's equality in Argentina, likewise had spent time in the United States. Buenos Aires became a glitzy world capital, attracting the likes of Theodore Roosevelt and Maria Montessori. Most of these foreigners marveled at the level of sophistication the country had achieved in such a short burst of time. One could mention Buenos Aires in the same breath as Chicago or San Francisco and not an eyebrow would be raised. Argentina appeared to be a worthy rival for greatness with the great metropolitans of America. The extensive similarities between the two republics appeared obvious. But, in the end, what they did *not* have in common proved more historically decisive.

Prosperity came almost too quickly to Argentina. Land, demand, and profit created an oligarchy that soon dominated politics as well as wealth. In the early decades of independence the United States ran the same risk. Fortunately, Thomas Jefferson, a Virginia oligarch but an enlightened dreamer, thought in terms of a small farmer agrarian democracy, and Andrew Jackson elevated the common people beyond the reach of a small privileged class. Argentina around the end of the nineteenth century attempted to do the same. But by that time it could not overcome an entrenched oligarchy intent on holding on to landed wealth and its export wealth. Voting reforms in 1912, had they been instituted much earlier, might have worked. But introduced at that late date totally failed. In Argentina the influx of immigrants remained outside of society, unabsorbed, while in the United States the early growth of political parties made voters of raw immigrants within hours of their arrival in New York. Argentina developed all the outer characteristics of a liberal democracy but failed to generate the motivational values to make it function. The desire to force it to work led to experimentation with authoritarian regimes in the 1930s, with Juan and Evita Perón in the 1950s and the mutilating excesses of the military in the 1970s. Failure to stumble on the solution engendered a destructive nationalism that sought scapegoats and hid behind victimization. While the role of the IMF, World Bank, and Inter-American Development Bank can be criticized, the roots of the problem are grounded in the Argentine experience. Frustration, resentment, and pessimism replaced promise and crippled effective action. Political paralysis lead to wide-spread corruption as desperate people attempted to extract personal success (i.e. money) from a failing system.

The oligarchy with its values grounded in landed wealth discouraged industrialization and economic diversification. They were too greedy and short-sighted for that. They feared that Britain, their largest market for foodstuffs, would insist that Argentina buy British manufactured goods or they would turn to the their bread colonies of Canada, Australia, and New Zealand for imports. You might say Argentina became an informal member of the British Empire. Once seen as the most promising country in Latin America, Argentina fell behind Brazil and Mexico in the sweepstakes to industrialize. State-run factories failed to propel the country forward. Central planning during the Perón era, while momentarily successful, soon collapsed. Neo-liberalism under President Carlos Menem failed to achieve reforms that might have made it work.

Argentina found itself mired in a horrendous downward spiral, a chain of political failures crippling the very *joie de vivre* of its hard-earned capitalism. Will Argentina be able to catch up in an era of globalization? That remains to be seen. My brilliant Tulane University colleague Colin MacLachlan has, however, written a book that captures the grim drama and pulsating excitement of modern Argentina. It is a book for the learned and one Borges—I think—would have admired for its erudition.

Douglas Brinkley
Tulane University
New Orleans
December 31, 2005

Acknowledgments

Many colleagues generously assisted at every stage of this project. Linda Rodríguez graciously read several drafts and made valuable suggestions. Sandra McGee Deutsch carefully read the work, commented extensively, and undoubtedly saved me from unnecessary embarrassment. Bill Sater went over a draft and made intelligent suggestions. Bill Ratliff called my attention to other sources, as well as provided access to questionnaire interviews with Carlos Menem. Bill Canek directed me to useful books as did David Castro. Ron Dolkart and Don Castro reviewed the work for coherence and suggested additions. Gregg Bocketti supplied information on Argentine soccer. Paul Lewis forced me to get to the point and sharpened my focus. Mim Graham Vasan selected the best publisher for the book.

Colleagues in the history department rallied around with books, ideas, and encouragement. Douglas Brinkley valiantly completed the foreword in spite of the evacuation forced on the city by Hurricane Katrina, its dreadful finale, and its continued agony. Trudy Yeager allowed me to read her unpublished work on Argentina. Susan Schroader, Dick Latner, Ken Harl, and Sam Ramer supported the project in different ways. Donna Denneen printed drafts and assisted as needed. Graduate assistants Nik Robinson and Charles Heath made innumerable trips to the library.

Hilary Claggett, Senior Editor at Praeger, coolly and professionally worked around the unexpected disaster and stressful aftermath of Hurricane Katrina to keep the manuscript moving. Marcia Goldstein, Permissions Coordinator, made sure everything was in order. Emily Johnston guided the project in its final phase.

My thanks to them all, and to the many generations of scholars whose names appear in the bibliography. They made this book possible.

Introduction

The world has judged Argentina a failure. Consequently, the first question people raise is, "What went wrong?" Underlying the question is an unstated worry: can it happen to us? Argentina speaks forcefully to a broad range of economic, social, and class insecurities. As a round table organized by the *Wall Street Journal* (January 2004) on the future of the American economy demonstrated, when one of the participants warned that the United States risked becoming another Argentina.[1] Clearly, an examination of what went wrong is needed to instruct, reassure and caution.

In Argentina, a modernizing elite turned to Europe for solutions to what they viewed as backwardness and primitive violence. They sought to sweep away the old Argentina, not just reform it. By the last decades of the nineteenth century the country's gross domestic product (GDP) came close to that of the United States, giving substance to the promise of a great nation.

Around the turn of the last century wealthy Argentines toured the continent, delighting and impressing the sophisticates of Monte Carlo, Nice, Deauville, the spa at Baden Baden and other fashionable spots where the rich gathered to play. The tango soon swept the exotic South American republic on to the world's dance floor and stage, from Paris and Madrid to New York and even Tokyo. Argentines saw themselves as part of the Atlantic world. Who did not know of Argentina? Unfortunately, the second half of the twentieth century administered a harsh dose of reality, and in fifty years Argentina went from an economic leader to impoverished survival, as the economy collapsed in the worst crisis in its history and the world's largest debt default.

For all the understandable fascination with the country's problematic trajectory it should be kept in mind that Argentines have a life and a contemporary culture. Buenos Aires is Latin America's third largest city behind Mexico City and São Paulo, with all the problems and creative energy of a major city. While Argentina's past is complex, it is not an enigma. The roots of Argentina's promise and problems are grounded in its history. The mystery unravels to reveal a very human story. Whether they remain trapped by history, ill-served by their politicians and themselves, remains for them to determine.

Chronology

1580	Buenos Aires definitively founded by Juan de Garay on the abandoned ruins of the earlier 1536 settlement called Nuestra Señora de Santa María del Buen Aire.
1776	Viceroyalty of the Río de la Plata established with its capital in Buenos Aires.
1816	Congress of Tucumán formally declares independence.
1844	Jorge Newton introduces wire fencing, making control of herds and selective breeding possible.
1853	A modified federalist constitution elaborated.
1857	First railway constructed.
1878–1879	Conquest of the desert destroys Indian tribes on the pampas, opening up new land for large-scale agricultural expansion.
1880	City of Buenos Aires separated from the provinces of Buenos Aires as a federal district and national capital.
1888	River Plate Fresh Meat Company ships consignment of frozen meat to England.
1891	Baring crisis creates financial panic.
1912	Sáenz Peña Law allows the oligarchy to withdraw from direct control of the government.
1916	UCR elects President Hipólito Yrigoyen under the rules of the Sáenz Peña Law.

1930   Military coup overthrows President Yrigoyen.

1932   *Concordancia* governs the nation until 1943.

1933   Roca-Runciman pact permits continued agricultural exports to Britain in exchange for economic privileges.

1946–1955   Juan D. Perón elected president. Forced into exile by the army in 1955.

1947   Women receive the vote.

1952   Evita Perón dies of cancer on July 26, 1952.

1973–1974   Perón returns from exile and is elected president only to die the following year; Isabelita, his wife and vice president, assumes power.

1976–1982   The *Proceso* intensifies the dirty war against guerrillas.

1982   Defeat in the Falklands War forces a transition to civilian rule.

1986   Divorce legalized.

1989   Carlos Saúl Menem elected president.

1999   Néstor Carlos Kirchner wins presidential election.

2001–2002   Argentina in the largest debt default in history.

CHAPTER 1

Fringe of Empire

Born, vaguely invented, only to be reinvented as an immigrant country, Argentina is both a new and old creation. When the country declared its independence from Spain in 1816, a little under half a million people inhabited what is now Argentina—some three percent Indians, about 20,000 blacks, 60,000 mulattos, over 100,000 mestizos, and perhaps 10,000 individuals of European descent. The demographic trend seemed clear: Argentina, in common with parts of the former Spanish American Empire, would be a mestizo nation. Events, never imagined at the time, created modern Argentina in Europe's image, while the old Argentina vanished, leaving only remnants in the interior provinces. By 1910, the country had few ties to its past except romantic illusions and cultural remnants in the interior.

Argentina emerged from the west to the east in the twilight of the Spanish conquest. Settlers from Peru founded Santiago del Estero in 1553, Tucumán in 1564, and Córdoba in 1573. From the then Captaincy-General of Chile settlers founded Mendoza in 1561 and San Juan in 1562. Finally, settlers from Asunción (Paraguay) successfully established Buenos Aires in 1580 on the failed ruins of the earlier 1536 attempt. Of all the region's outposts, Buenos Aires appeared to be the least important. The inland settlements, on the other hand, linked to the silver mines of Peru and Upper Peru (Bolivia) supplied mules, hides, foodstuffs, and rough textiles to meet the demands of miners. Buenos Aires existed on the far frontier of the Viceroyalty of Peru with Lima as its vice-regal capital. Lima to Buenos Aires required a journey of some 3,000 miles over rough and often dangerous terrain or a sea passage around the horn. Merchants in

Peru supplied Buenos Aires' limited needs, the great cost in transportation balanced by high prices and access to smuggled goods. Contraband and illegal trading with foreign ships helped soften prices but also gave Buenos Aires the reputation for being a criminal outpost.

The Spanish Bourbon monarchs, who replaced the Habsburgs in the early eighteenth century, respond to the ideas of the Enlightenment. Materialism became the measure of progress. Enlightened administrators, along with their new ideas, arrived with the establishment of the Viceroyalty of La Plata in 1776 with it capital at Buenos Aires. Vice-regal directives radiated out from Buenos Aires to take in all of modern day Argentina, part of Bolivia, Paraguay, and Uruguay as well as the settlements of Mendoza, San Juan, and San Luis, previously part of the Captaincy-General of Chile. The Viceroyalty of La Plata included the Intendancy of Potosí's long Pacific Ocean coast, making the viceroyalty a transcontinental entity. The interior cities—socially, economically, and psychologically linked to Upper Peru (Bolivia) or Chile, and in some regions with demographic and traditional cultural ties to those regions—resisted the pull of Buenos Aires. The port city-capital developed an Atlantic-centric outlook—ready for trade, legal or illegal, with the outside world. Distance limited the extent that interior cities could collect regional products and funnel them to Buenos Aires. At independence no interior city had a population of over 5,000. Two distinct trading spheres, with a hostile Indian frontier between them made the viceroyalty a political more than an economic entity.

The cultural divide between the enlightened outpost of the vice-regal capital of Buenos Aires and the reality of a frontier region could be measured in a few kilometers, barely reaching the horizon. Enlightened bureaucrats and those that adopted the new ideas shared a vision in which the lower classes functioned in a well-ordered society directed by an educated elite. The gauchos, rootless individuals who lived in primitive fashion on the margins of a frontier society, became the stereotype applied to a variety of interior inhabitants. Illiterate, violent when necessary and apparently self contained, they provided the armed force for regional caudillos and subsequently, competing armies. Their marginal expectations differed almost beyond compare with those of Buenos Aires. Interior inhabitants organized their life around a distant source of authority and their culture on folk religion veneered with Catholicism, anchored with faith healers and mystics. Marauders, Indians, fortified settlements, frontiersmen, and primitive ranchers, set the tone of the interior.

Landholders in Buenos Aires, Santa Fé, Entre Rios, San Juan and Córdoba did not command great wealth. While fifty families claimed some 4,600,000 hectares of land in the regional arc surrounding Buenos Aires, limited demand for agricultural products, salt meat, and hides made them more dependent on their presumed social position than on real wealth. Their ownership of land, contested by Indians at every turn, depended on colonial land grants. In contrast, the merchant community possessed a degree of wealth and political influence. The establishment of the Viceroyalty of La Plata and liberalized policies stimulated trade though Buenos Aires. Nevertheless, the Spanish trading system already showed signs of being politically and economically unsustainable. Dutch, French, English, and Portuguese traders transported products made reasonable by avoiding taxes, beginning the process of incorporating the region into the world economy.

Events detached Buenos Aires from the Spanish Empire. The British invasion of 1806, followed by a brief two-month occupation of Buenos Aires that ended with an uprising, damaged the legitimacy of the colonial regime. A second British attack the following year failed at the hands of a militia. Meanwhile in Europe, Carlos IV, under extreme French pressure, stepped aside in favor of his son in 1808. By the end of the year French troops invaded Spain. Political confusion engulfed the monarchy, and in America the empire began to crumble. By 1810, events in Buenos Aires had gone too far to be reversed.

The Buenos Aires elite hoped to maintain the physical and political integrity of the viceroyalty and perhaps pick up more imperial debris from the collapse of empire. They did not reject the idea of a constitutional monarchy but believed that only a nation rooted in Buenos Aires's intellectual and economic resources could accomplish the task of nation building.[1]

Two different visions of the nature of the state came into conflict—one based on the enlightened notion of a centralized entity directly responsible for material progress, and the other a continuation of the traditional negotiated arrangement between the Crown and the people with minimum state intrusion. Argentina's modern history revolved around these two visionary poles.

Conceptualizing the nature of the newly independent region required an imaginative feat as well as political skills. The term *Argentina*, as employed in the last decades of the colonial experience, referred to Buenos Aires and its surrounding frontier region, rather than the entire expanse of the viceroyalty. Another name for the envisioned new entity, the Provincias Unidas del Río de la Plata recognized Buenos Aires province as one of many, although the city would remain the center of union. *Porteños* often referred to Buenos Aires and "its" provinces, or this city and "its" province. In contrast, interior landholders preferred to be left alone to run their own affairs. They did not reject the colonial past, but accepted the utility of independence. Federalists by nature, they sought a slightly modified status quo.

Buenos Aires responded to the confusion attending the breakup of empire by defending its former political authority as well as the territorial unity of the old viceroyalty. In 1810, the Junta of the capital sent military forces into Upper Peru (Bolivia), Paraguay, and the Banda Oriental (Uruguay) to reestablish its authority. The forces of Buenos Aires conducted themselves as a conquering army, looting, abusing the inhabitants, and arbitrarily replacing officials as they advanced. A series of battles between quasi-royalist armies and those of Buenos Aires devastated the region and left behind a deep antipathy for the Porteños. In rapid order Paraguay formed its own junta, repulsed Buenos Aires twice, and went its own way. In the Banda Oriental a more complicated process led to the declaration in 1813 that Montevideo would join a larger union, but only on the basis of complete autonomy within a federal structure. Buenos Aires rejected the idea. The British imposed a solution in 1828, making Uruguay an independent nation.

The Constituent Congress that met in Tucumán in 1816 toyed with the idea of a monarchy under a descendent of the Incas with a national capital at Cuzco. Had the plan been implemented, Argentina would have tilted back to the west and Peru, leaving Buenos Aires an isolated Atlantic outpost. Provinces established their autonomy and drew up provincial constitutions to suit themselves. It became evident that the attempt to hang on to remnants of the old structure had failed, and with it had failed the territorial integrity of the former viceroyalty.

Buenos Aires turned inward to redeem itself. Bernardo Rivadavia, a *Porteño*, stepped forward, first as minister, then as president from 1821 to 1827. The well-educated son of a wealthy Spanish merchant, he married the daughter of Viceroy Joaquin del Pino. Rivadavia fought the British invasions of 1806–1807, became an avid supporter of independence, and advocated a centralized state. During a mission in Europe he became a disciple of Jeremy Bentham, embracing the philosopher's utilitarianism, along with liberalism . As president of the United Provinces of the Río de la Plata he established a parliament and state institutions; passed a series of liberal laws, including assuring private property rights; founded the University of Buenos Aires in 1821; and proposed a system of public schools.

Rivadavia shared the enlightenment's dismissal of cultures based heavily on religion. The objects of Rivadavia's strategy understood but rejected his notions. A satirical litany captured their reaction:

> From the marvelous future, deliver us, O Lord.
> From the Jacobin reform, deliver us, O Lord!
> From suppression of the religious, deliver us O Lord.
> From freedom of conscience, deliver us, O Lord!
> From Rivadavia, Deliver us, O Lord![2]

In 1827 Rivadavia resigned in the face of a revolt led by provincial caudillos.

The decline of interior trade with the silver mines of Peru after the destruction that attended the independence process narrowed the base of commerce. A trading economy based on hides and the natural bounty of the land rendered modest returns, enough to finance limited commerce in legal and smuggled goods. The brief occupation of Buenos Aires by the British indicated impending major economic changes that would reorder the region's trade and commerce. A flood of low-priced, high quality English-manufactured goods entered with the foreign troops.

Although the Argentine market appeared insignificant, in the early 1800s per capita income in the immediate Río de la Plata region slightly exceeded that of the United States. Both frontier societies hardly mattered in trade terms. Nevertheless, Britain's industrial output needed markets both large and small and had the ships and crews to carry on a worldwide trade. Immediately after independence, Britain absorbed 46.6 percent of exports. Nevertheless, the symbiotic relationship between Argentina and Britain did not begin to emerge until the 1860s. Hides, sheepskins, animal hair, wool, tallow, and dried salt beef met a mild export demand, but hardly a vital one.

Merchants with sufficient foresight transformed themselves into *estancieros* (commercial land owners). The trajectory of Juan Esteban Anchorena, a Basque who landed in Buenos Aires in 1751 as a seventeen year old, demonstrated the process. Anchorena established a rural general store, a *pulpería,* in 1767, expanded to a string of stores, married into a well-established Creole family, became a prosperous importer and merchant, and then bought land. His son Nicolas in turn owned several pulperias. The Anchorena family symbolized the fabulous wealth generated in the nineteenth century. Between 1810 and 1825 the price of exports increased in tandem with rising land prices by 350 percent.

PRIMITIVE FEDERALISM

Independence required a different relationship with the other pieces of the shattered empire. In Tucumán, for example, Bernabé Araóz, the governor of the Republica del Tucumán, called for elections in early 1820 to set the provisional rules by which to govern "ourselves." Nevertheless, the Republica considered itself part of the *Nación Americana del Sud* (Southern American Nation). Buenos Aires, the region's outlet to the nineteenth-century trans-Atlantic world, had resources not available to interior provinces; as the former vice-regal capital, Buenos Aires controlled the customhouse revenues and established the country's political legitimacy.

Powerful provincial leaders contended with Buenos Aires. Two issues constituted the core tension between the city and the interior. The centralists, known as the Unitarios, wanted a powerful Buenos Aires to govern the nation based on enlightened liberal principles. In opposition,

Federalist caudillos represented a counterforce—an American alternative to Europeanization within a centralized liberal regime. Federalist caudillos wanted provincial control within a loose federation, although willing to acknowledge a federalist Buenos Aires as a center of union. The other issue, the cultural transformation championed by liberal reformers, pitted them against the traditional culture defended by Federalists. Juan Manuel Rosas of Buenos Aires emerged as one of the most important Federalists.

Rosas became governor of Buenos Aires province in 1829. An ambitious individual from a respected family, married to María de la Encarnación Escurra, also from an important family, he had the proper social background necessary to unite the landholders. Equally as important, he had the respect of the lower classes. Raised on the pampas among gauchos, Indians, and rural workers, Rosas learned to fight, drink, and work alongside them. At sixteen he took over the several thousand acres of ranching and grain crops on the family estate. Four years later, he and his partners established the region's first *saladera* to prepare dry salt beef, adding to his wealth and increasing his economic stake in order and trade. Self assured and comfortable in his patriarchal superiority, he treated everyone with consideration, regardless of race. Both Rosas and his daughter attended Afro-Argentine dances and religious ceremonies. As a result, he enjoyed tremendous popularity among Afro-Argentines, in spite of the fact that he also held slaves long after legal abolition. He also patronized the informal demonstrations of horsemanship that served to entertain the still-frontier society. His mastery of virtually every gaucho skill impressed but, more importantly, indicated that he took their tasks seriously. Charles Darwin, on his voyage to South America, encountered Rosas and remarked on his horsemanship as well as his popularity with his racially mixed followers, including blacks, mestizos, and Indians. To Europeanized Unitarios, Rosas represented the gaucho *malo* (implying a dark, dangerous force) at the head of the vicious elements of society.

TRADITION AGAINST PROGRESS

The defeat of the caudillo Facundo Quiroga by José María Paz, the best of the Unitario generals, alarmed Federalists. Paz eventually controlled nine provinces, forming the *Liga Unitaria*. For the next two years Paz dominated the interior, while Federalists under Estanislao López in the littoral and Rosas in Buenos Aires remained on the defensive. As luck would have it, a hapless Paz, pulled off his horse by well-thrown *boleadoras*, captured and delivered to Rosas, no longer posed a threat. Nevertheless, Argentina hovered on the verge of splintering into a series of independent sovereign nations. Various provinces withdrew their agreement with Buenos Aires to conduct foreign affairs, even minting their own coins. In 1831, the resurgent Unitarios offered Bolivia the provinces of Jujuy and Salta in return for helping overthrow Rosas. Buenos Aires, fearing isolation, proposed a confederation of provinces within the same nation. The *Pacto Federal* of 1831 established an alliance between confederated provinces. Rosas succeeded in revitalizing the still-weak notion of unity. Nevertheless, as late as 1835 the Cuyo (the provinces of San Juan, Mendoza, and La Rioja) negotiated with Chile to join that nation.

When Rosas' term as governor of Buenos Aires ended in 1832, he refused reelection unless the government conceded him expanded powers. Meanwhile, Rosas campaigned against the Indians in the south. The frontier zone lay within 100 miles of Buenos Aires, creating insecurity of both life and property. Murder; kidnapping of men, women, and children; and destruction by raiding parties made campaigns against the Indians a popular activity. Settlers encroached on land beyond the frontier especially during droughts, in search of pasture for animals, guaranteeing constant warfare. Rosas penetrated deep into the interior, reaching the foothills of the Andes; established a new defensive line; and added thousands of squares miles of land to Buenos Aires Province.

While Rosas combined politics, security from raids, and economics on the pampas, his wife doña Encarnación campaigned to return her husband to power in the city. The *Sociedad Popular Restauradora* lined up political support invoking Rosas' contribution to the province and the need for a proven leader. The Society's paramilitary arm, the *Mazorca* (ear of corn), directed by doña Encarnación, intimidated the opposition. Violence created the conditions that supposedly only Rosas could deal with effectively. After two and a half years of turmoil, the governing committee agreed to Rosas' terms and he resumed office in 1835. A plebiscite returned an endorsement of 9,315 for and only 5 against. William H. Harris, the American representative in Buenos Aires, struggled to understand why the people submitted to one man. Harris underestimated the negative importance of the insecure frontier and its impact on politics as well as the cultural traditions that sanctioned what to him appeared to be an arbitrary government. When Rosas constructed his Estancia residence in 1838 (demolished in 1899) in what is now the Palermo barrio of Buenos Aires, its towers built on the four corners of the structure prudently provided an unobstructed view to the horizon and the Indian frontier.

Rosas retained the Sociedad Popular Restauradora as a proto-party and the Mazorca as its violent enforcement arm. Soon it would be known as the *Mas Horca* (more hangings) among Rosas' enemies as it went about its activities. In rural areas formal law and order depended on Justices of the Peace, an office established in 1821. They soon expanded beyond judicial function to include tax collection, organization of the militia, enforcement of the labor laws, and political responsibilities such as conducting elections. Rosas incorporated them as part of his apparatus of control. Elections, in theory open to all males of at least twenty years of age without restrictions, suggested a leveling equality, but in fact one overlaid by well-understood rules. Justices of the Peace served as the primary guardians of those rules.

Rosas, with full powers, abolished the Immigration Commission (established by Rivadavia), discouraging mass immigration from Europe. He also liquidated the *Banco Nacional* in 1836, ending commercial banking in the country. A colonial institution, the *Casa de Moneda* issued currency but did not make loans, discount commercial paper, or even accept deposits. Merchants, usually British residents, handled necessary foreign transactions and commercial services. Rosas believed in cheap money, a view popular with landholders but not the lower classes, who lost to inflation. The pattern of cheap money began before he came to power. The first authorized paper issue in May of 1820 met the demands of the independence era. A more systematic emission of paper began with the creation of a discount bank by the Province of Buenos Aires in 1822. Rosas followed this model, issuing paper note as he believed necessary. Paper money appeared to be necessary to keep modern commerce afloat. At times, a shortage of paper money pushed economic activity to primitive levels, including barter.

Rosas had two major constituencies, each handled in a different way. In the role of a paternal caudillo, Rosas directed the lower classes, who provided labor and soldiers and when necessary intimidated the centralists and provided a reserve military force in case of a Unitario attack. Meanwhile the landholders, the de facto aristocracy, received the resources to create an economy within a patriarchal system.

Property rights depended on Rosas' enforcement of colonial law (his title of Restorer of the Laws should not be seen as an empty honor) through the *Tribunal Commercial* that replaced the colonial *Consulado*. While the Tribunal drew upon custom as well as actual law, it favored social attributes such as honor, respect, and good reputation. Eventually, it enforced private contracts—a modern approach. The Tribunal contributed to the expansion of commerce until replaced by the national commercial code of 1862. Trade raised diplomatic issues with European powers able to muster significant naval force.

A fluid, far from solidified territorial situation fueled Rosas' distrust of foreigners. European powers and Brazil contemplated establishing protectorates on the Paraná River. Fructuoso Rivera explored the possibility of combining Uruguay, Paraguay, the Brazilian province of Rio Grande do Sul and the Argentine provinces of Entre Rios and Corrientes into a confederation strong enough to rival the one dominated by Buenos Aires. Foreign powers could tip the balance of power resulting in a reconfiguration of territory to the disadvantage of Buenos Aires.

In 1838, the French seized the island of Martín García at the mouth of the Paraná River and disrupted trade until they withdrew in 1840.

A joint British-French blockade in 1845, in cooperation with anti-Rosas groups, ended in 1848 with a reluctant agreement with Rosas. His successful resistance reinforced his popularity. José de San Martin, the Argentine hero of the independence era, directed that his sword be presented to Rosas in admiration of his firm stand against foreign powers. Nevertheless, Rosas understood that relations had to be mended in the interest of commerce.

FEDERALISM'S POLITICO-CULTURAL MACHINE

Rosas' order rested on a traditional patriarchal system. He provided a structure for his followers; incorporated their beliefs, values and fears; and enforced their observance. A series of popular patriotic celebrations called *fiestas federales* combined religious practices with support for federalism. Organized emotional displays, parades, and demonstrations implied the role of the people in defending their own survival. Rejection of foreign enemies and the Europeanized cultural impulses of the Unitarios could be invoked in simple terms in celebrations that identified the enemies. Papier-mâché effigies, burned with glee, symbolized the victory of the people and their culture over those who would destroy them.

Rosas elaborated the "federal look," a red ribbon badge or other device placed over the heart with a small image of Rosas and inscribed "Long Live the Federation." A red hatband, and for males a mustache and long sideburns, proudly completed the style. Red, the color of Federalism, represented the colors of St. Baltasar, the African king who attended the Christ child. Rosas made San Balthazar's day a provincial holiday, an act greatly appreciated by his black and mulatto supporters. Doña Encarnación dressed in bright scarlet, as did many other women. At the very least, red hair ribbons had to be worn. Soldiers in red uniforms mingled in the streets with red speckled civilians creating the illusion of Federalist monochromatic solidarity. Even gravestones bore the inscription at the bottom, "Long live the federation! Death to the savage Unitarios." Portraits of Rosas graced households, stores, and church altars. Songs and poems glorified the governor and his virtues. His daughter Manuelita collected them for the *Cancionero Federal* (Federal Song Book) in 1833. Federalism represented a way of life as well as a political system.

Rosas entwined religious notions in official acts to make the point that his regime represented the people's beliefs. A relieved Church appreciated Rosas' reversal of Rivadavia's anticlericalism. Restoration of property and official respect made the Church into an enthusiastic arm of the regime. The Bishop of Buenos Aires, dressed in vestments covered with Federalist symbols, instructed his clergy to support the regime and encourage loyalty among their parishioners. Nevertheless, Rosas continued to exercise colonial prerogatives that allowed the state to control appointments and restrict the application of papal decrees. When the Jesuits, invited back by Rosas, refused to cooperate, he expelled them again.

Loyal followers denounced the unconvinced as Unitarios. Victims executed and displayed decorated with ribbons of Unitario blue, served to deter plotters. Calibrated terror purged the ranks of possible conspirators while encouraging Federalists to demonstrate their loyalty. Cutting the throats of opponents, a skill associated with gauchos and Indians and much like the technique used to butcher hapless livestock, shocked the population. In certain periods, decapitated bodies lay discarded in the streets. Much of the terror occurred after dark, but the Mazorca on occasion dispatched suspects in daylight. The regime, confident that it enjoyed the support of the people, abolished the Mazorca in 1846. Nutritional well-being, a core indicator of overall social satisfaction, jumped after 1830, as indicated by the increasing height of soldiers. Trade in hides, tallow, and sheepskins resulted in a surplus of discarded meat, and the free-trade environment of the time, coupled with shipping efficiencies made imported staples less expensive. Nutritional prosperity under Rosas represented a recovery from a decline in average height in the generations born between 1790 and 1810.[3] Such well-being, among other factors, must be considered in assessing Rosas' ability to govern and the duration of his regime.

The Eurocentric liberalism of the Unitarios associated Federalism with the mixed-race lower classes and linked them to the lack of progress. Their struggle against Rosas had a strong racial component evident in their writings, particularly in José Marmol's novel, *Amalia*. Marmol depicted Rosas as barbarously evil, surrounded by vicious mestizo and mulatto "mongrels," unleashed like dogs upon the long-suffering elite; those of European lineage, the bearers of civilization. The Unitarios framed the struggle as one between good and evil.

The first notable anti-Rosas propaganda work, José Rivera Indartes' *Rosas y sus opositores* (Rosas and his opponents), published in 1843, set the tone. It claimed that Rosas killed over twenty thousand, roughly ten percent of the population. The author urged a "holy war" against Rosas and called upon the caudillo's daughter to murder her father. The virulent hatred of Rosas' enemies stemmed in part from his success in directing lower-class mestizos, blacks, and the various racial mixtures politically, psychologically, and physically against his opponents. The *Negrada Federal* symbolized the connection between the regime and the lower classes. A militia unit composed of blacks and mulattoes dressed in red uniforms, the Negrada served as a very visible indication of the ties between Rosas and the lower classes. At the time, Afro-Argentines constituted at least a quarter of Buenos Aires' population.

THE SCOTTISH DIASPORA

As the Spanish trading system went into decline in the latter half of the eighteenth century, Scottish merchants established a presence in the Viceroyalty of La Plata. In the early nineteenth century a number acquired land on the frontier fringes of the city of Buenos Aires. Daniel MacInlay developed the Estancia Espartillar, among other properties. His large house, now within the city, is today the National History Museum. A sense of community could be discerned as early as 1824, with a dinner celebration of Saint Andrew's day at the Faunch Hotel. John Miller directed the celebrants. Miller imported the first Shorthorn bull, beginning the process of commercial breeding that eventually transformed the beef industry. The other part of the transformation came when Jorge Newman introduced wire fencing in 1844, making selective breeding possible.

The first organized immigration from Scotland to Argentina occurred in 1825 with the arrival from the port of Leith (Edinburgh) of the sailing vessel Symmetry, which carried some 220 souls, including 78 children. As did many others, the ship's passengers responded to the socioeconomic changes that swept the country in the eighteenth century. The aftermath of losing the battle of Culloden in 1746 resulted in depopulating the Highlands, reducing the remaining inhabitants to impoverished tenant farmers and forcing the surplus population, unable to find an alternative to agriculture, to search the world for land and opportunity.

The passengers of the Symmetry had no idea of what to expect but hoped to obtain land. William Grierson, a farmer accompanied by his wife, three children, and sows that produced sixteen piglets during the course of the voyage, kept a journal of the 83 days on board the Symmetry. Most of the passengers listed their occupation as "servant," but their number included a scattering of artisans, farmers, a medical doctor, surveyors, and an architect. They had been warned of the advisability of carrying a loaded pistol at all times when they went ashore. A cautious Mr. Grierson noted that one look at the local inhabitants confirmed the wisdom of such advice.

Immigrants established the agricultural colony of Monte Grande, constructing houses, sheds, and animal pens. Production of salted butter to meet demand in Buenos Aires represented their first contribution. By 1828, 326 immigrants and 188 native-born inhabitants made the settlement a substantial one. Unfortunately, the following year the violent struggle between Unitarios and Federalists drove most of the settlers into the relative safety of Buenos Aires. Eventually, some of the refugees established Scottish settlements in Quilmes, San Vicente, and Chascomús, while others remained in the city.

Jane Robson left an account of her difficult and eventful life farming in the vicinity of Chascomús, which she titled, with understatement, *Faith Hard Tried.* Among other adventures, she and her young son rode for miles, crossing a river at full flood with the horses swimming across as their riders wondered if they would be swept away. When the exhausted pair arrived at a house they both had to be carried into the dwelling. On another occasion, she sold ten cows to a man who promised to pay after he sheared his sheep and sold the wool, but who left the area without paying. Jane and her small son rode after the man, riding all day and night, caught up with him, and extracted the money. She described a life filled with bandits, soldiers, false starts, failure, perseverance, and ultimately a dance on her 89th birthday, attended by her son, daughters, grandchildren, and great-grandchildren. The goings on of the community could be read about in the English language *Buenos Aires Herald,* founded in 1876 by William Cathcart, a Scot.

Andrew Graham-Yooll, *The Forgotten Colony: A History of the English Speaking Communities in Argentina.* London: Hutchinson, 1981. Iain A.D. Stewart, *From Caledonia to the Pampas: Two Accounts by Early Scottish Emigrants to the Argentine.* East Linton, Scotland: Tuckwell Press, 2000.

DISINTEGRATION

Conflicting political and economic interests brought Rosas down. Rosas needed the interior provinces more than the reverse. For the first half of the century the port city ran a negative trade balance with foreign partners and a positive one with the interior that financed the import trade. Buenos Aires' dependency on the interior underlay the political dynamics and explains Rosas' unceasing efforts to keep the notion of a confederation alive. Everything revolved around the preservation of Buenos Aires' role within the *patria grande.* Any restriction on imports to help the interior provinces deal with competition from foreign products would reduce Buenos Aires' import tax revenues. He failed to draw in allies by creating shared interests. Long-standing anger over Buenos Aires' monopoly of custom revenues and the desire of other ports to broaden trade with Europe fueled demands for changes that threatened Rosas, and which could no longer be ignored. Intimidation could not accomplish what became a political as well as economic task. At the same time, Rosas relied upon other provinces for military support. In the end, an unsatisfied ally, Justo José Urquiza, the caudillo of Entre Ríos, started the chain of events that lead to his defeat. By failing to devise a national compromise and develop a convincing rationale, he lost the battle that doomed his concept of Argentina.

A new generation of liberal intellectuals who came of age in the 1830s impatiently pressed for change. They wrote poems and essays, often in exile in Montevideo, Santiago de Chile, and elsewhere, that expressed their vision. Post-Rosas leaders came from the generation of 1837—Bartolomé Mitre, Juan Bautista Alberdi, and Domingo Faustino Sarmiento, among others. They adopted an unrelenting hostility to Rosas and what he represented. Rosas seemingly had outlived his time.

The immediate cause of the collapse of his regime resulted from his fear of Brazil and the centuries old competition between Spain and Portugal to control the Rio de la Plata river system. Rosas' notion of preserving colonial order had a territorial dimension. Paraguay had been a part of the Viceroyalty of La Plata until the collapse of the Spanish Empire. Rosas never recognized its independent status, referring to it as the Province of Paraguay. When the Empire of Brazil recognized Paraguay's independence in 1844, Rosa viewed it as a hostile act. The Brazilian Province of Rio Grande do Sul, bordering on Uruguay's northern frontier, facilitated meddling by imperial Rio in that country, just as Buenos Aires' location across the estuary from Montevideo drew Argentine interference.

Both Argentina and Brazil battled for influence, not actual occupation, because Britain supported Uruguay's buffer state role. Internationalization of the river system seemed crucial to Brazil in order to maintain contact with its western province of Mato Grosso. Free navigation on the Paraná and Paraguay rivers also concerned the Argentine littoral provinces as well as Paraguay. The river system brought all of them into an unlikely yet effective alliance against Rosas. Brazil broke relations with Buenos Aires in 1850. A formal anti-Rosas alliance emerged in 1851 that eventually included the Argentine provinces of Entre Ríos and Corrientes, along with Brazil, Paraguay, and Uruguay. The defection of Urquiza, with a force of 10,000 men equipped by Rosas, began the unraveling, soon followed by the capitulation of Buenos Aires' commander in Uruguay. Brazil's navy secured the entrance to the river and threatened to mount an amphibious invasion with troops from Uruguay. Rosas could not move in any direction without exposing his flanks. Trapped, Rosas, aided by the British *chargé d'affaires*, slipped aboard a warship for exile in England.[4]

Rosas left a mixed legacy. He governed without a constitution and handled the affairs of state as he judged fit. Equality, but only within one's class or station in life, resulted in acceptance of a stratified structure of privilege that could not be easily broken. During the Rosas era a patriarchal structure solidified as rising land values re-enforced by increasing export profits concentrated wealth. Nevertheless, he established a proto-state, headed off the fragmentation of Argentina and laid the groundwork for modern commerce that others built upon. Rosas used paper money to keep the domestic economy afloat, but he had little choice to do otherwise. Initially, Rosas financed deficits with bonds, but investors demanded such deep discounts that little revenue could be raised. Printing money allowed the machinery of Rosas' proto-government to function and kept real wages low, while merchants and landholders retreated as much as possible to the safety of foreign currencies, gold and silver, and credit mechanisms. While the amount of paper currency in circulation depended on perceived needs, Rosas cannot be blame for the lax emission policies of subsequent regimes.

CHAPTER 2

The Compromise

In early 1852 the victorious Urquiza arrived in Buenos Aires. He shocked returning Unitarios exiles by remaining a Federalist, even insisting on the display of red. He extracted vengeance on the defeated in a manner worthy of Rosas. Around military headquarters corpses rotted from tree branches. The remnants of the defeated elite Aquino regiment had their throats cut. As an observer noted, Urquiza is "more animal than intellectual."[1] Nevertheless, he had a vision beyond violence and the seemingly unbridgeable line between Unitarios and Federalists. Urquiza, drawing on his enhanced reputation, called all provincial governors together to work out an agreement on a political structure. The Pact of San Nicolas de Los Arroyos established a constituent congress to write a national constitution—an opportunity for Juan Bautista Alberdi, a prominent member of the generation of 1837, to influence the constitutional structure of the country. Alberdi, an uncritical admirer of England and the United States, wrote the *Bases and Points of Departure for the Political Organization of the Argentina Republic*. His ideas strongly influenced the Constitution of 1853. That document, modified in 1860, provided for a six-year presidential and vice presidential term; three independent branches (executive, legislative, and judicial); a senate elected for a nine-year term, with income and age qualifications; and a chamber of deputies elected for four years. A separate act subsequently set the minimum voting age at seventeen, without literacy or income restrictions.

Urquiza sought to eliminate inter-provincial trade barriers; nationalize customs revenues, including those of Buenos Aires; open the Paraná and Uruguay rivers to free navigation; and negotiate trade treaties with

European partners. As a provincial Federalist, Urquiza offered the compromises that Rosas could not bring himself to make. An irritated, intransigent Buenos Aires rejected his reforms. Taking advantage of Urquiza's absence to attend the constituent congress in Santa Fé, Unitarios seized control of the city and dropped out of the constituent assembly.

Urquiza, rather than plunging into an attempt to regain his grip on Buenos Aires, established the national government of the Argentine Confederation provisionally in Entre Rios' capital of Paraná, where he governed for the next eight years while Buenos Aires sulked and conspired. He appeared to be always one step ahead of the liberal Unitarios, stealing their issues and exposing Buenos Aires as more interested in power than principle.

President Urquiza opened the river to free navigation, recognized Paraguay's independence, and made it clear that he had no designs on Uruguay and expected Brazil to give up any claims it might have in the region. A new customhouse at Rosario began a period of growth for that city, in direct competition with Buenos Aires. For a while, Urquiza contemplated forming small independent nations, including combining his native province of Entre Rios with that of Corrientes. British disapproval ended that notion.

A tariff dispute in 1858 turned into a conflict. When Urquiza moved against Buenos Aires, the Porteños found it prudent to rejoin the nation. Nevertheless, the struggle between the port city and the interior required one more battle. Upset with the chosen successor to Urquiza as president of the Confederation, General Bartolomé Mitre of Buenos Aires attacked. The battle of Pavon in 1861, while it proved militarily indecisive, convinced an ill Urquiza to allow General Mitre to succeed him, but under his terms. Mitre preferred unification under Buenos Aires Province with centralized control over the other provinces. Realizing that he risked civil war and certain defeat if he attempted to impose his vision, Mitre accepted the structure of the Constitution of 1853 and its modified version of federalism.

The task of incorporating the Unitario desire for centralized control, provincial demands for a less intrusive political and cultural structure, and Buenos Aires' pretensions required a slow process. Semantics helped to blur conflicting demands. Article three of the constitution declared Buenos Aires the capital of the "Confederation" by a special act of congress, thereby eliminating historic claims to such status. In the 1860 modification, the term "Confederation" became the federal "Republic." Nevertheless, it seemed prudent to leave the political status of Buenos Aires ambiguous. Argentine federalism remained a fluid concept.

FOUNDING MODERNIZERS

With Bartolomé Mitre's presidency (1862–1868) the liberals and the Euro-modernizers assumed direction of the nation. Domingo Faustino

Sarmiento succeeded Mitre as president in 1868. The twelve years these two powerful personalities governed the nation swept the gauchos to the social and physical fringes, eliminated caudillos, confirmed the pattern of large land holding, and re-enforced the oligarchy. They did so in the context of the Constitution of 1853.

Bartolomé Mitre grew up in Buenos Aires under Rosas. He soon joined various anti-Rosas groups. As a young man he found it prudent to go into exile. Mitre spent time in Uruguay, Chile, Peru, and Bolivia and fought with Urquiza at the battle of Monte Caseros that toppled Rosas. Subsequently, he in turn fought Urquiza. As a soldier, he demonstrated courage but uneven military talent. As an intellectual he wrote constantly and well, including biographies of San Martin and Belgrano. As an orator he excelled, whether before a legislative body or a public gathering. Unfortunately, his polemics had a cutting and bitter impact that left opponents hurt and resentful. First and foremost he remained a Porteño, believing that the nation revolved around the port city and its province. He believed himself indispensable and tended to discount the contributions of others. Although virtually everyone recognized his talents, respect increased with distance.

President Mitre created a modern government out of Rosas' rudimentary structure. A stable government, coupled with an organized consular service, laid the groundwork for immigration. Federalized customs revenues, a national bank, and an organized treasury provided a degree of fiscal stability. Mitre cultivated the Vatican, to be rewarded with an archbishop for Buenos Aires under mutually acceptable terms. A judicial code, a court system with a Supreme Court, provided an illusion of a government of laws, with the occasional flashes of substance needed to assure foreign investors. Public education expanded and suggested that new values could transform the nation.

Argentina's participation in the War of the Triple Alliance against Paraguay diverted the nation's attention and drained away its energy. Mitre harbored the hope of reconstructing the greater Argentina that had existed under the Viceroyalty of La Plata, with its capital in Buenos Aires. He reverted to the general and led troops against Asunción. Argentina's war machine consumed conscripts with reckless abandon, resulting in resistance and a major riot in Mendoza. When his term ended, Mitre, constitutionally ineligible to succeed himself, stepped down. An election conducted as Sarmiento slowly made this way home from the United States placed him in the presidency. Mitre became a senator and founder of the newspaper *La Nación*, effectively disseminating his opinions throughout the nation. He remained an influential force until his death in 1906.

Domingo Faustino Sarmiento had much in common with Mitre—they shared a mutual dislike of each other. Unlike his predecessor, Sarmiento came from the interior Province of San Juan and a family of modest background. He grew up amidst the insecurity of Indian raids and the violence of regional caudillos, while yearning for a more refined life. He claimed to have learned to read with total comprehension at age five at a time when few in the province could read beyond a functional level. Sarmiento became something of a local oddity, touring to amaze and delight his neighbors with his reading ability. Indulged by his awestruck family, he virtually skipped childhood. Sarmiento reported that, while he never flew a kite or played other common games, he read everything he could get his hands on. The autobiography of Benjamin Franklin became one of his favorite books. He taught his two sisters to read and write, beginning a lifelong interest in women's education.

Drafted into the local militia at sixteen, he ended up jailed for insubordination. Subsequently, he fought against Facundo Quiroga, learned French, and then went into Chilean exile from 1831 to 1836. In Chile he taught school, clerked, worked as a mine foreman, learned English, and translated Sir Walter Scott into Spanish. With the death of Quiroga, he returned to San Juan, established a school for young ladies, and founded a newspaper that led to yet another exile in Chile from 1840 to 1845. In Santiago, he became a newspaper editor and founded another paper. In Chile for the third time (1848–1851), he published a completely uncritical article supporting European immigration. When Rosas read the piece he flew into a rage, but Sarmiento lay beyond his reach. While Rosas viewed him as a Unitario agitator, Sarmiento saw himself as a schoolteacher. Sarmiento believed his countrymen to be lazy, genetically debased, and perhaps beyond rescue. His solution: immigration from Europe, and the more the better. He argued for aggressive action to attract immigrants. Only much later did he express concerns about assimilation of the flood of newcomers.

He is best known as the author of *The Life of Facundo, or Civilization and Barbarism,* in which he listed all the evils of Argentina as he saw them, specially the barbarous gauchos and caudillos. In common with Mitre, he believed himself right and indispensable. The Chileans reacted to his inflated ego by calling him *don yo* (Mister me). Nevertheless, he introduced new ideas acknowledged to have made Chilean elementary and secondary schools more effective. In recognition of his talents, the Chilean government sent him to Europe and the United States to examine educational innovations that could be of use in South America. Sarmiento traveled extensively, visiting Spain, France, England, and then the United States in 1847. He made contact with intellectuals at every opportunity, including Ralph Waldo Emerson and Henry Wadsworth Longfellow, among others. In 1864 he became Argentine Minister to the United States. Bored with Washington, D.C., he moved to New York, renewing old friendships and making new ones. The University of Michigan conferred an honorary law degree on a delighted Sarmiento.

In 1868, he served as Argentina's second president under the Constitution of 1853. After leaving the presidency in 1874, he became a senator (1875–1880), Minister of the Interior, and subsequently, the Province of Buenos Aires Superintendent of Education. A sensual man, he had many affairs. He ate, drank, and lived life with gusto. His admirers and detractors agreed—Sarmiento's talents, virtues, and vices ranged from the exemplary to the abysmal.

Juan Bautista Alberdi (1810–1884), although never president, deserves to be recognized as a modernizer not only for his political contributions noted earlier, but for his belief in progress. Born in the Province of Tucumán, he won a scholarship to the University of Buenos Aires in 1824. Alberdi played a major role in shaping the belief that the Creole nation had to be replaced in the interest of progress. Alberdi's often-repeated statement that "to govern is to populate" captured only part of his beliefs. He asserted that only Europeans could construct a modern nation. In contrast, the Creole population, no matter how much they might be exposed to education, could not in a hundred years be anything more than miserable material. He observed that the United States, composed of Europeans, having excluded the Indian population, laid the groundwork of progress, even during its colonial period. He proposed the construction of railways as a mean of extending the immigrant's reach into the interior. Creole women married to Europeans, according to Alberdi, would eventually breed out the vices and leave Argentina with the virtues of Europe. He advised his compatriots not to be worried about national identify. Personally a dour man without the flair of either a Sarmiento or Mitre, he believed that Argentina needed to lay aside the heroic and pursue material progress. Although he could have become a soldier, he preferred his pen to the sword. His mixed political history, including supporting Rosas for a time and then Urquiza, much to the disapproval of others of the generation of 1837, gave him the perspective to help fashion the compromise inherent in the Constitution of 1853.

All three men reflected the liberals' elevation of Europeans and their culture to the pinnacle of civilization. Such notions relegated the interior's population to the bottom in terms of potential contribution to an independent Argentina. A people judged to be wanting merited little consideration. Mitre, Sarmiento, and Alberdi believed that their efforts had set Argentina on the road to becoming a cornucopia of wealth and civilized refinement. All represented *Argentina Atlantica,* with its emotional transatlantic terminus in Buenos Aires and it origins in Europe.

THE FEMININE FACE

In the early nineteenth century a political and social breakthrough occurred with the creation of the *Sociedad de Beneficencia* (Benevolent Society) in 1823 by Rivadavia, then a minister in the government. A man of the eighteenth century Enlightenment, Rivadavia believed that women represented an under-utilized economic and administrative asset. Education, the long- range solution, did not preclude an immediate female contribution. Drawing on a French model, he established the Beneficencia to break the clerical monopoly on charity and placed the direction of the society in the hands of elite women. Although Rivadavia sought to reduce clerical influence, most of the organization's directors—devout Catholic women—did not seek to challenge the Church. Eventually, a self-selected directive board of twenty-five controlled the organization well into the twentieth century. State funds and donations financed its activities.

The society took over principal responsibility for traditional charitable activities but also expanded services. The organization undertook responsibilities the state could not afford to fund or did not possess sufficient expertise to operate. In order to train female teachers, the society assumed operation of the *Colegio de Buenos Aires*, a secondary school previously directed by the Brotherhood of Charity. Until the 1870s, the society administered all female primary and secondary schools in the nation. Traditional notions of female responsibility for the instruction of children and the presumed need for gender segregation provided an opening for females. Primary school teaching became a recognized profession for women, and the creation of normal schools broadened teaching opportunities at the secondary level. Girls' schools required women teachers, but boys' schools had a mixed-gender staff.

In 1852 the Hospital for Women, then one of the largest such facilities, became the organization's responsibility, requiring training for medical staff until a nursing school opened in 1886. The association of women with social services broadened opportunities for females as directors of schools, orphanages, and other such agencies. The Beneficencia also assumed responsibility for providing natural disasters assistance. Together with the *Patronato de la Infancia* (Children's fund), elite women made a notable contribution.

Intellectual preparation for change depended on publications that carefully laid out the case for women. In the 1830s Patrona Rosenda de Sierra published a magazine, *The Tremor* (*La Aljaba*), that advocated educating women to make them less frivolous wives and better mothers. Rosa Guerra's magazine, *La Camelia* (1852), argued that educated women made better companions for sophisticated males, a theme common in such magazines worldwide. Her other magazine, *La Educación*, translated articles from French and English. Women's progress in more advanced nations reached readers within weeks. A children's book, *Julia y su Educación*, indoctrinated the next generation in progressive notions of women's roles. Nevertheless, obstacles remained. In 1888 Diógenes Decoud wrote that, "half of all women are hysterics, and in Buenos Aires, our professor of nervous diseases [Dr. Ramos Mejía] believes [that] the number is even higher."[2]

Sarmiento also played a role in expanding women's education. To a large extent he built on the foundation provided by the Beneficencia. Nevertheless, he believed the society had become an obstacle to educational progress. As director of Education of the Province of Buenos Aires in 1856, he appointed Juana Manso de Noronha as school supervisor of the province. The appointment caused a stir because it placed a woman, and moreover a Protestant, in a position of authority over men. In 1869, congress authorized a national normal school system to train teachers. Sarmiento convinced Emma Nicolay de Capfille to found and administer Normal School Number One. Mary Graham, an American teacher who arrived in 1876, established the National Normal School of La Plata. She devoted herself to Argentine education until her death in 1906. Her dream of a co-educational school never became a reality in her lifetime. Sarmiento also failed to convince the public that the French Delsarte system of physical education for girls and co-education would benefit the nation. Both ideas proved too daring to be accepted. Nevertheless, in 1876, the government transferred control of girls' schools in the capital and in Buenos Aires Province from the Beneficencia to provincial authorities, declaring the need for a modern approach.

The influence of American female teachers in the elaboration of public education resulted from Sarmiento's travels in the United States. Pioneer educator Horace Mann urged him to adopt the model that had worked so well in settling and schooling the American West, noting that women worked for much less than males, and, moreover, teaching offered unmarried women a respected profession.[3] Some sixty-five teachers arrived from the United States, most personally selected by Mrs. Mary Peabody Mann.

Minister of Education Nicholas Avellaneda worked tirelessly to overcome the country's alleged negative colonial heritage. School enrollment doubled to over 100,000 students attending 1,645 schools. Free public libraries, supplied with books by the national library commission, along with adult classes, provided culture for the lower classes and career roles for women. Significantly, by the second decade of the twentieth century females made up the majority of teachers. Women, as recognized agents of modernization, dominated a powerful agency for change.

Teaching provided status that weakened the obstacles that excluded women from other professions. The opening of professions began with occupations that drew on accepted notions of female nurturing, such as teacher, nurse, and medical doctor, in slow progression. Dr. Cecilia Grierson, a determined Scottish-Argentine women, became the first Argentine-trained medical school graduate in 1889, but it took years of legal wrangling before she could practice. Semi-professional occupations in commerce and banking also set the stage for further advances. A co-educational commerce high school established in 1910 provided entry-level white-collar careers in traditionally male dominated occupations. In 1905 the National Girls' High School began to funnel a small number of graduates into the universities. Distinguished foreign lecturers, such as Maria Montessori, encouraged women's education.

Foreign women not accountable to local cultural restrictions could ignore conventions without running the risk of being seen as impolite, boorish, or worse. Isabel King, one of the American teachers who responded to Sarmiento's call for normal school teachers, addressed the International Council of Women (ICW) in Chicago in 1893. On her return, she attempted to organize an ICW branch in Buenos Aires. With some frustration she turned to foreign women's clubs for help. Jean Raynes, an English woman, and Dr. Grierson attended the ICW conference in 1899. Encouraged by Clara Barton, founder of the International Red Cross, and others, Grierson won over Alvina Van Praet de Salas, president of the Beneficencia, who agreed to form an ICW branch, but one dominated by conservative values. Nevertheless, by 1910 the National Council of Women (NCW) had 1,000 members. More impatient women joined the Argentine Association of University Women (AAUW), founded by a profoundly frustrated Dr. Grierson in 1902. Thirty women made up the membership, including Sara Justo, the sister of the Socialist leader Juan B. Justo. The membership of the AAUW and the NCW, often the wives and daughters of influential people, pressed for political and social rights.

WORKING WOMEN

Urbanization brought changes, some easily accepted, but others encountered resistance because they conflicted with engrained values and attitudes. Patriarchal notions reinforced by law placed responsibility for family decisions on males, with the exception of widows and unmarried women. Society's Catholic orientation put home, family, and preservation of the male role as head of household far ahead of gender or wage equality in the workplace.

Low wages required all family members to work. Nevertheless, the physical separation from home and family members that factory work required suggested moral vulnerability. Increased levels of male supervision, absent from traditional agricultural labor when the entire family worked together, appeared to be a potential hazard. Waitresses, barmaids, street vendors, and others that dealt with transient customers became suspect. Police, under certain circumstances, assumed these women practiced prostitution. In 1875, the legalization and regulation of brothels theoretically separated legal sex practitioners from the chaste. Unlicensed

streetwalkers complicated matters. Suspicion became a disruptive everyday reality for women and a source of bribes for the police. In many bars
and in *café de camareras* (cafés with waitresses) male patrons could dance
with waitresses for a modest sum, and perhaps buy sexual favors. The
authorities, responding to such suspicions, required those that worked
in cafes to be registered as prostitutes. High license fees discouraged
employers from legally hiring waitresses. Respectable establishments
hired male waiters. While many evaded the laws and regulations, they
faced a hostile public perception that working women and prostitutes had
a common status and potentially a shared occupation.

Legislation to protect the "weaker sex" by limiting hours and jobs
in certain industries reinforced gender disabilities. Santa Fé Province
excluded women from 36 types of factory employment. By 1914 women
made up approximately 30 percent of the industrial workforce, mostly
at the low end of the wage scale. Gender competition for factory work
intensified as electrification reduced dependency on physical strength.
The number of female workers increased as technology advanced so that
by 1949 women made up 45 percent of the Buenos Aires industrial labor
force but earned 50 percent less than males.

Catholic women's organizations pressed for better working conditions.
The *Sociedad Madres Argentinas*, the *Sociedad Conferencias de Señoras de San
Vicente de Paúl*, and the *Cantinas Maternales*, among others enlisted women
in the struggle to change conditions. Women played an important role in
the functioning of mutual aid societies such as the *Asociación el Centavo* to
help women establish economic control of their lives. Some 400 belonged
to the Women's Catholic Benevolent Society, which pressed for improve-
ments as well as protective legislation.

The Anarchists, Socialists, and Argentine branch of the International
Association of Free Thought, advocated action. Working-class women
founded the Anarchist Women's Center in the capital. In 1898 the
Anarchist Union of Female Labor sought to draw workers together
in predominately female worker industries. In a similar fashion, the
Socialist Women's Center attempted to organize weavers and seam-
stresses. Gender segregation in the work place resulted in separate
campaigns for changes based on the sex of workers. Socialist Gabriela
Coni proposed a law enacted in 1907 that restricted women to a six-
hour day and permitted maternity leave of up to two months. In theory,
they could spend more time at home tending to their children; in reality
lost wages meant disaster for the household. In a similar vein, legislation in 1924 prohibited women from working the night shift or engag-
ing in unsafe tasks at a time when safety in the work place remained
primitive. Ignored and seldom enforced, laws based on perceptual
notions reinforced acceptance of gender weakness with its low-wage
implications.

RIVERS AND RAILWAYS

The traditional network of large wheeled ox- and horse-drawn carts that carried wool, tallow, hay, hides, and grain to Buenos Aires consumed time and exposed loads to weather, insects, and dirt. As exports became more diversified and quality important, modern transportation and processing became vital. Engineering reconfigured the export infrastructure and made an efficient export economy possible.

By 1910 the port of Buenos Aires consisted of four ship basins, over six miles of wharves with warehouses, flourmills, grain elevators, and pens for livestock. The port accommodated 1,400 ships, with more distant anchorage for many more. Observers compared it favorably to European ports.[4] In 1908, 84 percent of imports and over half of the country's exports passed through the port of Buenos Aires; other ports—Rosario, Santa Fé, San Nicholas, La Plata, and Bahia Blanca—received and exported the remaining volume. Channels allowed ships of 10,000 tons to proceed to Rosario, while smaller ships went up river as far as Paraná before linking with riverboats to proceed to Corrientes and beyond. Steep riverbanks with jetties for small boats made it possible to service the entire stretch of many waterways. Although the river network provided a natural outlet, railways maximized the profitability of large expanses of agricultural land. In Buenos Aires Province, not as well endowed with rivers, railways became indispensable.

Rail construction on flat pampas proved less expensive than in Europe but still required substantial capital. Railways offered speed to market and steady supply. Expansion of the rail network increased production and resulted in significantly higher land values. The first railway in 1857 ran six miles inland from Buenos Aires. A little over a decade later (1870), 455 miles had been completed, including a line from Rosario on the Paraná River to Córdoba. Freight trains soon made the run from Rosario to Córdoba in less than forty-eight hours, a trip that previously required over a week. Subsequently, construction began on a line from Buenos Aires to Rosario. By 1880 a trunk line from Córdoba to Tucumán added a far western connection. Subsequently, networks branched out from Buenos Aires, Santa Fé, and Rosario, reaching south a far as Báhía Blanca and west to Mendoza and Salta. In the latter decades of the century, the network ballooned from 2,300 to 25,000 kilometers of track. By 1912 rail connections to Paraguay and Bolivia had been completed. Mendoza connected with a line (since abandoned) on the Chilean side that provided transportation to Santiago and Chile's Pacific port of Valparaiso. Railways bypassed settlements that offered only marginal economic possibilities while turning others into prosperous collection centers tied into the Atlantic export chain.

No significant district in Buenos Aires Province lay more than 25 miles from a railway by 1920. The Southern line as early as 1868 carried some

28 percent of the wool, 48 percent of hides, and 89 percent of tallow and grease that entered the export chain. Sheep operations alternated between wool and tallow as prices dictated. Such flexibility depended on demand and rapid transportation.

Telegraph lines paralleled the rails. The Railroad Law of 1872 required that companies string and maintain telegraph lines along the right of way. An underwater cable connection to Europe, established in 1874, linked Buenos Aires to Montevideo, Uruguay, on to Rio de Janeiro and the Cape Verde Islands, and finally to Europe. From Europe cables from Argentina could be sent on to the United States. In the 1880s increased funding allowed the state telegraph monopoly to establish lines and offices in the interior, connecting previously remote areas with the world cable network. Another submarine cable linked Buenos Aires and Lisbon. Telegraph service across the pampas, through Chile to Valparaiso, then via submarine cable on to San Francisco, California, with a connection to Australia and China, linked Argentina with Pacific nations. Telegraph lines, some 31,251 miles by 1910, facilitated the flow of exports.

By 1900, 190,000 miles of submarine cable crisscrossed the ocean floor with innumerable access points. The formation of the International Telegraph Union (ITU) in Paris in 1865 obligated all members to accept messages and function as an international network. Argentina joined the ITU in 1889. In 1910 a cable to the United States through Galveston, Texas, and another to Europe via Madeira, along with technical advances, further accelerated contact. Initially, cable communication to Europe required five hours or more; by 1911 it took a mere 45 minutes. Telephone service in urban areas after the turn of the century linked Buenos Aires to Montevideo, Rosario, and Bahía Blanca. Major estancias, interconnected by telephone with each other and the urban processing centers, exchanged information, opinions, and gossip. Even in the remote south, a skeleton telephone communication network existed, in spite of winter conditions and high winds. Puerto Gallegos and Punta Arenas had contact with isolated telephones in the interior. The Chileans maintained a line in Tierra del Fuego from Cabo Dungeness to Punta Arenas, Argentina. Nevertheless, telegraph remained the most reliable and accessible communication medium.

Infrastructure development relied on foreigners. British investors supplied the capital by buying government-guaranteed bonds issued by provincial and national authorities or concession holders. Argentines preferred land, a rational choice given escalating property values. The newspaper *Buenos Aires Standard* claimed that land close to the city had increased in value 50 times over between 1850 and 1870, far beyond the modest returns on infrastructure projects. Even determined efforts to enlist Argentine investors in railways failed. In 1871 the majority of

Argentine investors had only minor interests. The immensely wealthy Anchorena family invested a paltry £200 in the Central and never added a penny more. Wealthy British investors put up 50 percent of the money, while the rest came from a scattering of widows, small investors, tradesmen, and assorted individuals seeking a modest but guaranteed return. The Argentine government became one of the largest holders of railway bonds. Most of the money borrowed or guaranteed by the government or otherwise pulled from the pockets of investors came from the same source—London.

Domestic capital financed production. Landowners used their influence to make sure that rail lines serviced their needs and extended as the frontier moved inland. Argentina generated insufficient capital to expand beyond agriculture.

MAKING OF THE OLIGARCHY

The struggle between the Federalists and the Unitarios damaged the republican ideal. Enlightened minds cast the contest as a battle between civilization and barbarism, or superior knowledge against an ignorant citizenry. Class divisions firmed around traditional culture at the lower levels and exclusive modernizing culture at the top. The promise of republican equality fell as an oligarchy emerged on the heels of prosperity.

Increasingly, the country's direction depended on a relatively small group with a tightening grip on land, the one productive asset. Although the elite had economic interests in common, their different roots made it difficult to merge into a unified and cohesive group. Merchant-landholders allied with former colonial officials provided the initial foundation. As the Indian frontier gave way, military men and republican politicians acquired sufficiently large land holdings to claim inclusion. Immigrants from Britain, northern and, to lesser extent southern Europe added another layer. National origins, generational roots in the country, and family names all counted in spite of intermarriage. Competition over resources and status, divisions by provinces, and camarilla politics at the provincial level resulted in differentiation within the emerging oligarchy. They strived for a reasonable political consensus through personal ties in clubs and associations. An elite culture modeled on that of Europe and reinforced by clubs and wealth legitimized their political role. By the 1870s the shift to an oligarchy had been accomplished.

Progressive European practices justified self-serving legislation behind the symbols of a liberal democracy, while the lower classes provided the façade of a pretend democracy. Immigrant labor fell into a separate excluded category. Meanwhile, the oligarchy negotiated alliances between families that enabled them to control their own province. Provinces and the federal district constituted electoral units with two national senators

elected by the provincial legislature and a chamber of deputies theoretically representing the people. Controlling the outcome of an election
posed few challenges in the absence of an effective opposition or a secret
ballot. Fixing the vote, stuffing ballot boxes, and other tricks might be
used as necessary.

The oligarchy directed the national government through the *Partido
Autonomista Nacional* (PAN) established in 1881. The PAN grew out of the
League of Governors organized by provincial politicians and their party,
the *Partido Nacional.* Julio A. Roca, an army officer and renowned Indian
fighter from Tucumán, made an attractive candidate. Typical of camarilla
politics, Roca's brother-in-law, Miguel Juárez Celman, active in politics in
Córdaba, organized the campaign. Córdoba, supported by the governors
of Santa Fé, Entre Rios, and the interior provinces of Tucumán, Salta, La
Rioja, Santiago del Estero, and Jujuy propelled Roca to the presidency in
1880. On the strength of Roca's victory the PAN emerged as a national
party that favored provincial politicians and commercial agriculture.

Julio A. Roca on assuming the presidency pronounced that his goal
would be "peace and administration," interpreted to mean social peace
through firmness and economic progress. It would not be that easy.
The outgoing government faced a rebellion by the governor of Buenos
Aires Province, Carlos Tejedor, an unsuccessful candidate for president.
The governor resisted the plan to declare Buenos Aires a federal district
detached from its province. Federal forces defeated those of Buenos Aires,
leaving some 2,500 dead or wounded. Congress approved the law creating the federal district just before Roca took office.

Within the PAN, factional demands, and conflicting interests could be
fought out or deals made. A presidential candidate had to obtain the backing of a viable number of governors to be selected. Political squabbles
subsided with the selection and election of the presidential candidate but
did not disappear. PAN presidents often confronted opposition from a
PAN congress. Party politicians agreed upon policy, but not the details
that had to be decided on the floor of congress. The president used the
power of his personality, family connections, federal patronage, and
threats to get his way or at least an acceptable compromise. Force served
as a last resort. Militias disbanded following the decree of 1872 left the
federal government with a military monopoly. Nevertheless, employing
force had risks, and phantom provincial militias could suddenly come
to life. A national camarilla independent of provincial politicians never
emerged to coordinate the system. Politics at the federal level remained
vulnerable to splintering into factions along provincial lines.

The nature of elite politics and divisions within the oligarchy made
social clubs important. The *Club de Progreso,* founded in 1852 by the
Buenos Aires elite, favored those families that played a role in the events
of the 1850s. Carlos Pellegrini, a prominent member of the immigrant

strata of the elite who favored a more inclusive elite, became the driving force behind the creation of the Jockey Club, established in 1882, the
same year as the *Yacht Club Argentino*.[5] Three years later the new *Círculo
de Armas*, with a focus on fencing, attracted elite members. The Círculo de
Armas restricted membership to 500 members, most from families considered to be the founding layer, with pre and early 1800s roots. The identification of clubs with sports—horses racing, sailing, and fencing—followed
the nineteenth-century European model.

The establishment of clubs paralleled prosperity. Memberships across a
number of clubs and associations did not create a unified elite. Pellegrini
envisioned the Jockey Club as the coordinating club, although it did not
succeed in drawing all layers of the elite together. Nevertheless, the Jockey
Club became an umbrella organization. Its European oval track, refined
betting, and thorough-bred animals made the sport a popular pastime.
A racetrack clubhouse, open to members and invited guests, became the
place to be seen and establish one's participation in high society.

In response to Pellegrini's inclusive notions, the club offered honorary membership to the president and vice-president of the republic, often
already members; the entire cabinet; federal senators and deputies; supreme
court judges; governors; the mayor of the capital and his chief of police;
and high ranking military officers. Foreign heads of legations or embas-
sies received memberships as soon as they presented their credentials.
Industrialists and important businessmen, often also members of the *Union
Industrial Argentina* (UIA) and the *Cámara de Comercio*, participated in the
Jockey Club.

The season's big racing event, the *Gran Premio Nacional*, occasioned a
flurry of parties, receptions, and banquets. Before the event, the president
of the republic saluted the crowd from his carriage before alighting at the
member's clubhouse. Closer to the Plaza de Mayo and government offices,
a lavish downtown club, constructed in 1897 on fashionable calle Florida,
hosted official receptions as well as provided a refuge for over-worked
ministers. Distinguished foreign visitors, including Theodore Roosevelt,
Anatole France, and others could expect to be entertained sumptuously
at the club. The building reportedly cost over two million pesos, with
the finest of materials and imported European furnishings and *objects de
arte*. When Georges Clemenceau, a future French prime minister, visited
in 1910, he described the building uncharitably as very American in its
ostentation. Nevertheless, the movers and shakers of Argentina inter-
mingled, discussed events, and set policy at the billiard table or over an
elegant dinner with well-chosen French wines followed by brandy and
fine cigars. From the overstuffed leather chairs of the Jockey Club, the
world seemed under reasonable control, in spite of recurrent anxieties
over radical excesses. The years between 1880 and 1910 came to be called

the "Golden Age" of wealth and privilege—a gloss that obscured a more fragile sociopolitical reality.

IMMIGRATION, LAND, AND PROSPERITY

A modest number of immigrants entered the country in the post-independence era in spite of Rosas' ambivalence about immigration. Over a thousand immigrants a year settled in Buenos Aires from 1853 to 1860.[6] As early as 1855, the foreign-born made up over one third of Buenos Aires' population. Fifteen years later, foreigners made up over half of the city's population. Between 1856 and the end of the century over two million newcomers arrived in the country as agriculture brought new land under cultivation.

Commercial agriculture crops and animal stocks required intensive labor. Expansion and the opening of new land required a constant flow of labor. Immigrants, mainly unattached males, along with a smaller number of females of working age, made a productive contribution. Abnormal age distribution, with fewer children and elderly to drain resources, made the wages offered acceptable. Moreover, the type of labor needed to maintain and expand agricultural exports attracted people in reasonably good health. Subsequently, the real social costs became evident as the labor force matured and a more normal age distribution emerged.

In the 1860s and 1870s, Indian attacks threatened to halt expansion. Bahía Blanca, anchoring the advance of Buenos Aires Province to the south, attacked by Indians in 1870, just barely survived. In 1872, a raid into Santa Fé foreshadowed an attack on Buenos Aires Province. Indians sold cattle and horses in Chile with no questions asked. More worrisome, foreign governments warned potential immigrants that their security could not be assured. The issue became an interrelated one of security, labor, and land for expansion. In response, the "Desert Campaign" of General Julio A. Roca (1878–1879), financed in part by promised distribution of land, broke the back of the tribes and ended the threat. Roca's campaign opened up new land at a crucial point in the development of the export economy and reassured governments that their nationals would be safe.

Proimmigration interests did not rely upon the need for labor alone to justify the flow. Economist Francisco Latzina elaborated a model based on an immigrant arriving with twenty pesos and muscle power equivalent to 1,500 pesos a year. Others supported immigration to replace the mestizo population. As late as 1904 sociologist Lucas Ayarragaraz wrote that mixed bloods could not grasp synthetic concepts or employ advanced reasoning. He advocated cross breeding with Europeans for at least three generations. Those concerned about occupying territory observed that only a large population could assure sovereignty, particularly in the northern and southern regions. A yearly average of some 240,000 immigrants landed in the period between 1900 and 1914. By that time the foreign-born made up one-third of Argentina's inhabitants. Along with the first and second generation, immigrants constituted 80 percent of the population of Buenos Aires.

British immigrants constituted a privileged group, inevitably linked to the export chain. They often had access to investment capital or personal assets, as in the case of British army pensioners and others with modest but dependable amounts. That British immigrants could just as easily have gone to Australia, New Zealand, or Canada, and in fact they represented an extension of the empire that consumed much of the country's exportable bounty. The government encouraged British immigration to balance the number of Italians in the country. Italian ships and sailors developed such an active trade and immigration route to Buenos Aires that many thought that Italy verged on establishing an informal colony in Argentina.

Mendoza, on the Andean fringe of the country, developed an immigrant-dependent economy centered on viniculture and light manufacturing. An earthquake in 1861 required the building of a new city to replace the destroyed colonial one. The new Mendoza, although rebuilt almost on the original location, reoriented its economic ties to the east and away from its former Chilean commercial links. In 1886 natural gas from the oil fields at Cacheuta provided energy for industrialization and powered the extensive irrigation system. Between 1895 and 1910, irrigated vineyards spread beyond Mendoza into San Juan and La Rioja provinces. The wine industry attracted Italians and Spaniards. In the dry foothills of the Andes, immigrant vintners produced wines to accompany the increasingly Italio-Argentine cuisine of the country. In 1913, 3,653 wineries produced 500,011,042 liters, exceeding Chilean production and far outpacing that of California at the time. In 1885 rail connections with Buenos Aires, and with Chile in 1910 (since abandoned), linked Mendoza to the national economy. In 1914 Mendoza had a population of 56,000, over a third of them immigrants. Land and labor could not make up for the lack of capital to enable wine makers to produce quality vintages. High production but poor quality wines restricted distribution and consumption to a regional market. A different type of immigrant pattern occurred to the east. Philanthropist Baron Maurice Hirsh established Jewish agricultural colonies in Santa Fé and Entre Rios provinces. By 1914 the baron had resettled some 25,000 Russian Jews in his colonies, and an equal number came on their own.

Export agriculture required an economy of scale that could be achieved by large holdings and sufficient capital. After 1880, large estancias emerged in the newly opened areas. Politicians and their families, those with useful ties and money, monopolized the land. Speculators snapped up land certificates originally sold to finance the Indian campaign and used them to acquire land. Rising commodity prices virtually guaranteed success. Wealth and influence ensured that railways would be provided. As the commercialization accelerated, many small operators abandoned agriculture.

Holders of prime agricultural land remained predominately Argentine. In 1914 foreigners made up only 4.4 percent of rural landowners, concentrated mostly in specialty agriculture such as vineyards (62 percent). Good agricultural land with transportation links to export points could not be purchased easily or cheaply. Land availability changed as family holdings gave way to management companies and indirect ownership, thus avoiding fragmentation among heirs. The government, more interested in stimulating export production than in creating yeoman farmers, made little effort to reserve land for immigrants. Small farms of approximately 125 acres numbered around 180,000 in 1895, some 60 percent of them worked by their owners.

Land use became more intensive. Most of the good land close to the coast had been appropriated in large blocks during the nineteenth century. Land on both sides of railways also transferred in large blocks. Prime land in Buenos Aires Province sold for £10,000 a square league (equivalent to three miles in length squared), falling in price as one moved further into the interior to £300 and lower a square league. Money bought proximity to railways and access to ports and provided operating capital and political influence.

The *Sociedad Rural Argentina* (SRA), established in 1866 to represent large landholders, lobbied for unrestricted immigration of agricultural labor in order to take advantage of what seemed an ever-expanding demand. The government created distribution facilities for foreign labor and in 1910 built a large, well-equipped hotel to receive new immigrants. Less admirably, it forced steamship companies to raise return fares to Europe by 100 percent to slow the number of returnees; referred to as swallows (*golondrinas*) because of their tendency to return to their original nesting place. Some swallows harvested crops in Europe, then did the same in South America, taking advantage of the reversed seasons.

The cities offered immigrants a chance to prosper. Foreigners owned the bulk of urban property, and their offspring dominated industrial activity, commerce, and urban activities in general. Immigrant-driven urbanization followed the course of the river from Buenos Aires to Rosario. The census of 1909 indicated that in Buenos Aires immigrants and their descendents owned two-thirds of urban property. The same held true in secondary cities. In Rosario, for example, foreigners controlled 62 percent of urban property. Nevertheless, cities functioned more as agricultural processing centers and exporting points rather than as independent commercial or industrial hubs.

Industrialists, a large percentage of first- and second-generation citizens, remained a weak interest group. Their association, the *Union Industrial,* unsuccessfully pressed the government to subsidize immigration of skilled workers who could introduce immediately new technology and the latest production methods. While urban employers complained about shortages of skilled labor, the flow of unskilled workers made it possible to break strikes. Railway companies imported workers from Spain and Italy with strike breaking in mind.

The oligarchy failed to consider the consequences of drawing a large numbers of immigrants into a socially restricted and politically static system. They did not make sufficient room for those they enticed into the country. Moreover, as technology reduced the need for rural labor, immigrants filled the cities, creating two very different Argentinas.

EXPORT BOOM

Rising living standards in Europe led to increased food consumption and meat shortages. Grain production began its ascent to record levels. In 1900, two million tons of wheat entered the market, making Argentina one of the world's largest cereal exporters. Wool became a major export commodity as flocks spread into Patagonia. By 1900, 100,000 tons of wool supplied the international market as merino sheep and mixtures displaced less productive breeds. At the turn of the century 75 million sheep made Argentina's flock second only to that of Australia. Replacement of the semi-wild cattle that roamed the Pampas by Hereford and Angus breeds provided more useable meat at better prices and stimulated stronger demand. New grasses, in particular alfalfa, increased growth rates. The size of the herd decreased, while production reached record levels.

Steamships made it possible to ship live cattle across the Atlantic, but disease limited the trade. In 1883 the English owned River Plate Fresh Meat Company shipped 7,500 frozen sheep to London, beginning a new export stage. Railways and the telegraph kept the flow of cattle and sheep constant, avoiding any scarcity that might idle meatpacking facilities or jeopardize the European market. By 1905 Argentina displaced the United States as the leading supplier of beef to the European market. Chilled beef, introduced in 1908, made it possible to preserve taste and export better quality meat. Exporters also began to compete in the mutton trade. In 1911 record exports of mutton and lamb to Britain made Argentine second only to New Zealand in volume, although Buenos Aires shipped mainly mutton. British breeds introduced in Argentina, such as the Lincoln, produced a preferred taste. Argentine exporters maintained a consistently reliable flow to the market and maintained meat cold storage facilities in various locations in England. In addition, they employed their own agents to handle distribution. Attention to detail and pricing allowed them to capture and hold market share.[7]

Chilled meat required rapid ocean transportation in order to reach European retail markets no later than 40 days after slaughter. Space on refrigerator ships had to be reserved in advance and processing as well as loading coordinated to meet schedules and fully utilize cargo capacity. British and German vessels that provided most of the transportation required at least 30 days to reach England, with stops along the coast of South America. After the ocean crossing only a week to ten days remained to distribute and sell to consumers. Freezing or canning, much less time dependent, met a different market with its own problems and peculiarities. In 1912, 4,333 ocean going vessels entered Argentine ports. Refrigerator and cargo ships, modern meatpacking and freezing plants (*frigorificos*), and grain storage facilities represented the export extension of the railway system.

By 1913 the country's per capita income slightly exceeded that of France, Germany, and the Netherlands, while far outpacing that of Italy, Spain, and other parts of southern and eastern Europe. Argentina trailed behind Britain. Somewhat overlooked, but a future indicator, the country lagged behind the United States and Australia. Equally significant, overseas meat and cereal demand unbalanced economic development. Manufacturing, with a small domestic market and subject to import competition, fell far behind. World War I import substitution did not develop sufficient momentum to move towards a reasonable balance between manufacturing and agriculture. Between 1913 and 1920 industrial output remained static.

BANKING AND SPECULATION

Banking constituted a weak reed in the preservation and allocation of capital. Almost immediately after the overthrow of Rosas, the Banco de la Provincia de Buenos Aires opened with the exclusive right to issue bank notes. In 1858, the Brazilian entrepreneur Baron Mauá established the *Banco Mauá* in Buenos Aires. He opened branches throughout the country and issued bank notes (notes backed by the bank that circulated as money) in the provinces. Mauá made short-term-loans and invested in land, industrial enterprises, and discounted commercial paper. Suspicion of Brazilian influence in the region marred Mauá's success and made it difficult to take full advantage of the services his bank offered.

With the arrival in 1862 of J.H. Green with two boxes of gold doubloons, letters of credit, and some account books, the London River Plate Bank began operations. When it opened in January 1863, it became the first British joint-stock bank in Latin America. The British bank avoided government loans, preferring nonpolitical commercial business, much to the displeasure of provincial governments. In 1872 the *Banco Nacional,* capitalized with 50 million pesos, offered financial services. The success of the *Banco Italiano del Río de la Plata* (1882) encouraged others to establish operations in Argentina, including French, Spanish and German institutions.

Inadequate and incomplete regulations that varied by province made banking excessively political. It could be highly profitable, but that could change overnight. Rapacious bank directors and politicians turned domestic banks into vehicles for speculation and uncontrolled emission of paper currency. A notorious example, the Banco de la Provincia de Santa Fé, controlled and protected from competition, functioned as a revenue source for the province and its political leaders. Always on the verge of insolvency, only to be propped up with new privileges, it misdirected and diverted capital, and hindered the efficient distribution of funds.

The suspension of the peso's gold convertibility in 1885 eliminated the metallic backing of the Argentine currency. Debts denominated in gold had to be met with a depreciated currency, requiring increasing amounts of paper money and exports to bring in hard currency. Nevertheless, the problem appeared manageable as new land came into production. The amount of land under grain cultivation increased from 580,008 hectares in 1872 to 2,459,120 in 1888, still only a small percentage of the country's potential. Coupled with increasing meat and wool exports, the financial future of the country appeared assured, but in the short-term the debt had to be serviced.

The difficulty of matching uncertain cash flows with concrete debt required luck and timing. Reckless gambles on the future, the government's inability to act independently of its oligarchic constituency, willing foreign investors attracted by high interest rates and unrestrained speculation by foreign and domestic banks proved a fatal combination. In Buenos Aires, London, Paris, and Berlin few considered the obvious— that market-dependent revenues could not reliably service fixed debts. Exports, imports, excise taxes, port fees, and land sales provided revenues that sagged or soared along with economy. A financial crisis and default became a possibility.

The development process accelerated as the central pampas, free of hostile Indians after the military campaign (1878–1879), would be configured into large commercial agriculture holdings that required investments in infrastructure. The cost of developing virgin land depended upon borrowed capital. Readily available money led to land speculation. Rather than paying down debts, profits and loan proceeds went into speculative land purchases.

In a burst of premature confidence, the government began construction of impressive civic buildings. Wealthy individuals indulged in mansions, polo horses, and European refinements appropriate for Paris or the French

Riviera. Many maintained European residences and spent almost as much time in France as on their estates. Extravagance made possible by the fruits of commercial agriculture led to the popular saying in Europe that an individual appeared to be as "rich as an Argentine." Successful agricultural enterprises generated wealth as well as status.

The promise of grandeur appeared to make all other considerations mere technicalities. What better way to make the point than participation in the Paris Universal Exposition of May 6, 1889; the year of the Centennial of the French Revolution. President Juárez Celman rejected any idea of sharing a pavilion with other Latin American republics. A planning committee constituted in 1886 included members of the SRA, appropriate government officials, and representatives of industry and culture. The government appropriated a handsome sum to construct an exhibit structure to impress the world and particularly the French, whose culture the elites embraced as the civilized ideal. A determinedly extravagant Juárez Celman spent a million francs. More mundane considerations, such as expanding the market for chilled beef and stimulating immigration, required that the Argentina Pavilion catch the attention of a broad segment of the public, including the French cultural elite, businessmen, consumers, and potential immigrants and do so in grand manner worthy of a modern, wealthy country.

Argentina opened the exhibit on the country's independence day, May 25. French President Marie François Sadi Carnot, escorted by Argentine Vice President Carlos Pellegrini, toasted Argentina and the ties of friendship between the two republics. Several stirring performances of the *Marseillaise* charged the atmosphere with excitement, overwhelming the more sedate Argentine anthem arranged and orchestrated by French composer Edmund Guion. Visitors entered the pavilion under a gilded statue of a nubile young woman reclining on the back of a bull. The predictable joke that it represented the "Bull *Époque*," surely could not have been resisted. Immediately inside the pavilion another exaggerated female figure represented the fertility of the soil. A plaster map of Argentina emphasized the wide expanse of the country and its limited population waiting to be reinforced by immigrants. Hard by the map an exhibit of frozen carcasses presented a macabre spectacle for those accustomed to confronting their meat covered with a delicate sauce and accompanied by fine wine. Occasionally, samples of cooked beef and mutton attempted to convince finicky chefs of the quality of meat shipped across the Atlantic.

The second floor, accessed by an elegant staircase, provided a view of Argentina's conquest of civilization. Displays of newspapers and literary magazines, photographs of modern mechanical marvels, and specimens of manufactured products, usually of leather, left little doubt that Argentina had a place within the modern world. As the exposition drew to its conclusion the government could take pride in winning a perfect score of 25 points. Even more gratifying, laudatory comments by distinguished visitors appeared to be a public relations triumph. British statesman and former Prime Minister William Gladstone commented to a member of the exposition committee at a banquet in Paris that, "You represent, sir, a country of wonders; your evolution in progress and wealth constitutes one of the phenomena of the present epoch."[8] The image so carefully constructed in the shadow of the Eiffel Tower crashed within the year, almost taking the Bank of England with it.

THE BARING CRISIS

Prosperity based on good harvests and strong overseas markets obscured a dangerous vulnerability. The trade balance did not provide a large enough positive excess over imports to build up sufficiently strong reserves. Moreover, the government directly or indirectly assumed responsibility for a significant proportion of debts managed by others. By 1875, debt servicing absorbed 25 percent of government revenues. Optimism and faith in the future had to be maintained in the face of fixed obligations, fluctuating revenues, bad weather, locusts, and unpredictable overseas economic conditions. Part of the problem came from an inflow of capital that could not be put to work in a productive fashion, but added to the debt burden the moment officials signed the documents. The availability of money stimulated loan activity and encouraged speculation. Foreign capital often underwrote unnecessary expenditures and financed excessive imports. Eventually loans had to be repaid, often at an inconvenient time.

Dependency on the British market emerged indisputably in 1895 when Argentine exports established a long-lasting favorable trade balance with Britain. Spread across its other lesser trading partners however, an overall favorable balance could not be certain. Swings from surplus to deficits made planning problematic. Accumulating sufficient reserves to ride out difficult times or invest in infrastructure without resorting to foreign loans could not be done. Argentina lived on the fiscal edge even during the so-called "golden years." Its international image as an amazing country that had gone from a primitive economy to modern prosperity, with an even greater future in store, jumped the gap between reality and fantasy for both Argentines and overseas investors.

Discounting bills during the periods of high export activity supplied credit to keep the financial system functioning. Deferred payment, usually for ninety days subject to renewal, providing both short-term and long-term options as needed. Mortgages, with loans in gold up to half of the property value for four years at nine percent per year, met some of the heavy credit demands of the export boom in the 1880s. Nevertheless, paper had to be transformed into gold or hard currencies to purchase foreign imports and repay loans.

An 1881 law established a national currency and prohibited the domestic circulation of foreign notes. A handsome five peso gold coin, the *Argentino* symbolically suggested that the country verged on monetary stability.[9] Companion legislation of 1887 attempted to coordinate provincial and national emissions of paper money by requiring provincial banks to buy gold bonds. They could then issue a set amount of paper notes. A subsequent adjustment allowed banks to provide a promissory note rather than actual gold, in effect backing paper with paper.

Foreign investors preferred fixed income rather than direct investments. The willingness of the national and provincial governments to guarantee interest payments made such investments attractive. In addition, two mortgage banks, the *Banco Hipotecario de la Provincia de Buenos Aires* (est.1872), and the *Banco Hipotecario Nacional* (est. 1886) made loans to individuals to buy land in the form of *cédulas* (bearer mortgage bonds) that could be sold to raise actual cash. Cédulas carried interest that could not legally exceed 8 percent, payable by the bank, even in the event the borrower failed to repay the loan. To reassure overseas investors, the government guaranteed interest and return of principal.

As the economy expanded, both in terms of trade, value, and complexity, its vulnerability became greater and more dangerous. European central banks, confident of the strength of their own gold-backed monetary system, and all too willing to believe in an Argentine cornucopia, ignored the warning signs. At some point, a day of reckoning would have to be faced. That moment came with the presidency of Juárez Celman.

President Juárez Celman's expansively impatient personality had a direct impact on events. As he declared, "We transform everything, we want to transform everything . . . we have launched ourselves onto the road of all these transformations and reforms with the unconsciousness of an adolescent who is not afraid of the unknown."[10] Loans made everything possible. From 1885 to 1890 the external debt jumped from 71.1 to 128 million in gold pesos. Sale of government investments in railroads provided more construction money. Buenos Aires began to be transformed into a South American Paris with the foundations laid for some of the city's most notable buildings, including the Colón Theatre.

While costs outpaced the economy's ability to generate revenues, most officials expressed confidence that expenditures could be balanced. New loans paid off old ones; exports, mortgage cédulas, and other sources of revenue brought in hard currency. They assumed that the pattern would continue. Rail lines increased by 60 percent with some 4,150 mile of track added. Construction depended on government guaranteed returns. Railroad guarantees soared from 840,000 gold pesos in 1887 to 2,919,000 in gold by 1890. In addition, the public debt at all levels of government doubled between 1885 and 1890 to some 200,000,000 in gold. By 1890, British investments in the country totaled some £157,000,000, much of it ultimately backed by the government. Juárez Celman gambled that revenues from new land in production would service debts. He lost.

The balance of trade turned negative, with a deficit of 56,000,000 in gold. The gold premium (the spread between gold or gold-backed currencies and Argentine paper money) widened, driving down the value of domestic money. Juárez Celman blamed speculation on the stock exchange (*La Bolsa*) and ordered it closed, shocking financial markets and angering investors. The decision to pay domestic holders of silver-backed peso debt with depreciated paper money came as another blow to investor confidence. After 1889, interest payments in gold exceed proceeds from all sources. The government scrambled to ward off default.

The suspension of restrictions on money in circulation flooded the country with cheap paper. Depositors withdrew their savings, and protesters took to the streets. A run on banks by depositors fortunately failed to bring them down. A decision in 1890 to increase customs duties and collect half the amount in gold and the remainder in paper soon changed to all gold. The price of imports rose sharply. The gold premium, an indicator of the falling value of paper money, reached 151 percent in 1890 and peaked at 257 percent in 1894. The *Banco Nacional* used hard assets to meet short-term European debts, depleting its balance sheet. It would be declared insolvent in 1891. It required recapitalization and reemerged as the *Banco de la Nación Argentina* still in existence. In 1890, more immigrants left than came into the country. Foreign governments worried about their nationals being stranded in acute misery.

The forced resignation of President Juárez Celman in August of 1890 and the assumption of power by Vice-President Carlos Pellegrini indicated the seriousness of the situation. With some £450,000 in gold to meet demands of £7.3 million in gold, the country could not pay its debts. Pellegrini feared a state collapse and anarchy. The government sought a loan to pay existing ones. The condition for such assistance included supervision of the disbursement of loan proceeds by the lending syndicate, no fresh loans for ten years, restricted emissions of paper money, and tight budgets. The government could not agree to such restrictions, particularly the end of cheap paper money that kept the domestic economy afloat. In 1891, with the price of gold continuing to climb, some 30,000 people left the country, but many more had no means of doing so.

Meanwhile, Baring Brothers, with a portfolio loaded with Argentine bonds, some £5,700,000 that could not be sold, faced bankruptcy. The Bank of England feared that Baring's collapse would set off a run on gold. Other financial institutions and stock markets throughout Europe held lesser amounts of Argentine paper. Baring's unraveling constituted the greatest threat to the intra-continental financial system. To shore up reserves in advance, Lord Rothschild transferred £3 million pounds in gold from the Bank of France to the Bank of England, and the Russians purchased Exchequer bonds (British treasury bonds) in exchange for a million and a half in gold. Baring, shored up by a now well-padded Bank of England, liquidated its assets to reemerge under Baring family control by 1896.

Debt moratorium and negotiations that lasted for a decade averted the immediate disaster. The 1893 arrangement required the transfer of 80 percent of export earnings to creditors, an amount that totaled 160,000,000 gold pesos between 1891 and 1900, making Argentina an exporter of capital. In spite of the return of capital to Europe, the national debt in the same period went from 204,000,000 gold pesos to 389,000,000. The assumption of all existing provincial and municipal (mainly those of Buenos Aires Province) foreign debts in exchange for the centralization of finances in the hands of the federal government accounted for much of the increase.

By 1895, land in production reached 4,892,004 hectares and along with rising prices made it possible to look forward to better times. The long anticipated cash flow from new land in production became a reality. In 1899, Argentina went back on the gold standard and internally made paper currency convertible at a fixed rate. The conversion law tied paper to precious metals and established a monetary agency to calibrate the amount of paper in circulation, issuing or withdrawing notes as economic needs required. It worked relatively well until world events provided the pretext for a return to a depreciating paper currency.

Debt servicing of the £74 million debt in the 1900s required almost 4 million in gold, apart from the dividends on railways and other claims on hard currency. Coal imports from Britain alone required over 3 million British pounds a year. Britain, Germany, the United States, France, and Italy (in the order of value of imports), and a long list of smaller markets supplied the country. In 1906, imports cost £53,994,104, balanced by exports of £58,450,766, rendering a surplus of ´£4,456,662—not sufficient to cover capital outflows. Even in a good year such as 1908, the cost of imports amounted to £54,594,547 while exports earned £73,201,068, rendering a surplus of £18,706,521 before debt servicing, dividends, foreign remittances, and other outflows. From 1862 to 1908, a positive balance of exports over imports occurred in only 22 of the 36 years, and even then in some cases just barely.[11] In 1907, for example, a little over 2 million surplus had to meet demands far in excess of that token amount.

Nevertheless, once again the demands of the international markets appeared to be insatiable. Exports jumped by 500 percent in the period between the recovery and 1912. The First Bank of Boston and the City Bank of New York (now Citibank) opened branches in Buenos Aires in

1910. On the surface all seemed well. A prideful lift to the once again confident modernizers came with the opening of Latin America's first subway in 1914, one of only thirteen in the world, with tiled stations and elegant wooden cars that connected the Plaza de Mayo with a rapidly changing city.

THE GREAT ESTANCIAS

At the heart of a modern estancia lay the luxurious country house. The estancia of Ramón Lopez de Alzaga in the 1920s, located just over an hour from Buenos Aires, presented a model. Turning off the main road one entered a forest of eucalyptus trees, drove past a walled area of formal gardens, and then, some five hundred feet further an impressive iron gate opened to two mansions, referred to as chateaus. Ornate towers, arched entryways, and mullioned windows suggested France's Loire valley. Señor Lopéz de Alzaga, dressed in gray flannel trousers cut to fit over handmade leather riding boots and a tailored herringbone tweed jacket over a white linen shirt open at the neck, could have been easily taken for an English lord of the manor or a banker relaxing on his rural estate. A red scarf, worn under a narrow brimmed, low crowned hat in the gaucho style, provided an Argentine touch. Don Ramón mentioned that "we Argentines love France." Predictably, the family maintained a home just outside Paris, often spending several months in Europe. Elaborating further, he noted that most of the large landholders spoke French, and that in his family they customarily hired British nannies in order to teach English to the children. Luxury overlaid and obscured their important administrative function. Not idle or absentee rent seekers, for all their personal wealth and pretensions, they constituted a managing class of commercial agricultural operations.

The agricultural oligarchy understood the importance of technology. Imported machinery from the United States and Europe had a ready market. El Condor, a southern estancia of 337,500 acres and 160,000 sheep, had 40 steam shearers, hydraulic presses, and heated sheep dips. Breeding stock purchased in Europe became a competitive status symbol. In the early 1900s, an American machine pulled by four horses, able to reap and thrash and then grade the grain and sack all in one operation made for an efficient harvest. Domestic farm machinery manufacturers also supplied estancias with more traditional items The *Anales* of the Sociedad Rural Argentina and innumerable magazines in Spanish, English, and French brought the latest agricultural findings and methods to their attention.

Nevertheless, large holdings could not be completely or intensely worked. Such economic reality lay behind the land law of 1907 that specified that one person could not own more that 6,170 acres. Easily circumvented, the law had little impact other than to express an ideal. Estanceiros preferred to rent to tenant farmers at a fixed rate for a limited time rather than sell excess property, or better yet attract share croppers obligated to spilt the harvest retaining from 50 down to 30 percent and deliver the rest to the land owner.

Land concentration and the wealth and influence it generated reached its zenith prior to 1930. The sheer size of estancias challenged the imagination. To grasp the size it should be kept in mind that a field of 12,000 acres would be four mile wide and four and a half miles long, and one of 50,000 acres seven miles wide and eleven miles long.[12] San Jacinto, one of the nation's largest estancias, comprised 244 square miles. Of this amount, 64 square miles planted in Lucerne (alfalfa) supported 100,000 Durham cattle, 100,000 sheep and 10,000 horses. The estancia San Juan, 25 miles from Buenos Aires, close to La Plata, covered 40 square miles of carefully tended meadows. Most estancias mixed animal breeding with supplying animals for the market and grain crops. The San Martín occupied some 30 square miles. It established a reputation for breeding draught horses— Clydesdales, Morgans, Hackneys, and Shires—to pull heavy machinery and the high-wheeled carts in the fields, as well as to transport production to the railway station. The San Martín also bred pedigreed Lincoln and Negrete rams and Yorkshire pigs, in addition to supplying most of Buenos Aires' milk and butter.

Carlos Casares' Estancia Huetel, some 150 miles from Buenos Aires on the Southern Railway, covered 240 square miles all enclosed with barbwire fencing. Subdivided into 42 units with 57 shepherd houses and 5 managers, it raised 62,000 cattle, 87,000 sheep and 4,200 Clydesdale horses. The estancia maintained its own school. One of its bulls, Aguinaldo, won the first prize ever awarded by the Sociedad Rural Argentina (SRA). La Vizcaina consisted of 183 square miles with the advantage of two railway stations on its land and another several miles away. Smaller specialty estates that did not merit the title of a gran estancia, such as that of Gregorio Villafañe (only 18,000 acres) raised breeding bulls and rams, collie dogs, fox terriers, and chickens.

To the south companies owned much of the land. The Patagonian Sheep and Farming Company covered some 734 square miles. Another estancia of 1,060 square miles belonged (1911) to the Bank of Antwerp. In Chubut and Río Negro, the Argentine Southern Land Company held some million and a half acres only partially in production.

A rough law of transportation governed the cultivation of crops and determined what would be grown or whether an estancia concentrated on livestock for beef, mutton, wool, or hides. Access to waterways or a rail line constituted the minimum, but the expense of transportation required that lower value products could be no more than 200 miles from loading to the final destination, a port or urban processor. Moreover, the nearest railway station had to be within 18 to 25 miles of the estancia. Few crops could absorb higher costs and still return a profit. Argentine exports had to compete with other sources, limiting the pricing power of producers. Nevertheless, cost controls, production, transportation efficiencies, and low-wage labor rendered a handsome profit for well-managed operations. Return on capital ranged from 13 to 16 percent.[13] All of which explains the pressure put on the government to guarantee railway bonds and a plentiful supply of labor.

CHAPTER 3

Urban Reality

Internal demands for everyday products created a market. Small-scale industries produced items of indifferent quality but at inexpensive prices to meet the needs of price-dependent consumers. Before the arrival of railways, the interior enjoyed a market inaccessible to foreign goods. Many engaged in local or regional trade with Chile, Bolivia, and Paraguay.

Railways made national distribution possible for a wide range of products and opened up the interior to competition from foreign goods. An 1877 tariff benefited regional agricultural items, as well as manufacturers of inexpensive shoes, textiles, and other consumer goods. The sugar industry in 1876 received the privilege of importing duty free machinery. Sugar plantations relied upon Indian labor recruited in the Chaco, paid at 2.5 pesos daily in scrip to be used in the company store. Ill-paid, exploited plantation workers provided an involuntary subsidy for domestic producers and consumers.

Initially, manufacturing tended to be labor intensive and relatively small-scale. Immigrant entrepreneurs founded and operated small firms. With success, they often adopted the management model of commercial agriculture with the family holding shares. Indirect ownership tended to broaden the focus of an enterprise encouraging diversification. Conglomerates, not necessarily efficient, provided more economic security for extended family members.

Agriculturalists believed that their activities represent the country's "natural industry," while manufacturing appeared to be an "artificial" activity. Only with World War I. and the depression following the crash of 1929 did this give way, but even then not entirely. The army saw the utility of an independent industrial base. They thought in terms of national security, however, not competition or profits. In 1895, a National Buying Act required the army to buy domestic products of equal price and quality to foreign goods, creating a market for domestic production of uniforms, blankets, and footwear. Establishing compulsory military service in 1901, implemented the following year, expanded that market considerably. Tariff policy selectively, but not systematically, offered some encouragement to manufacturers. A 1905 law set custom duties, but revenue concerns, not tariff protection, provided the impulse. Nevertheless, industrial production grew at an annual rate of seven percent between 1900 and 1913, but from a small base that depended on foreign inputs. Imports, including manufactured goods, rose by a similar amount.

In the initial stages of industrialization, characterized by under-capitalized small-scale industry, makeshift machinery, poorly designed buildings and a tendency to cut corners, workers labored under marginal conditions. Dust, chemical fumes, stench, and dangerous solvents assaulted the health of workers. Packinghouse floors covered with blood, entrails, and excrement made for ghastly work. Men who carried meat to the freezers covered their faces and hands with rags or old newspapers so that the fresh blood would not freeze on their bodies. Rheumatism disabled many packinghouse workers within five years. Child labor resulted in prematurely aged and wizened children. Employers, accustomed to the grim reality of factory life, demonstrated little concern for the health and comfort of their employees. The work-week varied, but was seldom less than fifty hours. Juan Bialet Masse (1904) reported to the Interior Ministry that employers could not understand that better working conditions made for more productive employees and avoided the social problem of exhausted and physically depleted workers. Industrialists dismissed labor legislation as the "ranting of Socialist professors in Buenos Aires who don't know what a factory or an industry is."[1]

Most workers inhabited slum tenements (*conventillos*) without plumbing or kitchens. Food had to be cooked on kerosene stoves or pans of hot coals set in the middle of the floor. The absence of sewers and the use of out-houses made disease a constant hazard and resulted in a perpetual foul odor. In the closed conditions of conventillos tuberculosis became a constant threat. Disease carriers infected others at work, in the tenements, and in the neighborhood; consequently, between 1869 and 1912, more people of all ages died from this disease than any other. In the nineteenth century, an estimated seven to fifteen percent of Buenos Aires' population died from tuberculosis. In 1883, one fifth of the capital's population lived in extremely poor conditions. In 1904, statistics indicated that 70 percent of Buenos Aires' inhabitants rented accommodations. Side streets became dusty or muddy, depending on the season. Horse-drawn vehicles added manure to the foul mix. Rotting garbage littered the unpaved streets, attended to by scavenging hogs, dogs, and chickens. Potholes collected refuse and filled with stagnant water, supporting mosquitoes and a plague of rats. Dead animals, particularly horses, remained to decompose after being torn apart by packs of dogs.

Conditions in secondary cities mirrored those in the capital. In Córdoba, municipal officials counted 2,041 rooms housing 6,494 individuals, without sanitary facilities or adequate ventilation. Flop houses (*fondines*) in close proximity to railway stations provided impoverish newcomers with shelter, with some ten to twelve individuals in a room. Men in small groups loitered outside sharing information about jobs available in the local area or perhaps further down the rails.

Industrial accidents and illness jeopardized families' survival. The marginal resources of urban workers did not allow for the unexpected. In a sample case, a worker with a family of four and employed as a common laborer in a glass factory earned 100 pesos a month. The family's expenses amounted to 107 a month (18 for rent, 53 for food, 20 for clothes, 6 for coal, and 10 for miscellaneous). Fortunately, a son earned 20 pesos a month as a messenger boy, leaving 13 pesos for emergencies.[2] In the four-year period between 1908 and 1912, 446 workers in Buenos Aires died in factory accidents. Those injured or incapacitated numbered in the thousands. Until 1915 employers could not be held responsible for accidents, and even after that date compensation did not replace lost income.

In rural areas conditions differed but presented their own hardships. Low wages, payment in script, inadequate food, and conditions of semi-servitude could all be found. Only an enlightened minority of employers paid reasonable wages. As one moved into the interior, wages dropped, encouraging people to move to Buenos Aires or other settlements. Internal migration joined with fresh inflows of immigrants, child labor, and low-paid female labor moderated wages and created a floating labor pool.

THE NATIVIST PERSUASION

Around 1905, philosophical support for mass immigration reached its zenith, slowly reversed, became ambivalent, then hostile. As the numbers of immigrants increased, they became increasingly urban. Hard working individuals became businessmen, manufacturers, and shopkeepers. Italians dominated the commercial and industrial sectors in Buenos Aires. In 1887, Italian immigrants owned a little over half of all industrial companies in the city and one third of commercial businesses. Including the first and second generation, Italians controlled the capital's economic activity. An extensive mutual aid network that included the Italian hospital, clinics, employment assistance, and other benefits supported the community. Newspapers, banks, and the membership of the

Club Italiano constituted a potential political base. Most Italian immigrants came from the entrepreneurial north and brought assets as well as organizational ability with them. They employed many of their compatriots, who between first and second generation workers made up well over 50 percent of industrial workers.

Spanish immigrants, collectively called *Gallegos,* generally came from impoverished Galicia, with language ties closer to Portugal immediately to the south. Unskilled Gallego labor concentrated in poorly paid, disagreeable jobs. *Gallegas* (females) provided a significant percentage of maids and domestic servants. They delighted in reminding Argentines that they had once been Spanish subjects. Critics portrayed them as doltish country bumpkins of limited intelligence—certainly not a social challenge. Gallegos became and to some extent remain the butt of exaggerated jokes. Unfamiliar groups considered less European encountered social suspicion and hostility. Syrian and Lebanese, collectively called *Turcos* because of their association with the Ottoman Empire, generally avoided rural areas and preferred street vending until they could afford a permanent retail store. Russian Jews and Volga Germans, both groups fleeing the oppressive Russian Empire, met with similar ambivalence.

Social criticism attempted to turn the immigrant virtues of hard work and thrift into less worthy materialism. Several immigrant groups allegedly acquired wealth with little patriotic concern for Argentina. Immigrant success stories, such as that of Gallego Santamarina, who arrived as a stowaway, landed in Buenos Aires penniless, eventually bought his own wagon for transporting wool, and then purchased some sheep and land, received mixed approval. He left a large fortune and the baronial Estancia of Tandril. Another tale of two Neapolitans who started with a *boliche* (a marginal bar) and parted company because the establishment could not support more than one, ended with the loser striking it rich in the commodity trade. These stories, apocryphal or not, implied that Argentina provided opportunity, but for the native born, immigrants could never quite give enough back in return.

Manuel Gálvez's books harped on the immigrant's repugnant materialism verging on greed, that supposedly corrupted the collective soul of Argentina. The financial collapse of 1890 would be blamed by many on Jewish speculators and to a lesser extent on Italians. Scapegoating and denigration served to push immigrants psychologically into their place. Crime and radical politics (Socialism and Anarchism) served the same purpose. To the more refined, Buenos Aires' rising crime rate constituted an immigrant problem. An Italian always had "his inseparable steel knife, his volcanic temperament and his excitable aggressive passions."[3] Subsequently, in 1924 an anti-Italian screed, *La Italianización de la Argentina,* by Carlos Néstor Macial, gathered all the poisonous bile together. Few mentioned the gaucho's ever-present long dagger, the *facón.*

Argentines, anxious to define the essence of the nation, decided that it resided in the interior, where the Hispanic heritage supposedly still could be found. Nobility of spirit and mind, idealism, and a refined sense of honor allegedly constituted their true inheritance. They believed that foreigners should be encouraged to become nationalized as a means of culturally integrating them. Yet, at the same time they remained suspicious of the immigrant's true loyalties. The fear that pseudo Argentines might take power lay behind the ambivalence to foreigners who adopted native ways. The common stereotype of the *Italiano acriollado* (Argentinized Italian) captured the ambivalence. An Italian who tried to be more Argentine than the natives became a stock character on the music hall stage.

Miguel Cané, a politician, diplomat, and one of the founding members of the Jockey Club, suddenly appreciated the allegedly servile mestizo population. He lamented the replacement of "the old and faithful servants like those I saw in early youth in my parents' home" by Europeans. Cané complained that the immigrant servants "rob us . . . dress better than we do and remind us of his status as a free man if one scarcely reprimands him."[4]

Journalists and others commented on the riffraff that inhabited the city; unsavory vagrants, the obviously deranged "crazy immigrant," and those engaged in disgusting forms of antisocial behavior. Their poor command of Spanish and use of *cocoliche* (a mixture of Italian and Spanish) and urban slang called *lunfardo*, which drew its vocabulary from various languages, set the urban lower class suspiciously apart. In 1922, Dr. Francico Veyga, employed by the police department, suggested a proactive locking up of all urban degenerates before they committed their inevitable criminal acts.[5]

Prostitution and the trade in women, inevitably became connected with immigration. The high percentage of males to females presented a business opportunity for the unscrupulous. Between 1857 and 1924, unattached young men made up 70 percent of immigrants. Buenos Aires authorities legalized bordellos, imposing some restrictions such as the prohibition of one less than two blocks from a school, and collected various fees. La Boca (the rough waterfront), filled with bars, wharves, and sailors, became the most notorious red light district. Unlicensed madams and pimps gathered, "hordes of prostitutes in furnished houses, hotels and directed their activities in the streets, theatres and public by ways."[6] Even the alleged nature of foreign prostitutes could be used against immigrants. Criminologist Eusebio Gómez claimed that native-born prostitutes had noble traits and true love for their clients, while foreign ones seemed emotionless. Given the high percentage of immigrants, foreigners made up the majority of pickpockets, thieves, pimps, muggers, beggars, and drunks.

Radicalism, equated with violence and foreigners, provided more fuel for anti-immigrant rhetoric, as well as justification for restrictive, repressive action. Skilled workers preferred Socialist unions, while the unskilled drifted towards Anarchism. Employers blamed outside agitators who infected workers with an allegedly European virus. By the 1890s, embattled employers confronted a militant working force. Thirty-five major strikes occurred between 1895 and 1896. Socialist railway workers paralyzed rail transportation for several weeks in 1896. The final straw came with the massive general strike of 1902. Anarchist workers carefully timed the general strike to cripple wheat exports.

President Julio A. Roca, alarmed at the threat to the country's international credit, called legislators into special session. Congress declared a state of siege, conferring emergency police power to put down the strike, then went on to pass the Residency Law of 1902. The law empowered the president to order the deportation of individuals believed a threat to national security or public order, or who had a criminal record before arriving in the country.

Nevertheless, violent strikes continued. In January 1907, 150,000 workers participated in a general strike. Two years later some 200,000 workers walked out to protest police violence. The government used 5,000 troops, heavily armed police, and mass arrests to break the strike. Special mounted units composed of mestizos and Indians from the interior proved effective in dealing with demonstrations by foreign workers. Ramon L. Falcón, Buenos Aires Police Chief, despised for his brutal suppression of strikers, died at the hands of a young Russian immigrant. The assassin, Simón Radowitzky, spent the next twenty-one years in semi-isolation, a caged monument to the notion that Anarchism constituted a contagious disease. Many feared that the country verged on social disintegration.

The apparently impossible situation on the eve of the centennial of Argentina's independence in 1910 dismayed the elite. The celebration, designed to impress the world with the country's amazing progress in the hundred years since the break with Spain, instead promised to be an embarrassment. Highly publicized disorders might scare off foreign investors, damage the perception of the country as a reliable food supplier, and lead to restrictions by governments on immigration. Anarchist groups announced their plans for yet another general strike to mark the centennial moment. An enraged congress responded by declaring a state of siege. On May 14, the police, joined by a citizen militia including politicians and elite members, sacked and burned Anarchist and Socialist offices and newspapers. Arrests and summary deportations followed. The next evening, vigilantes roamed through the capital's Russian district. Within a month a bomb exploded in the Colon Opera house, injuring several people. The police arrested a Russian Anarchist for planting the device. An outraged country demand protection—congress responded with the

Social Defense Law (1910) that prohibited the entrance of Anarchists and anyone who advocated the use of violence or assassination. It outlawed Anarchist meetings and demonstrations, regulated explosives, and provided for fines and penalties for steamship companies that allowed such people to embark. Immediate expulsion of those believed to pose a threat to order completed the law's sweeping provisions.

Continuing fears that embarrassing disruptions would mar commemorative events led to bouts of national hysteria. Political exclusion of immigrants seemed prudent to many in spite of constitutional provisions that guaranteed foreigners full protection of the law. The law enfranchised nationalized males without property or literacy qualifications, raising fears that radical immigrants might capturing control of the state. In reality, electoral law included provisions to discourage political fragmentation. A simple plurality in an electoral district took all the seats contested. The complete list (*lista completa*) made it difficult for small parties to elect deputies. In spite of the reaction to violence, immigrants did not endanger the government.

FROM NATIVIST TO NATIONALIST

The search for a sense of identity had contradictory strands. One focused on the a need to knit all classes and social groups together, including first and second generation Argentines, through recognition of a common national experience. It posited the existence of a spiritual nationalism able to unite all those willing to embrace *Argentinidad*—a psychological acceptance that did not depend on place of birth. Immigrants could choose to shed old loyalties and adopt those of their new country. That notion conflicted with one that blamed immigrants for the destruction of the old culture's traditions and values.

To those that lamented the passing of the Creole nation, the task required distinguishing Argentines from immigrants and identifying virtues on one side and assigning vices on the other. Following the resumption of relations between Argentina and the Vatican in 1857, nativists and subsequently Nationalists could draw on a powerful depository of tradition. In the *Syllabus of Errors* (1864) Pope Pius IX rejected progress and modern civilizations as false doctrines. In the 1890s the papal encyclical *Rerum Novarum* (1891) refurbished the concept of class harmony based on traditional paternalism and concern for the well being of the working class while supporting a hierarchical social structure. In 1903, the journal *Ideas* and, subsequently, *Nostros* in 1908, offered assurance that an almost vanished Argentina could be resurrected. Manuel Gálvez, a founding member of *Ideas*, noted that the foreign atmosphere of Argentina had not extinguished history. The colonial cities of Córdoba, Salta, Santiago de Estero, and others nurtured the spirit of Argentina's past, which could be employed to restore the Creole nation. Moreover, the efforts of Federalist caudillos to resist centralism and foreign influences had to be honored and understood. Liberalism, with its controlling centralism, thrust aside Hispanic municipal traditions and local government and transferred authority away from the people to liberal reformers. In his work *El Diario de Gabriel Quiroga: Opiniones sobre la vida Argentina* (1910), Gálvez noted that the Unitarios represented liberalism, pro-European and anti-Spanish. In contrast, the Federalists had a sense of the country's value without the desire to transform it by discarding its history and traditions. Gálvez defined emotional and cultural attachments as the true elements of the Argentine character, which when combined became Nationalism. Gálvez played a key role in the invention of Argentine Nationalism.

In 1909, Ricardo Rojas published *La restauración nacionalista* (The Nationalist Restoration), calling for a return to Creole values. Rojas attacked the influence of Buenos Aires and prophetically observed that future generations would have to decide between liberal progress imposed by foreigners or civilization that rested on the country's traditions and past. Carlos Ibarguren, another important Nationalist with provincial roots in Salta, lamented the brushing aside of the old native aristocracy that combined the best of religion, honor, and tradition for acceptance of a cosmopolitanism devoid of spirituality. In a series of lectures at Buenos Aires' Odeon Theater in 1913, poet Leopoldo Lugones (1874–1938) idealized the gaucho and the *payador* (storyteller) of the pampas as the true embodiment of the national character. He pitted the gaucho's legendary physical stamina against the overly civilized genes of Europe. Lugones eloquently scolded those that collaborated in the gauchos' disappearance as heedless of the loss of a central element of nationality. His lectures appeared as a book in 1916 with the title of *El Payador* (the storyteller). Carlos O. Bunge, previously given to denigration of mestizos as lazy, now joined in the rehabilitation of the gaucho as loyal, courageous, and patriotic. The 1926 novel by Ricardo Guiraldes, *Don Segundo Sombra*, completed the process of creating the gaucho archetype. Nostalgic cultural nationalism accepted the notion that when all the current racial amalgamation ended, the gaucho's spirit would remain.

The two poles of the Nationalist message had their manifestations in the mythologized Gaucho at one extreme and the stereotyped immigrant at the other. With the collapse of Rosas as their base, Nationalists interpreted events to re-enforce their reactionary message of resentment and cultural betrayal. They spoke to a broad audience that had been jarred by various aspects of change. Prosperity fell on the nation and on the different classes in an uneven pattern. The export economy and its wealth did not spread across the social structure but created sharp regional and class disparities. Several different Argentinas in various stages of development rubbed against each other. Nationalists' influence remained symptomatic of the troubled connection between the export economy and the society that depended on it but did not share equally in its fruits. People moved in and out of the realm of resentment and insecurity, depending on their circumstances and their level of confidence in the nation's course.

Nationalists often came from provincial families who perceived that they had lost economic and social ground after 1853. They emerged as an identifiable group with a recognizable core of proponents, yet they remained dependent on the fluctuating economic and psychological state of the nation. As a result, they never attracted a sufficiently large, stable constituency to become more than a movement. Nevertheless, the evolution from uncomplicated nativists to Nationalists had been completed by the outbreak of World War I. The economic shocks of the 1920s and 1930s convinced many others of the validity of Nationalists' complaints. Under post-1914 stresses, Nationalism became a semi-paranoid, inward, and bitter movement. Imperialism, imposed economic dependency, and other evils replaced the immigrant as the focus of the Nationalist movement.

A MYTHICAL CULTURE RIDES TO AN IMAGINARY RESCUE

The need to psychologically strengthen the concept of a nation required identifying elements of a unique culture that bound all together. Independence and the struggle between Federalists and Unitarios damaged continuity. The Unitarios, now reluctant Federalists, consigned all that went before, from independence to 1852, to historical oblivion as a dark age of barbarism. Even the Viceroyalty of La Plata, established in the twilight of empire in 1776 and which implanted liberalism, served only as a territorial template. Subsequently immigration submerged the frontier experience under layers of progress. Many wondered if Argentines shared a nationality. They looked to culture to place themselves in a national context. Cultural history had sufficient material to be reinterpreted, starting with *Gauchesca* literature.

Created by writers in Buenos Aires, *Gauchesca* literature appeared at the very end of the eighteenth century. Its practitioners considered themselves to be boldly departing from traditional literary forms. Written in verse, Gauchesca literature reproduced an urban version of the speech patterns and language of the pampas. It relied upon the tradition of *cantar opinando* (to sing a story) to give a voice to the marginal elements and their complaints. It would be recognized as a distinct literary form in the early 1900s.

Composers also appropriated music and placed it in modern form—not authentic but inspired by what they saw as traditional. Francisco Hargreaves composed his *Aires nacionales* (1880) for the piano, drawing on songs and dances of the interior. In a similar fashion Alberto Williams composed over 50 piano pieces in his *Aires de la pampa* in the last decade of the nineteenth century and into the twentieth. He incorporated the gaucho dance the *malambo*, into his *Primera Sonata Argentina*, Opus 74, written for the piano in 1917. Songs and dance melodies collected and arranged by Julian Aguirre (1868–1924) conveyed some of the emotional richness of the interior and opened the way for the tango songs of Carlos Gardel. Folk music arranged for the piano and orchestra, modified and Europeanized, suggested a font of inspiration in the heart of a vanishing Argentina, The process, similar to that which modernized gypsy melodies, used the rural interior to build a Europeanized modification suitable for city dwellers.

Cultural nativists, in the face of the immigration and urbanization, seized upon the gaucho. José Fernández's (1834–1886) epic poem, *El Gaucho Martín Fierro*, published in 1872 and 1879, provided a positive counterpoint to Sarmiento's *Civilization and Barbarism* (1845), which recounted the alleged vices of Creole Argentina. In contrast, Fernández chronicled the gaucho's heart rending but losing battle with the so-called civilized barbarism of governments and the emerging agricultural oligarchy. The gaucho as a romantic symbol arose from an urban reality that robbed life of romance. Journalist and writer Eduardo Gutiérrez's (1853–1890) semi-fictional *Juan Moreira* depicted the gaucho's life as a lost but heroic struggle against civilized progress. Dramatization of *Juan Moreira* marked the beginning of a distinctive Argentine theater performed before an audience anxious for roots.

Felipe Boero (1884–1958) composed operas with Spanish librettos. His first opera, *Tucumán*, premiered in 1918 at the Teatro Colon, winning the Municipal Prize. Boero had earlier won the Ministry of Culture's *Premio Europa*, which enabled him to study in Paris (1912–1914). Influenced by Modernism, he discovered the spirit of Creole Argentina while studying at the French National Conservatory. His most popular opera, *El Matrero* (1925), involves a gaucho bandit posing as a vagabond poet storyteller caught between the old life style and the new demands for respectability and social stability. El Matrero, also known as Lucero, passes himself off as Pedro Cruz in an attempt to court Pontezuela, a girl of the new rural generation. In the end, she is revealed to conserve the gaucho's independent spirit, while he, the traditional gaucho, dies in her arms.

The Gauchos' doomed frontier existence brought nostalgia into Argentine history, apparently permanently. Itinerent theater troups, the *zarzuelas criollas*, presented gaucho dramas, complete with folk dances and music. Clubs in Buenos Aires, the *centros gauchescos*, often with names borrowed from the mythical frontier experiences, resurrected what they believed to be traditional songs, costumes, and lore. Members practiced the art of being a latter day urban gaucho, fit to parade though the streets on festive occasions.

The invented gaucho mystique drifted down to the lower classes in the form of the urban *compadre.* A code of personal loyalty and attachment to a small group characterized the compadre. Compadres dressed in a fashion that suggested muted links with the pampas, yet clearly in the urban style. The imagined code of the frontier, honor and independence, became an attitude. A variant, the compadritos (street-wise young men) sported low crown, narrow brim hats, high-heeled boots, knives casually tucked into a broad leather belt, and an attitude that implied their readiness to resort to violence. At the other extreme, wealthy would-be gauchos could purchase the complete costume at the English department store Harrods, which took up most of a block on fashionable calle Florida.

Make-believe offered minor relief from the antiheroic sameness of urban life and its pedestrian foibles. Argentines ruefully laughed along with *Patorugú,* a cartoon character pampas Indian. Patorugú first appeared in newspapers and later as a comic book in 1935. He served as a bewildered foil for amusingly demonstrating some of the everyday oddities of life in the city of Buenos Aires. From 1964 to 1973 that role fell to a young, urban cartoon girl, *Malfada,* who commented on unfortunate world conditions.

Cultural nationalism's hunt for a unique heritage reluctantly recognized the tango. Originally a dance of men drawn from African traditions, it developed its heterosexual dance form on the steamy dance floors of brothels. The tango scandalized those who associated it with sexual looseness. Its classic form developed around 1880, drawing on the older *milonga* and Afro-Argentine influences, along with the Spanish *contradanza* and the Cuban *habenera.* The *Guardia Viejo* (old guard or fashion) tango improvised along the lines of American jazz, relying on the violin and the guitar. Tango bands played cafés in La Boca before the turn of the century. By the early 1900s, cafés and dance halls appeared on the slightly more respectable calle Corrientes, attracting a socially mixed audience.

The tango developed a song form, particularly under the influence of Carlos Gardel (1887–1935). Gardel refined the Creole (folk) song, seemingly penetrating the nostalgic and emotional reservoirs of the Argentine soul. *Mi noche triste* (My Sad Night) is considered the birth of the *Nueva Guardia* (new guard or wave) tango song performed in a standardized version. Better known, his recording of *Mi Buenos Aires Querida* (My Beloved Buenos Aires) is still popular around the world. As it evolved, the music added the German *bandoneon,* a modified accordion, as the key instrument, and the piano.

In 1913 and again after World War I, the tango craze swept Europe and then the United States. The Argentine minister to France, Enrique Rodríguez Larreta (1914), thought it necessary to warn the ladies that the tango represented "a pornographic spectacle," depicting "the obscene" (presumably the sexual act). Berlin and Vienna ordered soldiers not to dance the tango in uniform, and Pope Pius X warned the faithful that the dance encouraged immoral thoughts and actions. All of which made it irresistible.

The tango's acceptance in Paris appalled the elite. Nevertheless, after its overwhelming approval in Europe, they grudgingly acknowledged the tango's parentage. Argentina's upper class felt betrayed by their European brothers and sisters, an act that called into question their right and ability to represent the national identity. The idealized gaucho and nationalized tango represented a triumph of street over elite culture.[7]

Radio, introduced in the 1920s, began the process of diffusing the tango song far beyond the brothel and the traditional themes of male dominance, impossible love, and betrayal. The radio market demanded modifications to make the tango suitable for a general audience. Tango songs dealt with issues of everyday importance, in addition to the enduring but cleaned up heartaches of love and rejection. Tangos reflected an Argentina detached from the rural experience. Listeners wanted singers to address the hopes and expectations of an urbanized population anxious to embrace materialism.

A theme song for the 1920s, the *años locos* (the crazy years), could well have been the popular tango *La Mina del Ford* (The Broad with a Ford). The 1924 tango's lyrics expressed the modern women's desire to have it all: a balcony apartment, gas heat, carpets, beds with mattresses, and a maid to announce, "Madame, the Ford is here." Music expressed the young generation's rejection of social restrictions.

Girls cut their hair, wore short skirts and pants, drank and smoked in public, and carried on like men. Tango music fueled consumer-driven modernization. Raúl Scalabrini Ortiz, Nationalist author and critic writing in 1931, commented that women asked men for money to buy autos, outfits, and luxury items, never inquiring, "who are you, but only what do you do and how much do you earn?" Men, in turn, allegedly surrendered their true spirit to materialism, a sacrifice that modern women valued less than a doily on a piece of furniture.[8]

MOVIES AND THE GLOBALIZATION OF IMAGINATION

Movies arrived in Argentina in 1896, more as wondrous technology than entertainment. In 1897 Eugene Py, a Frenchman, produced, directed, and operated the recently introduced French camera to film *La Bandera Argentina* (The Argentine Flag), the first domestic film. He went on to direct a series of silent films, including the *Tango argentino* in 1900. That year, the first theaters designed and constructed specifically for film projection appeared. Nevertheless, most people experienced their first film in makeshift settings, from a farm structure to a café. Gritty, grainy, jerky, black-and-white, and short, silent movies strangely mirrored their awestruck spectators. People wanted to see semi-magical figures such as the Czar of all the Russians and the rich, powerful, and stylish, as well as exotic places and customs, some within their own country. Argentine silent movies initially concentrated on documentaries before moving to lighter fare.

Entertainment relied upon Gaucho themes, with such domestically produced films as the *Nobleza Gaucha* (1915). An instant success, *Nobleza Gaucha* (Gaucho Nobleness) became the first box office hit. Costing 25,000 pesos to produce, it made half a million pesos in six months. Itinerant projectionists joined the peddlers and medicine men, following the rails into the interior. Movie tents differed little from those of traveling circuses that provided dusty villages and towns a touch of magic. An attempt to break through into sound involved singers and even choral groups that did their best to reflect the action, hidden behind the screen, Pianos eventually gave way to organs, at least in the larger cities.

Filmmaker José Ferreyra, "El Negro," drew upon the drama of the barrio, occasionally accompanied by a tango band. Federico Valle produced Quirino Cristiani's and the world's first animated film, *El Apóstol*, in 1917. Domestic films relied on a flat fee paid by distributors, who in turn leased the film to individual exhibitors within an agreed upon region. At times, distributors also invested in film production. Argentine film production took off between 1916 and 1919 as the supply of European films decreased with World War I. When European studios recovered, they recaptured their share of the market. Nevertheless, domestic and European filmmakers could not compete with well-capitalized Hollywood productions.

American films entered the international market in 1910. By 1915, Hollywood dominated the screen through the star system, as well as by their technological advances and marketing strategy. Greta Garbo, Marlene Dietrich, Gloria Swanson, Mary Pickford, and others became household names. Fan magazines such as *Cinema Chat, Heroes del Cinema,* and *Hogar y Cine* kept the excitement alive between productions. The 1921 American film *The Four Horsemen of the Apocalypse,* starring Rudolf Valentino, marked the triumph of Hollywood in Argentina. Although the film presented an Argentina that few could recognize, it had the romance that audiences craved. In the 1920s, American film studios established distribution branches in Buenos Aires. The same terms demanded in the United States applied in Argentina. Exhibitors blindly rented films and agreed to share the gross receipts. Block rentals included productions bound to be popular with others of more doubtful appeal. American filmmakers recovered their costs and made a profit in the United States before they distributed aboard at attractive prices. They could easily meet local competition and make a reasonable profit, as well as cover minimum distribution costs. Moreover, American producers understood people's craving for fantasy at a time when materialism began to take hold around the world.

Talkies complicated matters. Sound synchronized with action became available in the late 1920s but required expensive equipment, new acting techniques, and scriptwriters. Initially, dubbing in other languages prove too difficult. A political issue emerged as Nationalists warned that sound movies would impose the English language and American values on their audiences, with nefarious consequences for national sovereignty. To meet such objections Paramount Films constructed a large facility in Joinville on the outskirts of Paris to turn out films in Spanish and other languages using native speakers when possible. Paramount cast Carlos Gardel to star in a series of successful tango films with plots that revolved around his voice and featured at least five songs per movie. For a brief period, films made in various languages attempted to preserve the market, but at prohibitive costs.

Fortunately for American filmmakers, audiences demanded Hollywood stars, glitter, and fantasy. Dubbing and subtitles eventually became technologically feasible and acceptable. Lumitón studio (1932) and Argentina's Sono Films (1937) filled the country's 600 movie theaters with tango movies, the only formula able to compete with Hollywood. Both distributed films to other Latin American markets and the American Southwest, creating a popular image of Argentina throughout the Spanish-speaking world.[9] Ferreyra produced talkies and succeeded in transforming Libertad Lamarque into a female star at the same international level as Gardel. Manuel Romero directed films that are among the best of the 1930s, including *Los muchachos de antes no usaban gomina* (Back Then, Boys Didn't Use Hair Cream) in 1938. Filmmakers created the enduring image of a sophisticated, tango dancing Latin lover strolling through the romantic streets of Buenos Aires, on occasion bursting into song in a dimly lit café.

By 1935, American films made up 76.6 percent of those shown in Argentina. Argentine productions made up only 2.5 percent, with European filmmakers and others making up the difference.[10] The Motion Pictures Producers and Distributors Association (MPPDA) in the United States constantly lobbied to ensure market access. The even more powerful Motion Pictures Export Association (MPEA) replaced the MPPDA in 1945.

Hollywood films suggested social and gender roles, as well as consumption patterns. For the first time, audiences had a glimpse of how the other half lived, loved, and consumed. While films portrayed an exaggerated lifestyle, they also suggested that certain items made the stars glamorous and could do the same for the discerning consumer. As Martínez Estrada noted at the end of the 1930s, Argentine women appeared worldly with short hair, exposed thighs, and penciled eyes. Yet, he expressed his belief that beneath the aphrodisiac exterior lay an incorruptible vestal. He may have exaggerated the triumph of virtue over form. Films presented a powerful fantasy dimension reflected in reality, and also stimulated expectations that helped shape modernity.

The young Eva Duarte (Perón) escaped her dreary rural poverty, at least for a moment, thanks to the imaginative genius of scriptwriters. Her determination to have lavish furs, jewels, lovely gowns, and stylish shoes grew with each movie ticket. Evita's career on radio and in minor movie roles drew on the hours spent in modest provincial theatres. Her husband hired a director to stage her state funeral. Juan Perón styled his hair to emphasize a physical likeness to Carlos Gardel and fancied himself a matinee idol of sorts. Dashing uniforms supplied fashionable props that added a touch of romance to politics.

PROFESSIONALS AND THE MIDDLE CLASS

The first census in 1869 reported a male literacy rate of slightly over 25 percent and a female literacy rate of just over 18 percent. A gender gap of only 7 percent seems typical of the equality of a frontier region. Twenty-six years later, the figures show a dramatic increase to 50 and 42 percent respectively. The use of the Lancaster method of successful students teaching others, who in turn taught more students, introduced at the suggestion of Rivadavia by the Benefiencia soon after their founding, deserves credit.

Support for education reflected the realization that modernization depended on complex knowledge across a number of fields. It lay behind the desire to flood Argentina with an idealized European culture as quickly as possible. New economic opportunities, commerce, light manufacturing, and the growing service industry created a small, still-weak middle class. The professions, teaching, the bureaucracy, and the army provided middle-class status and income for both nationals and the foreign born and their children. Those of immigrant origins moved into the middle class at a significantly higher rate than the native born.

Urbanization required myriad directive, supervisory, and technical tasks. Electrification of tramlines and construction of a subway expanded the capital city far beyond its traditional limits. Sewage and water systems and construction of all types pulled in capital and expertise and demanded more of both. Building the Paris of South America on the totally inadequate base of a minor colonial city provided opportunities for investors, developers, and the middle class. Railways carried new needs into the interior. Urban centers served as modernization demonstration points that radiated the possibilities out to all but the most remote parts of the nation. The nineteenth century appeared to belong to the engineers, from civil and mechanical to new sub-specialties. All the professional groups that industry and commercial agriculture depended upon required improved status and compensation.

The opening for women provided by teaching had its male counterpart in the creation of a professional officer corps. The War of the Triple Alliance (1865–1870) made it obvious that the days of frontier military tactics had ended. Both Presidents Mitre and Sarmiento acquired military skills on the battlefield; however, they realized that modern warfare required professionals. President Sarmiento founded the *Colegio Militar* (1870) and the *Escuela Naval* (1872) to train officers. General and President Julio A. Roca over a two term presidency equipped the army with the latest weapons and in 1900 founded the *Escuela Superior de Guerra* (Advanced War College). The War College emphasized knowledge that went beyond military skill. Roca further extended the military's social influence by instituting obligatory military service in 1901. Initially political patronage determined promotion but by 1910 gave way to seniority and merit. A selection board composed of division commanders and headed by a senior general removed politics from the process, except for the highest ranks. Control of advancement created a self-regulated, recognized professional group with its own interests.

Military schools offered free education and social status—attractive elements for sons of immigrants anxious to demonstrate their attachment to the *patria*. The military saw itself as the father of independence and an institution that predated the creation of the state. The officer corps had become part of the middle class and the senior generals honorary associates of the elite. Along with bureaucrats and teachers, the army represented one of the first state-created professional entities. Without economic assets to exert political influence, military officers learned that a monopoly on force constituted a useful commodity. Development of professions favored the army as an institution. It provided officers with a reasonably comfortable middle class lifestyle and upward social mobility. Institutional claims on respect and resources appeared beyond challenge. A sense of entitlement mixed with history, pride, and patriotism gave the institution a quasi-political mandate. Perceived responsibilities grew along with the realization that threats encompassed much more than invaders. Economic forces, including the structure of international trade, and foreign domination of domestic industries, capital, and technology could become menacing under certain circumstances. A perceptual expansion of potential dangers demanded vigilance and action, reinforced their place within society, and staked out an expansive notion of military professional concerns.

The establishment of military schools resulted in a critical examination of various organizational models. Consequently, the army abandoned the French model in 1904 and replaced it with a Prussian one. The Franco-Prussian war (1870–1871) ended French supremacy in Europe.

Prussian efficiency, a well-organized supply system resting on military-owned factories, appeared to be the key. The Argentine army realized that modern warfare required much more than forced enlistment of gauchos, men on horseback, and supply mules. Industrial strength became a military objective, but one that conflicted with the oligarchy's national vision.

Military involvement in industrial production and technical innovation began at a low level. Repair shops for basic weapons, including artillery along with some labor intensive manufacturing of weapons and a gunpowder facility, began in the 1880s. To provide expertise, the General Staff created an Engineering Department in 1884 that evolved into a military engineering school two years later, which lasted until 1895 as a distinct institution. The Prussian concept of a nation in arms had a reflection in the Ricchieri Law of 1901 that established universal military service. The first contingent arrived for duty the following year. Absorbing conscripts required better-trained noncommissioned personnel, resulting in a centralized school in 1908 that became in 1916 the *Escuela de Subofficiales* (Non-Commissioned Officers School), housed at the Campo de Mayo, the most prestigious army base.

The rapidity with which a professional middle class emerged between independence in 1810 and 1910 mirrored the trajectory of the economy. By the turn of the century foreigners and casual observers believed that Argentina had become a cultured, middle-class country with a level of material prosperity that rivaled that of European nations.

THE AGE OF MASS CONSUMPTION

Pressure for a share of the good life grew with the export boom and the "Golden Years." The largely European-created myth of fabulous wealth convinced Argentines as well as foreigners. Silent films and subsequently movies undoubtedly suggested possibilities. Elite demands, based on tastes often acquired during a European sojourn, conveyed their superior status to peers and foreigners alike. The wealthy dealt with approved suppliers or ordered French and British imports from the Buenos Aires branch of London's Harrods on calle Florida. Harrods carried everything the discriminating customer wanted, from the finest Norfolk jackets and Scottish tweeds to Carr's Table Water Crackers, "purveyor to Queen Victoria." The other classes made do with less expensive imports or domestic products. Many consumers had a direct connection with the producer of a product, often manufactured in small stores within walking distance. Consumption marked one's class, whether on the street or at home.

After the turn of the century demands for a share of the country's prosperity could not be denied, particularly to the middle class.

Expansion of the bureaucracy, university reforms, and the realization that tangible material benefits and politics went together created demands in keeping with change in real and perceived status. The poet-critic Leopoldo Lugones in 1913 described aspects of the national character that captured modern materialism. He observed that the gaucho's descendents liked to boast and let little stand in the way of acquiring material things, spending lavishly.

Foreign manufacturers, aware of the wealth produced by exports, encouraged modern consumerism. Creating needs associated with modernization relied on advertising agencies. Prosperity required a different approach to marketing. Argentine advertising agencies, following the British model, relied on subdued artwork, a subtle message, and polite encouragement. Good taste reflected on the company, while the product's virtues remained secondary. Stimulating sales of everyday items with a natural market seemed unnecessary to many domestic manufacturers.

Buenos Aires newspapers maintained representatives in London and New York to facilitate the sale of advertising space. Middlemen, such as the Foreign Advertising and Service Bureau and Gotham-Valdimir Advertising, Inc., arranged for local affiliated agencies to meet needs, but seldom to the complete satisfaction of clients. The drawbacks could be ignored in the early days, but not as demand and competition increased. Clumsy copy, grammatically correct but overly formal, conveyed a stilted message. Background art appropriate for New York, Paris, or London reached an elite group but did not convey a mass message that everyone in Argentina needed the product.

High-value products, luxurious and exotic, represented materialism's icons. While the furs and jewels might be beyond the reach of most, cigarettes, stockings, and a range of auxiliary items appeared both desirable and feasible, even if it meant squeezing limited resources in an effort to acquire them. Motorcars arrived in 1889, but the need for a mass market came with Ford's Argentine assembly operations in 1916. Marketing an increasing number of units required more aggressive measures. Ford Motor Company convinced a reluctant N. W. Ayers Advertising Agency to market the Model A Ford, introduced to South Americans in December 1927. Ayers had mounted a successful campaign for the model in the United States. The agency hired Boaz W. Long, a former Chief of the Department of State's Latin American division and a former Minister to Cuba, to survey the situation, along with a Ford employee. Both men spent five months touring Mexico, Central America, and South America, conferring with company representatives and assessing the difficulties. Nevertheless, another American agency, J. Walter Thompson (JWT), opened the first office in Argentina in 1929 to represent General Motors. Both Ford Motor Company and General Motors worked to establish an organized used-car market to spread the cost of a new model car across several successive owners and reach less affluent consumers.

Ayers opened an office in Buenos Aires in 1931 to oversee placement of copy initially prepared in its Philadelphia office, until they could hire a local staff and gather reliable data. McCann-Ericsson, pressed by their client Standard Oil of New Jersey to go worldwide, arrived in Buenos Aires in the mid 1930s. Considerable hostility had to be overcome from businessmen, publishers, and even Ford representatives that believed a foreign agency could not bargain effectively for prime space or understand local customs and tastes. In addition, a hard-pressed economy struggling with the depression and prone to antiforeign nationalism, made advertising foreign companies and their products a delicate task.

Occasional lapses, such as copy that presented an automobile with right-handed steering rather than the left- hand drive initially adopted in Argentina, could not be avoided. Eventually, all copy originated in Buenos Aires, designed, written, and placed by Argentine staffs. The expense of maintaining offices required the agencies to solicit both American and domestic business. Ayers hired Richard Puerrydon, from a wealthy estanciero family, the direct descendents of an important early independence figure. The young Puerrydon found the connection between advertising and psychology irresistible. American agencies hired women copywriters, assuming that they understood how to reach the female market.

One of the first successes involved a domestic company, Noel Chocolates. Noel produced a bar described simply as milk chocolate and bearing the name Noel. Ayers mounted a naming contest open only to children that led to the name Kilito, a new label, along with an ad campaign that resulted in a dramatic increase in sales. Magazines and newspapers often refused outright to publish ads that dealt with private intimate needs. Foreign agencies encouraged modern consumerism across a wide range of items, from the most mundane to the luxurious, creating demand rather than relying on the consumer's self-perceived needs. Their message, that a person could be redefined by consumption, spoke to aspirations that encompassed more than needs. Mass marketing eventually democratized consumption across a wide range of items as modern techniques and attitudes became standard.

Import substitution, implemented to deal with the country's inability to pay for imports after 1929, required industrial expansion and the shifting of consumers to domestic manufactured products. While many products enjoyed a captive market, advertising called attention to finer substitutes and made possible new plants and equipment. Swift and Company, formerly content to ship to the British market, turned to domestic consumption to offset the impact of the depression. Marketing inevitably stressed the patriotic aspects of buying what the nation produced. The next big move towards a mass national market came with radio.

Radio in Argentina attracted interest earlier than in other Latin American countries. Its utility seemed obvious to enthusiasts, who began to experiment with broadcasts to make culture readily available. The first broadcast (August 27, 1920) by Dr. Susini Romero Carranza y Guerrico, a medical doctor, and two medical students transmitted Ricard Wagner's *Parsifal* from the roof of the Teatro Coliseo in Buenos Aires. At the time few receivers existed and the audience of their friends and acquaintances numbered less than 50 listeners. The three went on to broadcast the entire opera season. That same year, the Radio Society of Argentina established the first radio station in South America to broadcast scheduled programming. Shortwave programs from Westinghouse, a major supplier of radio equipment and receivers, originated from KDKA in Pittsburgh, Pennsylvania.

The growth of radio receivers, some 60,000 existed by 1923, prompted the Ministry of the Navy to issue five more licenses to privately owned radio stations. Mixed ownership of stations by private enterprises, amateurs, and the government created some confusion. Authority for regulating radio communications transferred to the Ministry of Post and Telegraph in 1928. By the end of the 1930s, 42 radio stations broadcast, and the emerging networks began to focus on advertising. Three powerful networks, Radio El Mundo, Radio Belgrano, and Radio Splendid, formed in the early 1940s.

Radio advertising became attractive to advertisers as the technology improved and the number of receivers increased. Broadcasts reached a significant number of consumers by the mid 1930s. Programs penetrated into the most private spaces and did not require active listener involvement, unlike printed material. Radio's appeal cut across class lines to include listeners in the most luxurious estancias of Buenos Aires province as well as those in the dusty villages of the interior. Programs such as classical music conducted by recognized maestros received newspaper reviews. Depending on the cultural level of a program, certain groups could be reached.

Gardening and cooking programming attracted the middle class. Jazz programs appealed to the younger generation, anxious to be seen as participants in the modern world. Transcription discs, available in the 1930s, held 15 minutes of programming on each side, making the half hour program a favored length. Even remote radio transmitters could present technologically advanced sound and professional programs.

Tango songs, linked with inexpensive products, reached the middle to lower classes. Radical soap, subsequently promoted by Eve Duarte (Evita Perón), among others, did not compete with Lever Brothers Lux or the fine milled soaps available at Harrods but combined hygiene with a touch of middle-class politics. Soap operas and similar programs reached women as they worked in the home or cleaned the kitchen of their better-off employers. Men in bars and *pulperías* (a combination general store, bar, and pawn shop) relaxed, exchanged gossip, drank *caña*, and fought, sometimes fatally, to music provided by radio.

More expensive items, often of foreign origin, required an approach that mixed product promotion with status reinforcement. Items such as an English *eau de cologne* available in two almost identical forms, widely used in an age before modern deodorants, became in the hands of skilled agencies a daytime fragrance and an evening one with implied sexual allure. The sensitive consumer needed both.

Consumption engendered uncertainty and a desire to avoid embarrassment by consuming products appropriately. Upward mobility through calculated consumption created instant status, but one that had to be conspicuous in order to have the desired impact. Advertising suggested that a product could change the user's self image, attractiveness to others, and status. A comic strip character *Ramona* provided some relief. Ramona, a somewhat dense domestic servant employed by a pretentious, determinedly upwardly mobile middle-class family, struggled to comprehend the materialistic demands of an insecure class. Appearing in the pages of *La Razon*, Ramona allowed readers to laugh at themselves while seemingly amused by the lower class that served them.

THE COSMOPOLITAN CITY

Buenos Aires struggled to become a city. Its colonial status as a vice-regal capital appeared to be one of political convenience rather than one bestowed in recognition of urban grandeur. The all-too-close Indian frontier created a sense of encapsulation, with the only escape the watery expanse of the South Atlantic. A wider regional identification reached only as far as the horizon, and over time slowly extended to the boundaries of Buenos Aires Province. Buenos Aires functioned as a string of villages coordinated as a de facto capital in 1880, but in reality had only one commercial corridor along the buff overlooking the estuary of the Río de la Plata. To the south a small river port, La Boca, on the Riachuelo as it emptied into the estuary, eventually became the city's southern boundary. La Boca remained an isolated enclave poorly connected by roads and without a rail line until the 1860s. Across from La Boca, a companion settlement, Avellaneda, along with another salt meat center up river, Barracas, began the transformation of the Riachuelo into an industrial canal.

North of the estuary the villages of Flores and Belgrano emerged as frontier settlements. In 1806, San José de Flores formed around a mud chapel constructed by Juan Diego Flores, a local landowner. Travelers from the city reached the village by the *camino real* that linked Buenos Aires to Lima. A church constructed in 1831 contributed modern flair with a clock tower, a gift of Rosas. In 1857, the railroad arrived and less than half a century later in 1900, Avenida Rivadavia entered the village, instantly changing it into another Buenos Aires' barrio.

After the train's arrival in 1862, Belgrano began to be engulfed in the same fashion as Flores. Trams, inexpensive but slower, eventually provided access for the general population. The yellow fever epidemic of 1871 prompted many to take the train to where the fresh air offered some protection. The stench of the polluted Riachuelo, believed to be the source of the epidemic, and the dreary spectacle of some 13,614 deaths pushed people to the outer rings of the city. President Sarmiento made Belgrano the national capital for some three months, until the epidemic subsided. Fittingly, the Sarmiento Historical Museum is now located in Belgrano's old town hall, constructed in 1870 and overlooking the Plaza Belgrano and its church of *La Inmaculada Concepcion.*

Barrio Norte also took form with the 1871 yellow fever epidemic. New wealth created a district in the imagined likeness of Europe. It soon became associated, not entirely undeservedly, with pretension, as prideful *parvenus* signaled their arrival and exhibited the wealth that made it possible. Evita bought her first apartment here when she became a radio soap opera success. Not a true barrio but rather a state of mind, it arose out of the growing prosperity of the country.

After 1865, railway stations along the four rail lines that radiated out of the core provided a grid that facilitated the movement of travelers. Often compared with Chicago, before the city took on the aura of Paris, Buenos Aires also maintained roots in the cattle industry. Other barrios, some with touches of elegance, many almost interchangeable in their unremarkable sameness, rounded out respectable Buenos Aires. Less admirable and socially problematic barrios made up the remainder of a relentlessly engulfing city.

La Boca, on the lower end of the scale, built on flat tidal land reclaimed from the estuary at the mouth of the Riachuelo, emerged as a well-defined locality in the 1830s. Its shanties on stilts with makeshift walkways to higher and drier ground defied the turbulent waters that periodically washed under them. The Genovese, with their distinctive dialect, settled there, soon to be joined by Sardinians. A cross section of the world, a sprinkling of Finns, Koreans and Chinese added an exotic touch. It became a working class as well as a criminal barrio, with brothels, bars, gambling, and opium dens. In 1882, striking Genovese raised the flag of Genoa and declared the Republic of La Boca. President Julio A. Roca, ever the decisive soldier, personally tore the flag down. A chastened barrio changed the name of a street, both to honor and placate the president. Alfredo Palacios, the country's first Socialist deputy won his seat in the barrio in 1904.

La Boca offered innumerable challenges and, for the reckless, a short life. The Riachuelo, once a pleasant river, became the barrio's sewer, a place for all manner of refuse—offal, slaughterhouse remnants, tanning runoff, coal dust, and abandoned ships, beginning in the era of sail to the rusting hulks of the age of coal and steam. Slaughterhouses upriver polluted the water long before it flowed painfully past La Boca to its mouth. The 1920s represented the high point of prostitution in the barrio. A criminal association of pimps organized a synagogue, the *Zwi Migdal*, appropriately in a better area of town. It served its criminal community until shut down in the 1930. They controlled a large number of Jewish women from Eastern Europe obtained in a variety of ways, some purchased from their families in Poland, complete with a signed contract specifying payments over a period of years, or recruited from among the desperate. Perón, in the late 1940s, cracked down on La Boca's exuberant criminality, beginning its transformation into a picturesque artist colony with brightly painted houses and tin roofs. Calle Garibaldi still links the barrio together, but not with the dangerous tensions of the past.

The city began to take on monumental elegance with the federal building boom during the Juárez Celman presidency of 1886–1890. The government laid the foundation of some of the most impressive structures in the city. The inauguration of the Avenida de Mayo in 1895–1896, running west from the historic center of the Plaza de Mayo to a new Congress building completed in 1906, provided a ceremonial boulevard. The creation of the plaza and avenue is generally considered to mark the passing of the old city and its modern transformation. The areas to the south of the plaza, Barrio San Telmo, desirable until the 1871 yellow fever epidemic drove people to Belgrano and Barrio Norte, began to take on a rundown appearance made even worse as modernity's glitter moved northward.

In 1908, the Colon Opera House opened for its first season. Twice the size of La Scala in Milan, with a magnificent lobby modeled after Versailles' Hall of Mirrors, it became a cultural icon. Inside, dazzling balconies soaring six tiers to the ceiling decorated with gold leaf, created a sensation in the transatlantic world of opera. The inaugural season presented some of Europe's finest operatic talent in Verdi's *Aida*. Italian baritones Titta Ruffo and Feodor Ivanovic Chaliapin, both considered along with Enrico Caruso as among the most accomplished voices of the time, made the season a great success. Both Ruffo and "Fedia, who sang like Tolstoi wrote," had smashing successes at La Scala, on their way to performing in Buenos Aires. Titta, reputed to have a rubber face and able to physically become his role, stayed on for the next season. The Confiteria Paris, established in 1917, became the place to go after the opera to critique the performance.

Porteños referred to the semi-transformed city as the Paris of South America. French cultural influences showed in certain attitudes and ways of wearing clothes with a "European flair." Architecture, and copies (with a few originals) of French sculptures gracing important plazas, added to the Parisian ambience. A transatlantic mental template overlaid the city, conditioning the conduct of Porteños. Other Latin Americans found the pretension intolerable, aware that they fell outside the charmed circle of illusion. Certainly, Barrio Norte, Belgrano, and parts of Palermo had elegance. Nevertheless, the street names returned one to reality. The fact that so much of Argentina's history centered in Buenos Aires blurred the city's past into the present. Virtually every street corner, plaza, and building had a story.

As late as 1914, the city's buildings remained largely one story, with 105,000 such structures out of a total of 132,000. After 1920, a subway system(opened in 1914), a trolley network, and bus lines connected the city with urban outlying districts. Lots selling with monthly installments of as long as ten years attracted the lower middle class and skilled workers to the city's fringe, soon to become barrios. A lot and a one-room dwelling could be built on borrowed money, a major step up from the slum tenements (*conventillos*). With time a modest suburban home could be expanded and made more spacious. The city proper became a place for the rich, middle class, and the poor, each in distinctive districts. The more affluent spread out along the Río de la Plata from Barrio Norte at the edge of downtown through Palermo and Belgrano.

A city is a series of personal routines and haunts. Corrientes, named by Bernadino Rivadavia in 1822, became the street of the people—garish, crass, and never sleeping. Carlos Gardel centered his life in the Art-Deco fruit and vegetable market constructed in 1893 that sprawled over two blocks on Corrientes. When he died his body lay before the grieving crowd in Corrientes' Luna Park, where Juan Perón would meet Evita for the first time. While Gardel identified with Avenida Corrientes, Borges invoked Maipú in *el centro* (downtown).

At the opposite end of the social scale from Corrientes, Calle Florida, with its fashionable clothes and elegant women, attracted those with finer tastes. It became known for the *piropo*, the lustful gaze of ever-hopeful males accompanied by a verbal assessment of feminine beauty. Harrods lent a touch of imported style with its quiet British elegance. Calle Florida's Jockey Club, built in 1897, captured the street's sense of confident opulence. Cafes, designed to duplicate the ambiance of those of Madrid, Paris, and London, transported one to a distant serenity. Soft leather chairs and the aroma of cigarettes, coffees, and teas drew intellectuals, writers, and observers to sit for hours or read newspapers and literary magazines. From the 1880s to the present, calle Florida has been the street to watch others, gage their class and status, and approve or dismiss. Buenos Aires had style, and calle Florida served to demonstrate it. Nevertheless, the city could not avoid urban ills or the changing fortunes of the nation and region.

In 1940, squatter settlements (*villas miserias*) appeared to house migrants from the interior, as well as from Bolivia and Paraguay. They presented a different Buenos Aires of poverty, narrow twisting pathways, and bare survival. Some observers claimed that Buenos Aires, no longer a refuge for Europe's displaced, has become just another Latin American city. The lost viceroyalty came back with its people, but without its resources. Essayist José Bianco observed that squatters represented the "revenge that Spanish America has taken on Atlantic America."[11]

Unlike other mega cities, Buenos Aires seems more nineteenth century than relentlessly modern. In the twenty-first century, the city continues to generate character. Palermo Viejo (old Palermo) reemerged as a quaintly fashionable boutique district with a scattering of trendy restaurants. Adjacent parts of Palermo have become known as Palermo SoHo (after New York's SoHo, not London's Soho), close to Palermo Hollywood with its *avant-garde* filmmakers and low-budget TV production companies.

CHAPTER 4

Confronting the Oligarchy

THE IDEOLOGICAL CHALLENGE

Labor militancy achieved its first victory for better wages, shorter hours, and the end of piecework with the Typographers Union strike in 1878. Nevertheless, most workers had little ability to force concessions. Anarchism and Socialism as they took root sought to focus workers' demands. The first May Day celebration in 1890 featured speeches in Italian, German, French, and Spanish. It resulted in a premature attempt to form a labor federation and newspaper. The federation floundered on the philosophical divide between Socialism and Anarchism and the struggle between them for directive authority. The first organized group, the Socialist German Worker's Club (*Club Alemán Vorwarts*), established in 1882, appealed to a limited number. Typical of the early stage of radicalism, a flurry of short-lived publications sought to educate workers. In the 1890s the Anarchist newspaper *El Perseguido* (The Persecuted) distributed some 4,000 copies.

Socialism succeeded in going beyond ethnic divisions to appeal to second and third generation workers. Spanish provided the language unity necessary to bring groups together. The newspaper *La Vanguardia*, established in 1894, gained readers as Socialism spread beyond Buenos Aires. Its editor, Juan Bautista Justo, instrumental in the founding of the Argentine Socialist Party in 1895, crafted both the newspaper and the party. In 1895, the national party had 803 members, but only 348 had citizenship. Many immigrants hoped to return to their native land and hesitated to become citizens. The eight-hour day, women's suffrage, equal pay for the same task, workplace safety, and other issues became party objectives. The party opposed immigration because employers used new arrivals to break strikes and hold down wages. A seven-person executive committee, including Justo, ran the national party.

A strong personality from a third-generation immigrant family (with Italian and Spanish immigrant roots), Justo grew up on the pampas, where his father worked as a manager of various estancias. While he had a relatively privileged childhood, he understood the social and economic gap between the elite and everybody else. Professional school offered the best possibility of status and economic stability. Young Justo graduated from medical school in 1888 with a gold medal for his thesis. The following year he traveled in Europe to study surgery. On his return, he enjoyed almost immediate professional success as a professor of surgery and clinical chief of a major urban hospital. He pressed for proper sanitation and equipment sterilization to bring medical establishments up to European standards. Nevertheless, Justo, as did many professionals, understood that elite politics limited social and economic possibilities regardless of individual accomplishments.

In common with many of that educated generation, Justo absorbed the basic principles of Comte's positivism that posited a technocratic elite and a society based on virtue and merit. He concluded that the system, blocked by effective barriers of privilege and class, had to be modified. He became a member of the directive committee of the Unión Cívica de la Juventud in 1890. The violence of the *Noventa*, to be discussed later, convinced him that the Unión Cívica represented traditional politics in a different garb. Socialism, in contrast, appeared to offer a clear break from a corrupt political system, with the ability to eliminate class limitations and the oligarchy's economic control. It proposed the nonviolent rearrangement of wealth in a scientific manner that meshed with positivism. He acknowledged that his conversion to Socialism in 1893 resulted from his own experiences. Only later did he read the philosophical literature. In 1895, he returned to Europe to study Socialism in action.

Justo's single-minded dedication to the cause and his editorship of the *Vanguard* made him an indispensable man. He seldom joked, although he used irony and sarcasm to cutting effect. He read six foreign languages and could speak several. Justo's intelligence and education impressed associates as well as opponents. He had little patience with nonbelievers and possessed the scientist's certainty of truth. Dressed and groomed in the fashion of a businessman with a hat and cane, Justo, a short stocky man, presented a reassuring image. Socialism attracted more professionals and intellectuals than workers.

Anarchism, in contrast, appealed to workers. In 1885, Anarchist Enrico Malatesta arrived from Italy intent on convincing adherents to focus on collective organization rather than individual direct action. When he returned to Europe four years later, another Italian, Pietro Gori, took his place. A Spanish-born woodworker, Inglan Lafarga, who participated in the founding of the newspaper *La Protesta Humana* in 1897, became a convert to this view. Along with another Spaniard, Antonio Pellicer Paraire, he shifted the movement from direct action to organizing. Anarchist leaders accepted the notion that a disciplined working class could force the state to concede under a general strike. Anarcho-syndicalist unions soon dominated the labor movement.

The Socialists, on the other hand, viewed strikes with ambivalence. They agreed that at times a strike became necessary, but such action had to be carefully considered. The philosophical notion that Socialism emerged from capitalism as the final stage inclined them towards preservation of the state, not its destruction. In 1902, a new electoral scheme divided the country into districts, making it possible to elect a Socialist to the chamber of deputies. In 1904, Alfredo L. Palacios, a native Argentine, became the first Latin American Socialist elected to national office. He represented La Boca, a heavily immigrant and socially marginal barrio of the capital. While he labored alone, he legitimized the strategy of political participation. Palacios ran again in 1908, but under the reinstated rules of the lista completa the PAN swept to victory.

THE NONIDEOLOGICAL CHALLENGE

What would be an effective challenge to the PAN began with violence under the leadership of Leandro N. Alem. A veteran of the Paraguayan war, congressman, and lawyer, Alem had long rallied against the perversion of the ideals of the Constitution of 1853. In his view, the amoral pragmatism of the governing elite and its transformation into a self-serving oligarchy violated the agreement that constituted the foundation of the federal republic. Outrage provided a revolutionary cast to Alem's conservative response.

Alem organized a protest movement in 1889 called the *Unión Cívica de la Juventud* (Youth Civic Union). The organization attracted the nonstudent opposition, including the senior statesman Bartolomé Mitre, Catholic groups opposed to introduction of civil marriage and educational reforms, and others that sought a platform. The movement, born in part out of a reaction to President Juárez Celman's policies and his abrasive personality, became the reactionary vehicle for a wide spectrum of individuals and groups with little in common except that they perceived themselves to be ill served by the PAN.

A renamed *Unión Cívica* protested the government's failure to alleviate the economic misery as the Baring crisis loomed. Some 30,000 protesters gathered to demand the resignation of the Juárez Celman government. With some military support, the group attempted a coup, the *Noventa*, in

1890. Only an estimated 5,000 took to armed insurgency, but 800 to 1,000 wounded and dead bloodied the streets of Buenos Aires before it ended. The violence sought political influence within the existing structure. Although the attempt floundered, a rattled PAN, already concerned with debt default, forced the resignation of President Juárez Celman in August of 1890.

The PAN, naturally prone to factionalism because of the lack of a coordinating national camarilla and weakened by the policies of the deposed president, confronted a crisis. Prominent PAN politicians threatened to withdraw from the party, further adding to political instability. The PAN, through its official newspaper, *La Tribuna Nacional,* rushed to remind its readers that order permitted material progress and with it the moral advances to embellish civilization. With the debt crisis of 1890, the PAN's already weak legitimacy began to wither, as even its beneficiaries questioned whether it could or should be sustained. Some PAN members deserted the party to join factions within the UC and the Catholic party, only to return to the PAN in a chaotic search for political direction.

Carlos Pellegrini (1846–1906), a prominent member of the generation of 1880, came to the conclusion that the PAN should surrender its governing role. Never a strong unified party even when it did not confront a challenge, it could not co-opt the opposition or suppress it. Before his resignation, as he realized his regime hovered on the verged of political crisis, President Juárez Celman , introduced legislation to make minority representation in congress easier. Pellegrini had to follow through decisively.

Pellegrini viewed the reform movement in the United States as a model. Both nations contended with immigration, Anarchism, and labor unrest. Pellegrini believed that American political parties effectively defused the dangers posed by an alienated working class. Similar reforms in Argentina could end the threat of revolution. He considered joint labor-employer committees to negotiate contacts and balance productivity and wages but laid the notion aside. Pellegrini's ideas helped frame the reforms of 1912 discussed later.

In 1891, the UC split into two. Mitre formed the *Unión Cívica Nacional* with the idea of reaching an accommodation with the oligarchy. Alem, ever intransigent, headed the *Unión Cívica Radical,* now referred to as simply the Radicals. Having failed in Buenos Aires in 1890 and frustrated elsewhere, the Radicals set off a series of revolts in the provinces in August of 1893, followed by another wave in September. Electoral gains in Buenos Aires Province in 1894 gave the Radicals a sizeable bloc in congress. Additional electoral victories in the capital and Buenos Aires Province increased the influence of Alem's nephew, Hipólito Yrigoyen, who assumed a more directive role in the party. The two men did not work well together. A reorganization of the UCR to eliminate divisions promised to make the party more effective. Then, on May 19, 1896, Alem committed suicide. He called a meeting of his closest friends, then took a carriage to the *Club del Progreso;* when the driver opened the door he found Alem dead from a shot to the head. Letters sent to his friends did little to explain his actions.[1] By the end of 1898, the UCR scarcely existed. Most of Alem's group joined other parties, including the PAN. Nevertheless, the UCR would be resurrected by Hipólito Yrigoyen, but in a form that his uncle probably would not have approved. The new UCR recruited different social elements, including recently established families in their second and third generation. It attracted a middle class anxious for political representation, as well as elite members, particularly from the third layer of the oligarchy, as discussed earlier.

Hipólito Yrigoyen (1852–1933) can only be described as odd. Originally from a modest background, the illegitimate son of a blacksmith, Yrigoyen acquired an education and wealth. He purchased land and continued to add to his holdings, eventually becoming a large landholder. He had one foot, perhaps psychologically the most secure one, in the lower middle class, and the other foot in the economic elite. Yrigoyen evolved into a middle-class champion and posed as a patron of the working class while maintaining his good standing in the SRA. He joined the Jockey Club in 1897, the year the club opened its luxurious building on calle Florida. Although he never became active in the club, he developed friendships and acquaintanceships with many of its members.

Yrigoyen, a mystical figure possessed a low-key intensity that, when combined with patronage, entranced followers. He lived in an austere, ascetic fashion, largely immune to the materialism he disdained. A confirmed bachelor, he nevertheless enjoyed the company of a number of interesting women and had a number of children by a series of mistresses. A man unable to give into flights of fancy, suspicious of advice, and unable to empathize, he had few obvious political skills. A terrible orator, he reputedly made only one public address during his political career. Yrigoyen excelled, however, in striking backroom deals. The Socialists referred to him a conniver. His rigid grasp on the party made his own personality central to its success and failure.

To Yrigoyen, the coarsening of culture appeared to be a danger inherent in liberalism. He admired the ideas of the German philosopher Karl Krause (1781–1832). Krause spoke to the desire to be modern without rejecting Catholic beliefs or breaking with the Church. Yrigoyen mixed liberal, traditional Catholic, and Krausist ideas into a personal synthesis. He viewed materialism as a threat to the common good, particularly the individualistic materialism of the United States. The UCR and its leader mirrored the confusion of a society torn between outmoded values and economic desires. Argentines accepted Yrigoyen's political and philosophical confusion because it mirrored theirs.

Yrigoyen started in politics as a police superintendent—an experience clouded by accusations of rigging elections. In 1879, he won a congressional seat and the following year served on the National Council of Education. He joined the Unión Cívica in 1890. By 1898, Yrigoyen controlled the remnants of the Unión Cívica Radical and began to rebuild its membership. Constantly flirting with insurrection, he believed that the political system had a corrupt moral dimension that made participation in elections abhorrent.

In 1905, the Radicals attacked government offices. In a matter of hours the authorities suppressed the violence. UCR leaders went to prison or fled into exile. An amnesty the following year allowed a chastened UCR to contemplate new tactics. The party pressed for electoral modifications and a larger share of political power and the patronage that it provided— change, but hardly revolutionary. Meanwhile, it refused to participate in the electoral process.

Catholic worker groups also applied pressure to change the system. Dedicated to working-class material and spiritual well being, they presented themselves as a moral alternative to Socialism and Anarchism. Father Federico Grote arrived from Germany in 1884 and eight years later founded the Central Worker's Circle. In the aftermath of the papal encyclical *Rerum Novarum* (1891), the number of Circles grew to forty with 10,000 members. In addition, Catholic Women's Centers sponsored housing projects conducive to family formation. In 1884, Catholic layman José Manuel Estrada organized a weak *Unión Católica* Party. Estrada articulated positions that the Nationalists subsequently embraced. He viewed liberalism's "egalitarian delirium," as destructive to an organic society. He believed that liberalism, by transforming the workers into the masses, made them vulnerable to radicalism. For many Catholics the inability of the Church to sponsor an effective party meant that the Radical Party presented the only viable alternative to the PAN, Socialism, and Anarchism.

A NEW POLITICAL CONFIGURATION

Violence and general strikes concerned the governing elite at the moment that exports reached new levels. Between 1907 and 1910 some 785 strikes occurred, drawing in over 200,000 workers. At the same time, frozen beef exports climbed by 1910 to 245,994 tons, a 90 percent increase. Meanwhile, an embattled political system facing continuous strikes appeared increasingly unstable. Although rural workers also engaged in work stoppages, the labor problems of urban Argentina threatened processing and exports. Producers worried that confidence in an uninterrupted supply of meat and agricultural products to the European market might be damaged, encouraging them to increase imports from the competing food colonies of Canada, Australia, and New Zealand.

Labor unrest obscured the problems that led to strikes. Complaints about wages and working conditions tended to be pushed aside in the eagerness to blame foreign agitators. Politicians and newspapers lamented the failure of many immigrants to become citizens, but when a growing number chose citizenship, voted, formed parties and organizations, and ran for public office, they expressed fears that the country would fall into foreign hands.

In 1908, the *Liga del Sur* emerged with the objectives of transferring political control from northern Santa Fé Province to the southern part and moving the capital to Rosario, where most of the province's 300,000 immigrants lived. Congress predictably considered a more restrictive naturalization policy, debating the possibility of a prolonged residency requirement. A failing political system, not responding to the old methods of control, appeared to be on the verge of collapsing in violence. Restricting immigration might solve the problem of order and political control, but many worried that it imposed unacceptable economic costs. A pervasive sense of an accelerating loss of control gnawed at elite confidence.

Conceding political authority and patronage to the UCR appeared to be a feasible solution. The Radicals already attracted the sons of immigrants and seemed better prepared to deal politically with the urban working class. A carefully structured political system could preserve control over productive wealth, minimize the dangers of Socialism and Anarchism, and form a socio-political alliance with the more acceptable and responsible elements of urban society.

The individual responsible for managing the hand off of political authority, Roque Sáenz Peña, established a new party in 1909, the Unión Nacional. The UN sought a consensus for electoral reforms. Sáenz Peña, from an old Buenos Aires family with a distinguished diplomatic and political reputation, ran for president, assured of election. During the campaign he positioned himself as a viable choice between reasonable reforms and revolution. The old corrupt methods assured his victory. Two months after the election he sent reform legislation to congress. Reluctantly, congress passed the Sáenz Peña Law in 1912. In spite of opposition and alarmist editorials, the plan won by a substantial margin.[2]

The law provided a secret ballot, compulsory voting, and minority representation for the party with the second largest number of ballots. No property or literacy requirements restricted participation. The federal judiciary assumed the task of organizing elections, while the army supervised polling. The voter list, derived from the registration for military service compiled since 1901, included all male citizens eighteen years of age and older. The reforms drew in citizens, only 40 to 45 percent of the male population, and excluded women and noncitizen immigrants. Nevertheless, the reforms encompassed a large enough number to be functional. Sáenz Peña understood that Hipólito Yrigoyen, a fellow SRA and Jockey Club associate as well as the leader of the Radical party, concerned himself with constitutional democracy, not the redistribution of wealth or the destruction of the export elite.

Compliance and enforcement received its first test in the governor's race in Santa Fé Province. When the parties involved in the election claimed procedural irregularities, the president appointed a special representative to supervise the election. The UCR won. The results erased most of the Radical party's doubts about political participation as their candidates swept the 1912 congressional elections in Buenos Aires. The Socialists won two seats and showed strength in number of districts. Predictably, when the Socialists increased their representation the following year, many conservatives renewed calls for restrictions, alleging that the electorate lacked a mature sense of responsibility. Nevertheless, the oligarchy drew considerable comfort from the Radicals' rhetorical attacks on the Socialists and the immigrant Liga del Sur as "foreign scum." The Radicals portrayed their party as homegrown and its members as responsible citizens.

The Socialists became the most avid critics of the Radicals, concerned that they would lose members to the UCR. Their critique of the Radicals became a well-reasoned attack on the political system that the UCR appeared poised to inherit. Justo attacked in direct terms the government's responsibility for the rising cost of living. Justo noted that the problem resulted from an increase in paper money that eroded the value of wages at a time when the country enjoyed prosperity. Moreover, nonproductive government expenditures and the creation of positions for relatives, hangers on, and middle-class petitioners consumed revenue. The number of bureaucrats grew significantly between 1895 and 1914. Special appropriations for various groups drained resources. Moreover, protective tariffs for privileged industries, including sugar, kept consumer prices artificially high. Justo pointed to the distribution of funds to cover provincial budget deficits without any federal restrictions on how the provinces spent resources. Federal money appeared to underwrite the corrupt patronage for the camarillas that governed the provinces. Agricultural land, only lightly taxed, burdened middle and lower class tax payers.

The Socialists faced the problem that many of their supporters could not vote. Many immigrants hesitated to give up their native citizenship to enter a society that viewed them with suspicion. Subsequently, when World War I broke out, a significant number returned to their homeland to go to war. In the 1913 election only 13,300 naturalized citizens voted out of 109,000 ballots cast. The Socialists attempted to introduce legislation to simplify the naturalization process, but failed. The 1914 election indicated a trend, as middle-class voters flocked to the Radical party. Bureaucrats, professionals, and university students became the key groups needed to win. The Radicals had 28 deputies, as a result of wins in the provinces as well as the capital. Increasingly, the Socialists and the Radicals ignored the conservatives to attack each other, as it became obvious that the UCR would capture the presidency. The Socialists charged, with some reason, that the Radical party constituted a branch of the elite "oligarchic trunk." Indeed, the new political structure rearranged the previous one, and in effect the UCR shared power with the oligarchy. Sáenz Peña's death in August 1914 marked the end of an era perhaps too generously eulogized as a peaceful political revolution.

The Radicals met two weeks before the election to select Yrigoyen as their presidential candidate. The UCR's congressional ticket included three SRA member, but no working class candidates. Yrigoyen remained in seclusion and did not convey even a remotely suggestive platform, but his fellow candidates promised change. The PAN's retreat from power left conservative and Catholic voters only two options, supporting the Radicals or the Progressive Democratic party (PDP), established in 1915 by Carlos Ibarguren. A reformed conservative party, the PDP criticized the oligarchy for accepting French and British ideas without questioning how such notions met the needs of the country. The PDP accused the oligarchy of making the nation economically dependent. In addition to antagonizing the elite, the PDP's secular approach alienated the Church and Catholic voters. Of more significance, Ibarguren laid out complaints against the oligarchy that the Nationalists endorsed. Nevertheless, Yrigoyen's election in 1916 appeared preordained.

Unrealistic expectations became evident at Yrigoyen's inauguration, when the crowd surged, unhitched the horses and pulled the president's carriage down the Avenida de Mayo. During his first term (1916–1922), nine Jockey Club members served in Yrigoyen's cabinet, as did three from the SRA, including the president, and four Circulo de Armas members. The oligarchy retained sufficient elements of power at the upper levels of the UCR administration to further their interests or counter unacceptable reforms. Indeed, legislation during this period favored the agricultural elite. Moreover, the Sáenz Peña law required provincial legislatures to elect senators, allowing elite camarillas to determine the selection.

Many UCR supporters expected sweeping changes, perhaps the beginning of a new era. The absence of a program made disappointment inevitable. Yrigoyen talked of economic and social reforms, but what he had in mind remained unclear. He seemed to imply changes in land policy or some other means of distributing wealth. He did not follow through. Yrigoyen used the old methods, including the device of federal intervention in the provinces to break the control of uncooperative provincial politicians. In his first term he intervened 20 times, including 15 by presidential decree. Employing constitutionally questionable practices, he gained control of the Chamber of Deputies but still faced opposition in the Senate, elected for a protective nine-year term.

The Radicals governed reactively. Only after protest or large-scale violence occurred did they act. Nevertheless, the president changed the image and social posture of the presidency. He projected a man of the people persona willing to listen and even help on an individual basis with money or employment. He dressed in the fashion of a worker in his Sunday best and acted without class pretensions, although employing patriarchal methods. Less positively, he failed to concede the legitimacy of his political opposition and embraced the same negative practices that he had challenged during the early days.

THE EXCLUDED WORKING CLASS

The urban working class found little in common with the middle class. They resented the economic privileges of factory owners, landholders, and exporters, as well as the Radical party's patronage of the middle class. Strikes became more disruptive as industry attempted to deal with material shortages caused by World War I. The war disrupted coal imports from England, forcing industry to operate at reduced levels. Railway companies struggled to maintain schedules while imports plunged. Real wages fell between 1914 and 1917 by a third as shortages forced industries to dismiss workers. Use of agricultural wastes compressed into briquettes for heating and cooking symbolized wartime hardships and the decline in living standards. Frustrated workers clashed with factory owners as strikes became violent. Employers with links with vigilante groups formed the Labor Association (*Asociación del Trabajo*) to break strikes with replacement workers. The meatpacking strike of December 1917 ended bloodily, as the police stormed union headquarters armed with sabers slashing anyone unlucky enough to be in the way. A railroad strike earlier in the year resulted in damaged and burned equipment. The government usually intervened against strikes mounted by supposed radicals, while moderate union leaders often received Yrigoyen's support. In the case of the rail strike the president imposed a generous contract on the companies, including an eight-hour day, annual paid vacations, and sick and overtime pay. Yrigoyen's tactics undercut the Socialists and pushed the Anarchists into confrontation, with grim consequences. Two violent clashes, the January 1919 *Semana Trágica* (Tragic Week) and the *Patagonia Trágica* (1921–1922), rank among the worst labor disturbances of the early twentieth century.

The Semana Trágica began with a strike against a metalwork factory by an Anarchist union late in 1918. Fighting broke out between strikebreakers and workers. Heavy-handed police tactics added to the violence. Over the course of the next several days, events spun out of control. The

Anarchist Labor Federation's call for a general strike provided the pretext for vigilantes, who subsequently provided the core of *Liga Patriótica Argentina* (Argentine Patriotic League). Thugs swept into the Jewish barrio of Buenos Aires (popular perceptions associated Jews with Anarchists) and by the time the destruction ended, 700 to 1,500 people died and another 4,000 had been beaten or injured. The army, without orders from the president, assumed control of the capital. Property damage and lost production and wages cost the economy millions of pesos.

Yrigoyen offered to arbitrate between the parties. In the end, an alarmed government forced the company to settle the strike. Lingering police and vigilante violence slowly played itself out and the Semana Trágica ended. Upper class perceptions that the government lacked the will or ability to discipline workers resulted in the formation of the *Liga Patriótica Argentina*. The LPA responded to fears that foreign ideologies, and labor organizations influenced by them, would shred the social fabric and damage the economy. Manuel Carlés established the League in 1919 with the idea of using physical force to root out radicals. Organized as a paramilitary organization, the LPA drew much of its leadership from the Jockey Club. The league's mission to indoctrinate the working class to counter radicalism had the support of the Church, the elite, and the middle class. A female division labored to bring the League's message to working- women. While the upper and middle classes became more concerned, labor became increasingly desperate and militant.

In Patagonia, violence came on the heels of a momentary improvement in working conditions. In late 1920, employers, mainly British sheep operators, organized as the *Sociedad Rural de Santa Cruz*, responded positively to demands for better wages and conditions. Workers wanted a limit on the number of occupants per hut, a mattress for each person, and salaries in hard currency to protect the value of wages. Unfortunately, a drop in the price of wool on world markets led to deterioration of labor and living conditions. A general strike drew a sharp line between owners and workers. The issue came down to which side would bear the burden of hard times. Angry workers seized property, while landowners formed white guards to defend their interests. Local Radical party officials sided with the owners. Unbalanced reports picked up by the press presented an alarmist and distorted picture. After local muscle failed to break the strike, the army arrived in early 1921, believing that it faced an Anarchist insurrection. The Tenth Cavalry, commanded by Lt. Colonel Héctor Varela assisted by LPA members, shot suspected Anarchists in cold blood, tortured strikers, and dumped their bodies into mass graves. After some 2,000 victims, the strike collapsed. In a gruesome aftermath, Colonel Varela died in a bomb blast, his assassin subsequently murdered by a guard, who then in turn died violently: a chain of death that shook the nation.

A SHIFTING CULTURAL BASE

The middle class viewed a university education as a means of upward social and economic mobility. They wanted professional schools and the status of a university degree but without the humanistic learning that the children of the wealthy acquired. University curriculums reflected traditional academic values with little practical instruction. The University of Córdoba, a Jesuit institution founded in 1622, symbolized education as class adornment. It had been reformed several times, by both the Jesuits and secular authorities. Nevertheless, an impatient middle class saw little value in learning not directly connected to immediate economic and social advancement. Worldwide, a new educational age appeared to have dawned, a notion subsequently reinforced with the transformation of education in Russia. In the view of the middle class Argentina needed less elegance and more applied learning. With the election of a UCR president in 1916, pressure turned to demands.

Córdoba's students protested in 1918 with strikes and passionate manifestos. They demanded student participation in all areas of the university, including its administration. Strikers called for a less humanistic curriculum, practical examinations, and an end of faculty selection based on what they considered arbitrary criteria. Student strikes spread to the universities of Buenos Aires and La Plata. A combination of complaints mixed with class frustrations fueled the reform movement. A rapid increase in university enrollment also played a role. From some 3,000 students in 1900, enrollment surged to 14,000 by 1918. Although a small number in today's terms, the influx of students overwhelmed institutional ability to meet new expectations and blend them with the existing university culture.

The Radical government supported the strikers, forcing their demands on the universities, including establishing autonomous universities with power shared equally between students, faculty, and alumni. Financing responsibilities remained with the state. All institutions functioned under charters elaborated by the government. Two new universities, in Santa Fé and Tucumán, received similar documents and regulations. The university reforms in 1919 ended traditional higher education and shifted the emphasis to professional training.

Reforms brought economic and social benefits but politicized higher education as students became active political participants with their own interests. While professional advances failed to close the social gap between the middle class and the oligarchy, the middle class achieved a status separation from the lower classes, complete with their own professional associations and clubs. Politically, they relied upon the UCR to promote their class interests, although many students from immigrant families preferred more militant groups.

University reforms also created a new type of intellectual perceived to be grounded in reality, with only a mild interest in humanistic learning or professional training. For many the Russian Revolution of 1917 signaled the dawn of a new social science age. Marxism appeared to offer an explanation of Argentina's problems. Many of those attracted to Marx accepted some of the complaints advanced by the Nationalists. A Socialist party splinter group established the International Socialist party, which became the Communist party when it joined the Third International in 1920.

Marxism's intellectual development began with Aníbal Ponce (1898–1938), a psychology professor at the National Institute of Secondary Education, who became one of the most important Marxist writers. As did many, he had intellectual roots in positivism before turning to Marxism. A product of the 1919 university reforms, he considered humanism to be too abstract to be useful and advocated a rigorous analysis of reality and the acceptance of humans as concrete beings rather than spiritual abstractions. In his book, *Humanismo burgués y humanismo proletario* (Bourgeois Humanism and Proletarian Humanism), published in 1935, he declared that true humanities could flourish to the fullest extent only in a classless society and on the basis of absolute equality. Ponce viewed the Church as a supporting pillar of the oligarchy because of its desire to preserve hierarchy based on a class structure and passivity through social harmony.

Another influential Marxist, Rodolfo Ghioldi (1897–1985), directed the National League of Teachers between 1910 and 1921. After a visit to the Soviet Union in 1921 he became a party loyalist following the Comintern line. He accepted the Nationalist notion of a conscious alliance between foreign imperialists and the oligarchy but rejected the separation of interests between Buenos Aires and the provinces. Victorio Codovilla (1894–1970), a close associate of Ghioldi, attacked the Pan American Union (subsequently, the Organization of Americas States) as a tool of Washington. Rabidly anti-imperialist, he warned against the seduction inherent in the Good Neighbor policy that created collaborators and clients. He also cautioned against the creation of exclusionary regional blocs.

Others who offered a Marxist interpretation included Silvio Frondizi (1907–1974,) the brother of Arturo Frondizi, elected president as discussed below. Silvio had a national reputation as a history and political science professor and prolific author. His 1956 multivolume work, *La realidad argentina* (The Argentine Reality) offered an interpretation that placed the country in the context of the global spread of capitalism. He approved of the activities of radical priests and lay followers and their amalgamation of Catholic social thought and Marxism..

Liborio Justo (1902–2003), another product of the university reform of 1919 and a Marxist gadfly, had the distinction of being the son of Augustín

P. Justo, who served as president of the republic from 1932–1938. Liborio, referred to as Quebracho (a hardwood tree reputed to break the axe of those that attempted to cut it down), published short stories, tracts, and brief histories, including some on imperialism. He explored the relationship of the pampas to the nation's history and believed the destruction of the Indians could only be seen as a racist act. Influenced by the writings of American writer Waldo Frank, he called on Argentines to resist the crass, grasping values of the United States, along with its expansive economic reach.

In an amusing incident during a 1937 visit to Buenos Aires by the American President Franklin D. Roosevelt, a voice in the back of the hall shouted "Down with Yankee imperialism" as Roosevelt rose to speak. Policemen subdued the interloper and ejected him. After the event, a mortified President Justo whispered to a policeman: "Was that my son Liborio?" And as he feared, the officer replied, "Sí Señor Presidente."[3]

Marxists condemned imperialism, colonialism, liberal democracy, capitalism, and materialism. They rejected religion, class harmony, nationalism, the importance of a unique Argentine spirit, and the cherished Nationalist notion of a natural aristocracy. Unlike the Nationalists, their nostalgia had utopian roots that dismissed Creole Argentina as a colonial episode. Both Nationalists and Marxists supported authoritarian governments and did not accept the finality of elections or the existence of a legitimate opposition and a critical press. They agreed on who controlled the means of production and shared the anger and resentment the Nationalists directed at the oligarchy. Conspiracy theories supplied the same degree of energizing victimization for both groups. Nevertheless, Marxists submerged the country's complaints in the broader context of internationalism. University professors introduced Marxism to generations of Argentine students. It would soon be reflected in literature as well as in social science. Marxism's ability to define terms and break processes into component parts with a convincing degree of clarity had much to do with its acceptance. Marxist thought, like Nationalist thought, entered the mindset of Argentines as a means of comprehending their history.

In spite of their deep antipathy for each other, Marxists and Nationalists shared many common enemies, a reality that had a major impact on popular attitudes. A siege mentality developed among the middle class, who felt bombarded from both sides on core issues such as imperialism's hold on the nation, the oligarchy's destructive economic alliance, victimization by external forces such as foreign multinational corporations, and betrayal by the elite. Many learned to address their concerns using the rhetoric of both the Nationalists and the Marxists.

The cultural shift diminished the influence of the oligarchy. Nevertheless, agriculturists continued to direct the economy. The oligarchy revealed its vision at the annual agricultural fair held in the heart of the city. The popular event, sponsored by the Sociedad Rural Argentina (SRA) and held in late July in Buenos Aires' Palermo Park, displayed prize livestock and modern devices of every sort, and demonstrated new animal husbandry techniques. The fair entertained and instructed. Urban and rural families, along with their children, admired the exquisitely groomed animals and enjoyed their brush with the estancia mystique that made Argentina famous throughout the world. The association's presidential address set the political tone and outlined the organization's objectives. Politicians listened, and newspapers carried extensive coverage. Links between the SRA and the *Union Industrial,* which represented factory owners, the *Camara de Comercio,* bankers, national and foreign owned packinghouses and grain shippers, constituted an important political and economic force when a consensus existed.

THE COLLAPSE OF 1929

Yrigoyen's term ended in 1922. Unable constitutionally to seek a consecutive term he selected Marcelo T. de Alvear as his replacement. Alvear (1868–1942), a member of the SRA, the Jockey Club, and the Circulo de Armas, and from one of the richest families in the nation, joined the Radicals as a law student. Yrigoyen appointed him ambassador to France in 1916. Generally considered a *bon vivant* and socialite, Alvear appeared to be a controllable successor. Yrigoyen selected him over other more obvious possibilities with the idea that he would not overshadow or threaten his control of the party. Moreover, Alvear's presidency would help reassure the oligarchy that the UCR had not moved too far to the left.

President Alvear (1922–1928) inherited a large public debt and a swollen bureaucracy, both a result of Yrigoyen's use of patronage to build support. As a first step, the new president replaced Yrigoyen loyalists in the government and the military. Alvear selected his cabinet from his friends, including eight Jockey Club members. The rift between the two men contributed to the split in the party in 1924. The majority stayed with Yrigoyen, while the dissidents formed the *Unión Cívica Radical Antipersonalista.* President Alvear did not support the split in the UCR. Nevertheless, the Radical Party lost momentum and creditability, and the balance of power in the lower house fell to Socialist deputies.

Divisions among the Socialists made it difficult to take full advantage of the UCR's troubles, and in 1927 their party also split. It represented the party's fourth schism. Ironically, class differences within the party led to the breakup as middle-class lawyers defended their right to represent clients opposed to Socialist principles. The Independent Socialist Party (*Partido Socialista Independente*), representing an upwardly mobile segment of the party, had more in common with the UCR than with the Socialists.

The decline of economic liberalism after World War I posed a serious challenge. The ability to raise investment capital and maintain export-based expansion became less certain. Markets changed as consumption declined along with prices. By 1925, this became evident in wheat as Europeans increased domestic production. That same year Benito Mussolini announced the "Battle for Wheat" in Italy to increase self- sufficiency. Agricultural prices began a long period of weakness.

Moreover, Britain, the country's source of investment capital, emerged from the war bankrupt. In 1927, talk about imperial preference favoring agricultural imports from British dominions and possessions concerned the agricultural producers. The British Ambassador made clear that his country would buy from those who purchased its manufactured goods. That same year the United States, in spite of the fact that it could not meet its own demand for beef, imposed a blanket ban on Argentine meat as a consequence of an outbreak of foot-and-mouth disease, effectively ending the hope of entering the American market.

The presidential elections of 1928 predictably returned Yrigoyen to office. Yrigoyen rebuilt his popularity by promising a return to the free spending patronage of his first term. Yrigoyen cultivated the Catholic hierarchy also, on occasion involving clerics indirectly in his administration. The president's opposition to divorce served as the foundation of the de facto alliance with the Catholic hierarchy. Not all approved. The army long resented Yrigoyen's meddling in army affairs and the weakening of discipline that he encouraged by favoring his own military supporters. Concerned officers disliked what they believed to be demagoguery.

Yrigoyen used his own Nationalist issue—the state petroleum monopoly—to deflect criticism. During his first term, Yrigoyen established a petroleum board, the *Direccion Nacional de los Yacimientos Petroliferos Fiscales* (YPF). Supposedly, revenues would eliminate public debts, provide cheap power, and make other taxes unnecessary. The Radicals trumpeted their commitment to a state monopoly from drilling, refining, and distribution. Standard Oil became the emotional focal point of an antiforeign campaign. Trade difficulties with the United States provided a sub agenda for the conflict with Standard Oil. Yrigoyen, to make his displeasure evident, supported the SRA's campaign to buy British goods. Herbert Hoover, President-elect of the United States, visited Argentina in 1928, only to be rudely ignored.

By the late 1920s the electorate doubled over that of 1912, potentially providing the Radicals with a mass base. Nevertheless, the unappreciated immigrant and first-generation working class citizens had not been accommodated politically or economically. Yrigoyen concerned himself with the population core of Buenos Aires and its province, ignoring provincial politics. The interior remained peripheral to the nation and the party. The UCR became a Porteño party rather than a national party, with a governing committee composed of Buenos Aires politicians who met in the capital. Presidential intervention in the provinces reminded them of Buenos Aires' historic self- interested desire to subordinate the interior.

With the 1929 Wall Street crash, the regime began to unravel. The bureaucracy, central to Yrigoyen's patronage system, could no longer be supported; income declined, unemployment rose, and the Radicals began to lose their core constituency and elections. A torrent of rumors regarding Yrigoyen's mental state reflected weakening support. Disenchanted Radicals, and a growing number of political enemies, referred to the president as el Peludo (the mole), an image suggested by his excessive hairiness and reluctance to appear in public, but one that also implied isolation. The absence of a party structure able to go beyond personality proved fatal. A far-too-domineering leader failed to recognize how much the world economy had changed. The president, like many others, including Raúl Prebisch, who subsequently helped pull the economic situation together, thought that the crash of 1929 represented just another economic cycle and recovery would soon follow as orthodox remedial measures took hold.[4] Newspapers, including *La Prensa* and *La Nación*, assured their readers that it represented a temporary break in prosperity.

As what had initially been seen as a routine economic cycle deepened, the sense of unease mounted. A contracting economy and shrinking resources stripped away illusions reducing everything to economics. The elite, anxious to use their influence to mitigate the negative economic impact, coveted government assets. At the same time the middle class, with its sense of entitlement nurtured by the Radicals, wanted tax revenues to prop up wages and employment. In the scramble for resources, the middle class and workers could not win. Apprehensive Radicals unintentionally captured the extent of their concerns in the ritual greeting that posed the question, "*Radical?*" And the response, "*Hasta la muerte!*" (until death).

The threatened collapse of exports exposed the vulnerability of raw material producers. Britain, the major agricultural market, held all the cards—it could buy elsewhere or strike a favorable deal with a desperate country. The times appeared too critical to allow a continuation of ineffectual government and what many believed to be Yrigoyen's destructive politics. Nevertheless, the 1912 compromise could not be annulled without creating further uncertainties. The solution appeared to be an authoritarian government that could manage the crisis. A coup in September 1930 ended the regime. That same month and year the anarcho-syndicalists and Socialist labor confederations joined to form the *Confederación General de Trabajo* (the General Labor Confederation—CGT).

THE PRINCE OF WALES IN ARGENTINA

The Prince of Wales' visit to Argentina in celebration of the centennial of the Treaty of Amity and Commerce between the two countries presented the opportunity to strengthen ties with Great Britain. President Marcelo Torcuato de Alvear carefully prepared for the visit of the future Monarch of Great Britain, soon to be Edward the VIII. The handsome young man from the House of Windsor arrived in Argentina in August 1925. The Prince of Wales may have been the most sought-after celebrity visitor of the era, but also represented Argentina's most important trading partner. He had a reputation as a charming person who did not stand on ceremony—an approachable and very modern prince, and one of the world's most eligible bachelors. All understood that the country had much to gain by receiving him in style and seeing to it that he left with fond memories of Buenos Aires, the Paris of South America, the pampas, the tango, and the warmth and generosity of a proud modern nation. Every comfort would be provided. Daniel Ortiz Basualdo placed his elegant Buenos Aires residence at the prince's disposal.

The royal visitor had a hectic schedule. A typical day consisted of a morning visit to St Andrew's College, followed by a tour of the British Hospital, then lunch with the British Chamber of Commerce, a short break, then polo at the Hurlingham Club, all before the evening's entertainment. Minor moments, such as a quiet coffee and pastry at the Confiteria del Molina, must have seemed a relief to the prince. The Confiteria del Aguila, with an imperial eagle above the entrance, catered a celebration in honor of the prince. The Jockey Club constructed a squash court to enable the prince to keep up his game, and showed him every consideration.

President Alvear, a sophisticated man and a former ambassador to France, came from one of the country's most distinguished families. He knew how to entertain in the roaring twenties manner, mixing elegance and wealth and a touch of street culture. The president moved in show-business circles (his wife had been a singer in Portugal) and understood the mutual attraction of princes and entertainers. The high point came at a private dinner at Huetel, the magnificent estancia of Doña Concepción Unzué de Casares, for the Prince of Wales and his escorting party of three cabinet ministers, a general, a rear admiral, the British minister to Argentina, a British vice-admiral, the Maharaja of Kapurthala, and assorted important people. After an elegant but supposedly typical Argentine dinner accompanied by carefully selected French wines and fulsome toasts, the evening's entertainment began.

Carlos Gardel and José Razzano, dressed as gauchos, supplied the popular touch. Just on the verge of becoming an international star and with a reputation as one of the country's finest singers, Gardel and his partner Razzano, accompanied by two guitarists, launched into the evening's entertainment. An enthralled prince tapped his feet and nodded his head in time to the music, then rushed up stairs to get his ukulele and join the performers. At the stroke of midnight, the prince shook hands, autographed photos for the singers, and retired. The party went on without him until two in the morning.

Subsequently, a dinner in honor of the Prince of Wales at the Savoy Hotel in London celebrated the successful visit. Lord Farington presided over a distinguished gathering attended by the Argentine Minister and a glittering array of prominent British and Argentine guests, including military dignitaries, commercial figures, and others with connections with South America. The ties between the two countries required toasts, reference to the number of congratulatory telegrams, and amusing comments about their common interest in sports, horses, and Polo. At the time, few could have imagined that within a decade ties between the two nations would be strained almost to the breaking point.

The Times, December 11, 1925. Simon Collier, *The Life, Music, and Times of Carlos Gardel* (Pittsburgh: University of Pittsburgh Press, 1986), pp. 85–86.

CONFRONTING THE CRISIS

The leader of the coup, General José Felix Uriburu served as provisional president from 1930 to 1932. From an important family in Salta, his uncle José Evaristo Uriburu, a prominent member of PAN, served as president from 1895 to 1898. General Uriburu supported the PDP's failed attempt to defeat the UCR in the election of 1922. Under President Alvear, General Uriburu became inspector general of the army. A member of the Jockey Club and *Círculo de Armas*, he shared elite concerns but also those of the army. Uriburu understood the utility of nationalism as a means of rallying the nation to confront the crisis but did not share the passion of the Nationalists.

Provisional president Uriburu exiled or imprisoned those he viewed as a threat to stability. The government controlled the press, intimidated students, and violated university autonomy. Even some of Uriburu's elite friends from the Jockey Club felt his heavy hand. Victoria Ocampo (1890–1979), a complex personality from an upper class family, a feminist and

Radical Party supporter, established her influential literary journal *SUR* in 1931, as a voice for liberalism in the face of the authoritarian regime. Fortunately, the government ignored her.

Prior to the crisis the government derived slightly over 60 percent of its revenues from land sales, customs duties, harbor and moorage charges, and fees and licenses. After 1929 import tax collection dropped by 10 percent and export taxes fell by 45 percent. A frantic government cut expenditures throwing an estimated 20,000 federal employees in Buenos Aires into the streets. Exchange controls and a general 10 percent increase in tariffs forced a contraction in imports. Previously untaxed items, including gasoline, lost their exemptions. Fees raised on every conceivable service and a business and income tax put in place in 1932 squeezed out barely enough revenue.

Fear of food riots prompted the introduction of soup kitchens in some of the hardest-hit districts of Buenos Aires. A police unit, the Special Section, monitored alleged subversives. The Special Section's usefulness endeared it to successive presidents until its elimination in 1955. Uriburu joined Nationalist groups together, forming the Argentine Civic Legion. Members, attired in brown shirts after the model of the German S.A., carried weapons and received military training. The Argentine Civic Legion promoted a strong military to confront their ideological and psychological enemies. The Special Section, the Legion, and the police constituted the enforcement structure believed necessary to ensure internal stability, while the army remained responsible for foreign threats.

Lt. Colonel Manuel Savio, a central figure in the creation of military industries, rose to an influential position as part of the Uriburu faction. Well aware of the dangers posed by the world depression, General Uruburu pressed forward with an expanded role for military factories. He built on the World War I experience, which demonstrated the nation's dependency on foreign suppliers for vital goods and material. Even before 1929 much of the foundation for a state owned industrial sector had been laid. The state petroleum agency (*Yacimientos Petroliferos Fiscales*—YPF), placed under the direction of General Enrique Mosconi in 1922, already aimed at self-sufficiency in fuel oils as a security objective, and in 1923 congress mandated the establishment of defense industries, including a steel mill.

Crisis measures by a provisional president could be tolerated in the short run, justified by the emergency. Nevertheless, long-term legitimacy required the preservation of a liberal-democratic façade no matter what shady manipulations it required. General Augustín P. Justo assumed the presidency.

DEALING WITH THE DEPRESSION

President-General Justo (1932–1938) represented a return to the pre-1912 political realty. A former minister of war, Justo relied upon the oligarchy, provincial politicians, dissident Radicals, and the army. The *Concordancia* brought together the conservative National Democratic Party, Anti-Personalist Radicals (Justo belonged to the Anti-Personalist Radical party) and the Independent Socialists in what constituted a national unity government. The notion that a faltering liberal democracy needed to retreat and regroup unpinned the Concordancia, although some believed that it had been fatally wounded. Electoral manipulation and disqualification of orthodox Radical Party politicians assured the desired results while maintaining a civilized façade.

Justo terminated some of the heavy handed practices of his predecessor, ended the state of siege, released political prisoners, and permitted pro-Radical professors to reclaim their positions. Yrigoyen, allowed to return to his Buenos Aires home, died several months later. Justo preferred gentle repression, whenever possible. President Justo dispatched General Juan Bautista Molina, an admirer of Nazi Germany, to Berlin in an attempt to remove him from contact with the Legion. Over 10,000 Legion storm troopers constituted a force potentially able to challenge the government. When politically feasible, Justo reduced the Legion's influence.

The balance-of-payments deficit and the external and internal debt would be managed by a series of almost day-to-day adjustments. By 1934 taxes almost balanced the budget. Federal budget procedures, already addressed in a preliminary way by the previous government, became much more exact and able to identify shortfalls and surpluses in time to redirect revenues. Nevertheless, internal measures had to contend with international trends. Predatory trade policies threatened primary product exporters worldwide. In 1932, Britain, struggling to keep afloat, adopted imperial preferences that supported their colonial food dependencies over noncommonwealth suppliers. The Ottawa Pact favored New Zealand and Australian wool and meat and Canadian wheat exports.[5] Moreover, technology increased yields and resulted in higher animal carcass weights, further weakening Argentine prices, quite apart from the deflation that accompanied the depression after 1929.

An almost panicked government agreed to the Roca-Runciman treaty (1933) that tied the country economically to Britain. Many Argentines angrily opposed the treaty as an infringement on the nation's independence, but the government saw no other option. Under the agreement, Britain promised to purchase the same amount of beef as in 1932. In return, Argentina reduced tariffs on British imports to 1930 levels and made other concessions. Argentina exported six percent less in 1934 than before the economic collapse, and for the same money purchased 40 percent fewer imports. Even an all-out export program could not compensate for the reality that raw materials prices fell more than prices of manufactured goods. Foreign exchange controls allowed the government to restrict imports of necessary items. In 1936, the agreement, reworked and renewed, reduced the British quota and, disquietingly, allowed for limited imports of chilled beef from Australia. Argentina appeared to be helpless and unable to bargain as an economic partner. In 1933, Finance minister Federico Pinedo worried that that crops would not be planted because producer returns fell below costs, in part because of exchange rate restrictions, so he guaranteed a minimum price for agricultural exports. Fortunately, prices improved as a consequence of droughts in Canada and Australia in 1934 and the droughts and storms that created the dust bowl in the United States. By 1937, the support program could be dropped without endangering production. Many noted that the trade concessions favored foreigners and propped up the domestic agricultural elite. Nevertheless, chilled beef alone represented 16 percent of the country's exports. Agriculture directly or indirectly supported a significant number of urban workers. Moreover, the guaranteed market for agricultural exports under the terms of the Roca-Runciman agreement made it possible to convince bondholders to accept new bonds with lower interest.

State intervention, no matter how distasteful to agricultural producers, appeared to be the only solution to the collapse of the presumed-to-be-natural economic order. Although Yrigoyen's petroleum policy, along with elements of European fascism and FDR's New Deal, provided precedence, finding an acceptable model required experimentation. The Roca-Runciman agreement allowed the importation of more expensive British textiles but shut out inexpensive Italian and Japanese imports. Domestic textile producers supported by a subsidy now had a protected market. Demand for textiles overwhelmed manufacturers. A twelve-month backlog guaranteed future work and profits. Some 65 percent of industrial activity concentrated on food, beverages, and textiles to meet basic needs. A public works program created consumers for domestic goods. Purchases of surplus machinery at cut-rate prices in distressed industrialized countries made it possible to meet light manufacturing needs without imports. A 1930 decree that favored national firms in public contracts spurred domestic production of concrete, dramatically reducing demand for the imported product. Between 1933 and 1935, import substitution driven industry grew at a 16 percent annual rate, then slowed to a still respectable 5.5 percent annual rate through 1939.

A small number of large firms such as the *Sociedad Industrial Americana de Maquinarias* (SIAM), which manufactured appliances under foreign licenses, and the major beer producer, the Bemberg consortium, had considerable influence on industrial policy. Reasonable economic stability and tariffs attracted American subsidiaries, including General Electric, American and Foreign Power, International Telephone and Telegraph, Dupont, and others. By the late 1930s, American companies employed 14,000 workers.

Finance Minister Pinedo built on the foundation of confidence created by earlier reforms to restructure the banking system and prop up the paper peso. Revaluating the country's gold reserves (virtually the only asset that appreciated during the depression) made it possible to provide capitalization for the Central Bank, established in 1935 under the direction of Raúl Prebisch. Gold revaluation allowed the government to return the money it had withdrawn from private banks and provide liquidity to back up deposits. Although in the early years of the depression unemployment surged, by the mid-1930s it returned to its 1929, level indicating that the country had regained its economic balance.

Migration into the cities, as a consequence of mechanization and a soft market for export agriculture, stimulated the urban economy. Buenos Aires grew to 3.5 million inhabitants by 1936, and migrant flows transformed villages into towns and towns into cities. Pinedo proposed to raise wages to support more demand for domestic production and increase the rate of industrial expansion beyond the import substitution market. His grand plan of 1939–1940 anticipated a European war and planned to build upon it. Pinedo envisioned a free trade zone with neighboring countries to absorb exports disrupted by hostilities, and as the situation stabilized and wartime oversea exports returned, the country and its free trade partners could exploit regional as well as global industrial opportunities. Nevertheless, the Central Bank cautioned that without access to inexpensive raw materials, reasonably priced energy, and improved transportation, insufficient production could not soak up the proposed higher wages, which risked elevated prices and inflation.[6] The opportunity to pursue socio-economic viability would be missed. The political relationship between rural and the urban areas continued to be more or less as it had been in the earlier decades, in spite of the growth of cities.

The interior provinces remained mired in backwardness, poverty, malnutrition, and disease. A few economically viable industries, such as the wine industry in Mendoza, cotton in the Chaco, and sugar in Tucumán, flourished amid working-class poverty and nineteenth-century labor practices. Cotton supplied demand in Germany, Japan, and England, and government incentives, including free land, seed, and technical advice, increased production to some 70 to 80 thousand tons with an estimated million acres under cultivation. Nevertheless, by the end of the 1930s, per capita income levels in Catamarca and in Santiago del Estero barely amounted to ten percent of that of the City of Buenos Aires, with other interior provinces not much higher. In more favored provinces 20,000 owners controlled 70 percent of the best land. In Buenos Aires province 3,500 owners controlled 50 percent of the land. The softening touch of paternalism disappeared as commercial agriculture became ever more impersonal. Machines reduced the number of seasonal workers, while managers dealt with employees. The socio-economic gap between the upper class, the middle, and lower classes widened as the exports recovered from the crash of 1929.

As the troubled 1930s drew to a close, President Justo chose Roberto Ortiz, a former minister of public works and an anti-personalista Radical, as his successor. Ortiz supported a more open and honest political arrangement. His election in 1938 promised action to resolve the urban-rural stalemate. Unfortunately, a series of problems led to indecisive drift. Complicating matters, the president's health deteriorated. Chronic diabetes forced Ortiz to turn over the presidential office to Vice-President Ramón S. Castillo. The new president had few ideas to put forward, knowing only what he opposed. Nevertheless, Minister Frederico Pinedo proposed to press ahead with industrial investments in favor of urban Argentina. The conservative opposition derailed the plan. As his term drew to a close, Castillo backed Robustiano Patrón Costas, a wealthy sugar businessman from the interior, as his successor.

Manufacturing offered the best hope of employing the urban working class. Nevertheless, industrial employers received only cautious encouragement in the 1930s. Agricultural producers viewed import substitution and manufacturing as undeniably useful under the circumstances but limited in the long run. The idea that industrial goods might be able to compete on the world market, as did agricultural exports, appeared highly unlikely, if not impossible. Prudence suggested a continuation of the emphasis on agriculture. Economic policy reflected the negative influence of the agricultural oligarchy, unwilling to confront the need to employ a growing number of urban workers.

NATIONALIST PERSUASIONS

By the 1930s Nationalists expanded their critique from defense of traditional culture to a more complex mix heavily laced with economic concerns and anti-imperialism.[7] Their support of the Catholic concepts of social justice and harmony firmed into an advocacy of a political structure to direct and regulate society. A system of government based on liberalism appeared unnatural, because as a Church spokesman noted, Catholics "cannot be liberal." [8] Nationalists warned that tyranny resulted from anarchy, but only as a consequence of authoritarianism's failure to perform its functions. Most Nationalists viewed the army as the institution best suited to provide a stable foundation for such a system, but not necessarily suited to govern directly.

The disruptions of the 1920s and 1930s and uncertainty over the outcome created a near-perfect environment in which to influence a public anxious for explanations. Raúl Scalabrini Ortiz published his critique of what had gone wrong, *El hombre que está sola y espera* (Man Alone and Waiting) in 1931. The spirit of Argentina, constantly evoked by the Nationalists, took

on aspects of a secular "Holy Ghost," a source of unchallengeable legitimacy. Scalabrini Ortiz offered an image of what he termed the "el espiritú
de la tierra," a giant so large that he could not be seen, who devoured
and assimilated vast numbers of immigrants. The giant knew what he
wanted and where he needed to go. Argentines, mere microscopic cells
of the large body, could not use their puny intelligence to understand the
destiny that the spirit had in mind.[9] Only the Nationalists had an inking
of what stood in the way of an acceptable destiny.

Scalabrini Ortiz, as both a writer and historian, contributed to a wave of
revisionism that reinforced the notion that Argentina had been a victimized by foreign ideas. Alien notions prevented the population from drawing on the true spirit of the country. Scalabrini Ortiz accused the oligarchy
of betrayal and corroboration with the British imperialists at the expense
of their own nation. Scalabrini Ortiz's denunciation influenced Rodolfo
and Julio Irazusta's book, *La Argentina y el imperio británico: Los eslabones
de una cadena* (Argentina and the British Empire: The Links of a Chain),
published in 1934. The Irazustas cast the British as conniving villains
bleeding profits from the work of others while exploiting the country's
resources. The Roca-Runciman agreement, conceded by a misguided ruling class according to the Irazustas, exposed the colonial relationship and
endangered the nation's sovereignty. A long dormant issue, the British
Falkland Island colony, came back to life on the centenary of the British
occupation, which conveniently coincided with the signing of the Roca-
Runciman agreement. The Nationalists adroitly fashioned it into an
enduring anti-imperialist cause.

In their opinion, Liberalism led to communism, and materialism to a
mechanistic view of human beings that destroyed their spiritual quali-
ties. Nationalists rejected populism as a force that destroyed the natural
hierarchy. True democracy lay with the community and underpinned
everything, making democracy at the upper levels of government unnecessary.[10] Influential Nationalists believed that the country, by subordinat-
ing the question of social justice, jeopardized the nation. Nationalists
drew on selected elements of Catholic doctrine presented in the papal
pronouncements of *Rerum Novarum* (1891) and *Quadragesimo Anno* (1931)
to justify their demands for social justice and class harmony. Externally,
that meant throwing off colonial and unequal relationships. Internally, it
required altering political and moral values and their incorporation in the
governing structure, preferably under an authoritarian regime. A government functioning for the common good had to be corporatist. Justice
and discipline depended on a natural hierarchy and an authoritarian
government.

In place of liberal democracy the Nationalists offered traditional culture
as they defined it. Government by the competent meant a hierarchy that
included all citizens, but with functions consistent with their place in the

social order. Their basic source of inspiration became the Creole spirit and values of old Argentina, both imaginative creations. The Nationalist movement moved in tandem with a Catholic revival that reached a high point with the 1934 *Congreso Eucarístico Internacional* in Buenos Aires. The conference emphasized social justice as a basic step toward an organic, functional society and government able to address the problems of uneven distribution of wealth.

Acceptance of Catholicism as a major element of tradition excluded non-believers from the Nationalist concept of Argentina. Nationalists indulged in anti-Semitism, and in some cases embraced notions drawn from the infamous *Protocols of the Elders of Zion.* Jews, democrats, communists, and Masons served as internal scapegoats, while Britain and the United States became the external forces that preyed on the country's wealth.

Foreign companies came under pressure to justify their presence. The West Indian Oil Company (WICO), the Argentine subsidiary of Standard Oil of New Jersey (Exxon), shifted its advertising away from selling their products to emphasizing the company's social contribution. Their advertising agency dispatched Juan José Soiza-Reilly, a writer for the photo and features journal *Caras y Caretas* (Faces and False Faces), to the Province of Salta, the location of the company's drilling operations, to report on its impact, write a booklet, and over a period of weeks present a series of 15 minute radio broadcasts. Soiza-Reilly reported on community projects; including a 50-bed hospital; the number of people happily employed; and the capital invested by the company—all emphasized WICO's positive participation in the national economy. The campaign confronted irrational, emotional politics that thrived on villains.

Nationalist influence became insidious, molding attitudes accepted broadly across society. Young radicals within the UCR accepted many Nationalist notions. In 1935, they formed the *Fuerza de Orientación Radical de la Juventud Argentina* (FORJA), whose manifesto declared the existence of an ongoing struggle for sovereignty and against imperialism. In 1938, with the establishment of the Juan Manuel de Rosas Institute, the Nationalists created a research organization able to develop policy as well as provide revisionist history to support their agenda. Nationalists created a poisonous mass that metastasized across the culture, but did so in an uneven manner across the political spectrum.

RELATIONS WITH THE UNITED STATES

With the fall of France in the spring of 1940, a British naval force sealed access to European markets, except for Spain and Portugal. Exports plunged to levels below those experienced during the depression, threatening an abrupt economic collapse. Crop financing kept producers afloat until the export market eventually stabilized.

VICTORIA OCAMPO

If there is one person who captures the contradictions of modern Argentina it is Victoria Ocampo. Born in 1890, the year of the Baring debt crisis, she grew up with wealth and status. Victoria came of age on the eve of the Sáenz Peña reform's attempt to create a viable socio-political compromise.

One of six sisters, she grew up with a sense of privilege mixed with impatience at social limitations imposed on her gender. Money, social standing, boundless energy, and an education based on the study of languages and history propelled her into the world of letters. Anxious to escape family restrictions and expectations, she married impulsively and badly. The absence of divorce during her lifetime protected her from further social pressure to marry while providing the opportunity for a series of semi-concealed affairs. She understood that economic independence and a lively mind could place a creative woman at the center of a self-constructed world.

Victoria Ocampo approached Argentine history with the intimacy of a person related to those who played prominent roles in the creation of the nation. To her, street names had faces; she knew the families sometimes well, but always by reputation. Taught French from early childhood, much of her education revolved around the great works of French history. Her education subordinated Spain, its language and its heritage, to the extent that she felt insecure writing in Spanish. Her life with books and languages, family stays in Paris, and the cultivation of an exquisite taste in music, prose, and poetry drew her to writing and literary criticism.

Rich, beautiful, and gracious, she had the soul of an intellectual, a combination that made it easy for her to mingle with intellectuals and accomplished visiting foreigners, absorb their ideas, and test her own. She published her first article in *La Nación* in 1920. Her article on Dante marked a declaration of intellectual confidence. Subsequently, she expanded it into a short book published in 1924 in the Spanish journal *Revista de Occidente*.

José Ortega y Gasset, the force behind the *Revista de Occidente*, became a friend. Although she did not share his traditional views of women, Victoria accepted his belief that intellectuals could never overcome barriers between them and the masses but had a natural affinity with the educated elite. Ortega y Gasset urged her to found a journal drawing on the strength of ideas across national boundaries. The American writer Waldo Frank also nudged her to publish her own journal. Frank met her in late 1929, on the eve of the publication of his *America Hispana*.*

The first number of *Sur* appeared in 1931, financed by Victoria with articles contributed by her friends and acquaintances. It would take a few years to establish *Sur*'s character and gather a core group to create its guiding culture. By 1935 the pattern had been set, and *Sur* provided a link between Latin America, the United States, and Europe, but one that favored European culture. Translations into Spanish introduced many to foreign literature that otherwise they would have been able to experience only in an indirect fashion. Afro-American poet Langston Hughes, translated by José Luis Borges, would be made known to the journal's readers. William Faulkner, at the time poorly received in the United States, appeared in *Sur* (1939), and its supporting publishing house published his translated works. José Luis Borges, Octavio Paz, Ernesto Sábato, Gabriela Mistral, and other accomplished Latin Americans appeared in *Sur*. It became one of the most important cultural journals of the twentieth century.

Victoria Ocampo sought to mold herself as well as advance culture. While she had no interest in undoing her treasured formative childhood experiences, she consistently added elements. She met Virginia Woolf but could never develop a relationship. The Bloomsbury group, drawn from the British upper class, appealed to her notion of the importance of privileged intellectuals to culture. José Luis Borges translated Woolf's *A Room of One's Own*, publishing it in installments in *Sur*, making the work available to a small but influential Latin American audience. She saw Virginia Woolf's gender rebelliousness of word and deed as her own. Victoria Ocampo caused her own Woolfian stir in the Buenos Aires Jockey Club; commenting on a marble statue of the goddess Diana, that she could not imagine menstrual fluid staining the smooth white marble of a goddess's thighs.

She opposed the authoritarianism of the *Concordancia* in the 1930s. When President and General Augustín P. Justo proposed a bill in congress to limit the rights of married women by classifying them as minors, she helped create the Argentine Women's Union to defeat it. She viewed Juan Domingo Perón and Evita with disgust and the post-war regime as antidemocratic, in spite of Perón's victories at the polls. *Sur*, while recognized as hostile, continued to publish without experiencing Perón's heavy hand. Nevertheless, when a bomb attack rocked the regime in 1953, the police rounded up Victoria among others for questioning.

An appeal from the Chilean Noble Prize Laureate, Gabriela Mistral, led to her release, although her innocence seemed obvious.

Victoria Ocampo died in 1979, an important transitional figure in the elaboration of Argentine and Latin America culture. An oligarch by wealth and education, but also a cautious democrat, she mirrored the confusion of the socio-political compromise of 1912. As a woman she participated in the partial redefinition of gender that characterized the 1920s and 1930s. As an elite woman she failed to understand that, while she had "a room of her own," others could not so easily move beyond tradition.[†]

* Waldo Frank, *America Hispana: A Portrait and a Prospect* (New York, Charles Scriberner's Sons,1931). Frank believed that American pragmatism, "a degenerate Protestant religion" (p. 329) in his view, represented the total submission of men to machines. He predicted that unless the United States turned to humanism it would run out of initiative and collapse into disaster.

[†] John King, *Sur: A Study of the Argentine Literary Journal and Its Role in the Development of a Culture, 1931–1970* (New York: Cambridge University Press, 1986). Doris Meyer, *Victoria Ocampo: Against the Wind and Tide* (Austin: University of Texas Press,1990). Jason Wilson, *Buenos Aires: A Literary Companion* (New York: Interlink Books, 2000)

Europe no longer could be relied upon for imports, and exports became uncertain. Prewar coal imports of three million tons, mostly from England, fell sharply, requiring rationing and the use of marginally effective alternates much as those used during World War I. Argentina produced petroleum sufficient for only 50 percent of its requirements. The war partially closed the transatlantic market. Submarine warfare reduced the availability of vessels as well as the reliability of delivery. The United States appeared to be the only alternative source of manufactured goods and a possible market for agricultural products, although American agriculture rebounded from the drought by 1939. Few appreciated the difficulties of trade with North America even under wartime conditions. The U.S. Senate rejected tentative moves by the FDR administration to reach out to Argentina, including plans to buy canned meat for the U.S. Navy. Offers by Washington to extend credit for the purchase of manufactured goods did not provide for the trade necessary to pay for them. In fact, wartime needs led to an increase in exports to the United States, but all understood that it constituted a temporary situation in spite of a 1941 commercial agreement. Argentina's frustration encouraged paranoia. Rumors of a planned invasion of the southern port of Comodoro Rivadavia by U.S. Marines to secure a base on the South Atlantic seem silly in retrospect; nevertheless, had the war gone badly for the Allies or Argentina offered facilities to the Axis, that could not be ruled out.

A group, mainly of lower ranking Nationalist army officers including Col. Juan Perón, formed the United Officers Group (*Grupo de Oficiales Unidos*—GOU). Strongly anticommunist, the GOU planned a Nationalist revolution to end what they viewed as a dysfunctional political situation. The fact that Patrón Costas favored the allies also threatened to reverse Argentina's policy of neutrality. The public's dismay at the prospect of more political drift by an ineffectual regime, the army's doubts about the government's commitment to neutrality, concern over geo-political changes in the southern cone, and impatient military politicians led to the overthrow the government on June 4, 1943.

The military regime's favoring of neutrality reflected the general national consensus at the time, although the implications and consequences had not been thought out. Buenos Aires' refusal to join the anti-Axis Pan-American Alliance meant that little of the American military supplies sent to its members went to Argentina. Brazil, traditionally Argentina's rival for hegemony in the southern cone, received the bulk of war material. Nationalists worried about the balance of power in the region, and some entertained the idea of seizing Brazil's industrial heartland. They envisioned a resurrected Viceroyalty of La Plata as the core of a commercial sphere, along the lines of the predatory empires of the late 1930s.

Nationalism strengthened with the continuing pressure from the United States. In the end, the government retreated from negotiations with Washington and reaffirmed the country's neutrality. Pressure intensified with the freezing of Argentine assets in the United States, charges of fascism, increasing arms shipments to Brazil and export restriction. Argentina avoided isolation with a series of trade treaties with its Southern Cone neighbors that provided an outlet for the country's light manufactured goods. President-General Ramírez attempted to placate the United States and avoid a Nationalist reaction by breaking diplomatic relations with Germany (January 1944) but holding back from declaring war.[11] Nevertheless, those that favored neutrality forced Ramírez out of office. The United States withdrew its ambassador and pressured others to do the same. American public opinion viewed the country as pro-Axis and a source of danger. Overlooked in the desire to separate a world at war into friends or enemies, Argentina provided refuge for an influx of Jewish immigrants between 1933–1945.

The Argentine army began a broad mobilization of men and material. Industrial plants directed by the army provided a military industrial base. Armed strength went from 30,000 in 1943 to 100,000 by late 1945, with defense spending absorbing 40 percent of the federal budget. Continued external pressure from the United States, and that country's apparent favoring of Brazil, provided a growing element of insecurity. Argentina, excluded from most international postwar planning conferences, repaired relations just in time to take part in the creation of the United Nations in 1945, but the relationship with the United States had become chronically dysfunctional.

CHAPTER 5

The Age of Perón

Juan Domingo Perón had roots in the old and new Argentina, as well as the upper and the lower middle class. His family traced its origins to a Sardinian immigrant of the Rosas era of the 1830s. Perón's grandfather became a noted physician and a prominent public figure. Unfortunately, his premature death at fifty sent the family into a downward spiral. Juan's father became an overseer on a Patagonian sheep ranch. He fathered two sons, Mario and Juan, by an Indian girl, Juana Sosa Toledo, barely a teenager at the time. Juan (born in 1895) and his older brother, left to their own devices, mingled with an array of doubtful characters on the Patagonian frontier. In some respects, his formative experienced mirrored that of the young Rosas, and like that caudillo he learned to understand those who struggled to survive in rural Argentina. The family arranged for him to be educated in Buenos Aires. Originally, Juan hoped to follow in his grandfather's footsteps and become a physician, but insufficient resources forced a pragmatic choice on the family—Perón entered the military academy at age fifteen.

In Buenos Aires, the young cadet put his Patagonian days behind him. The boy disappeared amid the cosmopolitan experience of army life in the capital. Subsequently, he selected bits and pieces of his early years to establish a useful political connection with the Argentina that lay beyond the urban core of Buenos Aires. He carefully controlled the family's contribution to his public persona. When he became president his mother remained in the interior. Juana lived to be 80 years old, visiting her son in Buenos Aires only once. Perón explained the separation as her preference for the countryside, describing his mother as *la Vieja* (old gal), very much a *gaucha* and also described her, with some admiration, as an Amazon who rode and hunted with the boys. His older brother, Mario, who shared Juan's professed love of horses, allegedly spent his days with his dogs and animals. Fittingly, Mario became president of the Zoological Society of Buenos Aires. When asked about his own few visits to the region of his birth, Perón commented that one could get to Europe easier than to Patagonia. In reality, he became a Porteño, both in a physical and psychological sense. Nevertheless, he used his past to connect politically with Creole Argentina, among other things fondly recalling his first friend, a broncobuster called Chino. He sprinkled *criolloismos* in private conversation and referred to colleagues from the region as his *paisanos patagónicas*. He expressed his love for folklore and an attachment to traditional songs, dismissing modern American music as jarring.

Perón never had children by any of his three wives, a problem in a society that elevated family and male sexuality to exaggerated levels. Jokes about his impotence circulated among his opponents. He compensated for attacks on his masculinity by speeding in small boats and riding motorcycles. In his taped recollections he recalled a number of affairs. He claimed to have lived with an Italian actress in Barcelona while awaiting a ship to Buenos Aires in 1941. She returned to Italy rumored to be pregnant. How many of the anecdotes about Perón's mature life represented useful image building is difficult to determine, as is how much Perón believed his own efforts to craft himself. It is clear however, that the cadet years from 1910 to 1913 and early army service had a formative impact that overrode his abbreviated childhood.

As a cadet he distinguished himself physically but not academically. An avid sportsman, he excelled in boxing and fencing. Commissioned as an infantry officer at age eighteen, he slowly moved up the ranks. His prospects brightened with a teaching appointment at the Sargento Cabral School for noncommissioned officers. Perón's ability to motivate students caught the attention of the high command. Selected for the Superior War College, Perón now had an opportunity to move into the upper levels of the army.

A mature Perón spent more time in the library than on the sports field, graduating at the upper level of his class. His next posting to the General Staff Headquarters placed Captain Perón at the nerve center of military politics. As an inexperienced politician, he fumbled his first gambit. Invited to join the conspiracy of General Uriburu to topple the government, he first agreed then backed out to join another group that planned a coup under General Justo. Uriburu's coup succeeded, and the reluctant Perón found himself serving on the Bolivian frontier. Fortunately, friends arranged for his transfer back to Buenos Aires, a promotion to major, and a teaching appointment at the Superior War College. Perón had survived his misstep well.

The Superior War College provided a political haven and time to think. As a professor of military history, Perón reflected on the role of the army within a modern nation. A stream of publications secured his reputation as a military intellectual. Perón's political opinions emerged clearly in his *Apuntes de historia militar* in 1932, a second edition two years later, and a third edition in 1951. The book won a medal and a certificate of honor at the Rio de Janeiro Exposition. Perón shared the general notions of many officers, but added a few twists that made him appear to be forging new ground. Charts, outlines, and graphs made a professional impression.

As he saw it, a nation had to be ready to defend itself or be incorporated into a stronger power's sphere of dominance. Moreover, an army by itself could not guarantee survival. A nation with a poorly organized government could not sustain a war. The entire republic, its human resources both military and civilian, and its industrial might, had to be continually strengthened and made ready for war. Modern wars, such as that launched by Imperial Japan in China, represented an impending worldwide struggle over markets and material resources, not an abstract threat. While technically at peace, the modern nation had to be on a war footing if it hoped to escape predators seeking to exploit weakness. The ever-present shadow of war, conquest, and subordination justified the guiding role of the army as civil society prepared for the inevitable. Leadership, the personality of an individual in the service of the people and *la Patria*, appeared crucial to future prospects. From Caesar to Napoleon the lesson seemed clear—a people must rely upon a decisive man at the head of a mobilized nation.

In early 1936, Perón went to Chile as a military attaché, returning once again to the Superior War College. A rumor circulated that he left Chile suspected of espionage. Ordered to Italy as a Lieutenant Colonel in 1939, he studied the deteriorating European political situation, traveling to Germany and Austria as well. As part of his tour he studied with the Italian army's elite mountain troops and at the alpine school in Innsbrück. Italian fascism's apparent emphasis on class harmony influenced him greatly, as did National Socialism. Subsequently, he claimed to have read *Mein Kampf* in both Spanish and Italian translations. An audience with Mussolini made a powerful impression on the admiring colonel. Perón concluded that both German and Italian ideologies offered valuable ideas and techniques, but not as a template for Argentina. On returning home, as he later asserted in his taped recollections, he reported his opinion (1941) that the Axis powers could not win the war—an unpopular prediction that resulted in a posting to the mountains of Mendoza to teach skiing.

THE CONQUEST OF POWER

The officer corps agreed on the coup of June 4, 1943, but little else. Factionalism stemmed from different opinions about what needed to be done and who should head the government. After a false start, but one quickly resolved, General Pedro Ramírez, the leader of the GOU, replaced General Arturo Rawson, who lasted a bare three days in office. President Ramírez implemented the first stage of a modified Nationalist revolution.

As part of the GOU's strategy, Perón assumed the directorship of the inactive National Labor Office. In his official capacity he offered union leaders assistance in return for political support. Perón expanded his office into the Secretariat of Labor and Welfare to mobilize and direct union power. As Perón made clear, he intended to make sure that workers organized and benefited directly. Alleged agitators, the "agents of destruction and unrest, who are often not even Argentines but foreigners," had to be pushed aside.[1]

The objective, to raise the standard of living of workers without social conflict, required a spiritual revolution—a well-established Nationalist objective. In 1944, the *Consejo Nacional de Postguerra* (National Post War [planning] Council), chaired by Perón, set industrial policy. That same year, the Bank of Industrial Credit opened to extend long-term, inexpensive loans. Perón pressed for development of the domestic market to provide jobs, stimulate consumption, expand manufacturing, and establish a self-sustaining momentum. The government, with the approval of the Church, decreed various populists measures: freezing apartment rents in Buenos Aires, cutting fares on the British-owned tram systems, and setting tenant farmer rents.

Military governors administered the provinces, and by the end of 1943, the regime abolished political parties, appointed Nationalists to university positions, and repressed perceived radical groups. Rumors of a concentration camp under construction in Patagonia reflected the fear that anti-Semitism among Nationalists and pro-German sentiments among army officers might result in such steps. The forced disbandment of several Jewish groups, the selective stripping of naturalized Jews of citizenship, and other types of harassment created fears that even more harsh measures would be introduced. Liberals, Jews, communists, democrats, the entire "Masonic cabal," in the Nationalist's lexicon, felt under pressure.

Under President (General) Farrell (1944–1946), Perón consolidated his power as minister of war and as head of the National Labor Department. Perón placed military supporters in key posts, mobilized unions, backed them in workplace conflicts, enforced labor laws, and became the champion of workers and the confidante of labor leaders. An executive decree of July 1943 prohibited unions from becoming involved in politics or advocating ideas opposed to Argentina's national interests. The decree's vagueness made it possible to replace labor leaders who refused to cooperate. Wage increases, rhetorical respect for labor, and the promise of more concessions to come generally did the trick. The Law of Professional

Associations, modeled on the Italian code, declared that only unions recognized by the state enjoyed legal status, protection, and benefits. Following the corporate model, each union limited itself to representing workers in a single defined economic activity. Perón selected which union would represent each activity. Unauthorized action by either the employers or workers violated the law. The government collected union dues through payroll deductions and doled them out at the union's local and national level. Pensions became political assets to be awarded or withheld, as deemed useful. Perón grasped the importance of molding a supportive national mentality. He advised the regime that, "We should try advertising, propaganda is a powerful arm especially, when one controls the media."[2]

Perón addressed the problems of rural workers, long ignored and exploited under conditions that in certain regions seemed nineteenth-century at best. In 1944, the Statute of the Peon set a minimum wage and fringe benefits, including reasonable housing, medical attention, and appropriate clothing and food. The law's detailed requirements eliminated any possibility of employers cutting corners. Rural workers could not be fired, and in the event of layoffs, they received severance pay based on years of service. Regional Labor Commissions closely inspected conditions and enforced regulations. By placing the government between rural workers and their employers, Perón extended political control into the countryside. Rural labor unions affiliated with the CGT to complete their inclusion in the national labor movement. The CGT, with its 500,000 members, made a formidable political force. Only migrant workers remained outside the circle of privilege and political obligation. Perón accomplished what the Socialists and Anarchists had failed to do for the working class. The workers had been formed into a political constituency, but not yet a party.

Meanwhile, as the war in Europe moved towards its conclusion, the military government and Perón in particular came under criticism from the oligarchy and the middle class. Some hoped that the victorious United States would force the regime out. Improbable rumors circulated that Perón planned to establish a Fourth Reich in Argentina in collaboration with Hitler's successor, Martin Bormann. Such an event certainly would have drawn the attention of Washington had anyone believed it.

EVITA

Juan and Eva Perón represented the two halves of a political whole. Nevertheless, they functioned in separate spheres. Evita went beyond the practical to transform Perón's political maneuvering, and at times overly cautious tactics, into a mystical, quasi-religious movement that meshed with what the Nationalists had elaborated in the 1930s. As a woman Evita demonstrated Peronismo's emotional side, in spite of her cool, calculating personality. Her skills as an actress enabled her to create a powerful emotional matrix within which Peronismo flourished. Almost perfect political symmetry made it possible for Juan and Evita to posture as the father and mother of the shirtless ones (the *descamisados*) and by projection all those who needed a protective state.

Evita's life experience and shrewd intelligence made her perfect for the role that she played. She understood the deep moral imperatives of human beings, knew their boundaries and strengths and how to articulate a vision in terms of good and evil. Evita brought to her role a deep appreciation of corruption, its seductive satisfactions, its power to turn life into a game, and how it could be rationalized to re-enforce power in the name of the downtrodden. To her formidable perceptional talents she added an instinctive understanding of the role of women in Argentine society, with its imposed social burdens and its compensatory expectation of compassion, sincerity, feelings, emotions, and empathy with others. The accepted relationship of women to masculine power—the suffering, public subservience, and self-denial that concealed manipulate powers—became a powerful weapon in her hands. She also understood the lower-class attraction to style. They might be poor, but they wanted a queen as their benefactress. Evita's elegance, her gowns, jewels, furs, shoes—all the good things in life—became religious adornments for the "Madonna of the Americas."

Evita codified her personal tactics and complementary political strategy in her autobiographical book, *La Razon de mi Vida* (1951). A Spanish journalist wrote the first draft—deemed totally unacceptable by Perón. One of his trusted speechwriters revamped it removing a section on feminism and adjusting the details to fit political needs. The book presented President Perón as a generous, fatherly figure complemented by an all-loving, adoring Evita who had forgone having children so that she could take care of the helpless and downtrodden. The book served as a script projecting the ideal public persona in its feminine manifestation.

Evita's ceremonial prominence at times came close to overshadowing Perón. Government officials, including the vice-president and cabinet ministers, conceded her importance, occasionally using the title *Señora Presidente*. Perón's willingness to allow his wife such prominence reflected her usefulness and vital presence, but also his understanding of her insecurities and emotional vulnerability. Her early life left emotional wounds that underpinned both her anger and energy. Her book observed that as far back as she could remember she had been tormented by injustices that have "hurt my soul as if a nail had been driven into it." Her personal history deeply influenced her and for a period molded history.

Born sometime in 1919 in the small village of Los Toldos, about one hundred and fifty miles from Buenos Aires to the mistress of Juan Duarte,

Eva María Duarte entered a life of insecurity. When less than a year old, her father abandoned his mistress and the Los Toldos children, returning to his wife in another village—a traumatic event made even worse by the family's decent into poverty. Villagers viewed the abandoned Duartes as objects of malicious gossip. When the father died in an automobile crash his illegitimate family, after traveling some distance, received a shabby reception by the relatives. The almost complete absence of status and respect scarred the children beyond recovery. Evita dealt with it by blotting out the past from her memory but could do little to ease the psychological pain that left her vulnerable and emotionally dependent.

Doña Duarte earned an income from sewing and saw to it that her children dressed well and avoided the slovenliness of many of the village's poorer children. She constantly drummed into them the notion that their poverty resulted from injustice. When the family moved to the village of Junín some twenty miles away, Evita's mother took in guests, while her sister Elisa worked at the post office and her brother Juan became a traveling salesman selling household products, including Radical Soap. In Junin, two movie houses, the Roxy and Crystal Palace, offered movies, mostly from Hollywood, that opened up a wider world of illusion to girls such as Evita. Fabulous cities and sophisticated ladies and gentlemen filled the screen, contrasting sharply with village reality. In the movies beauty became an asset that resulted in furs, jewels, lovely dresses, and, if handled properly, power.

Evita's movie idol, MGM star Norma Shearer, came from a once privileged Canadian family made poor by financial miscalculations. Norma specialized in such themes as the faithful, upbeat romantic women thrown into squalor and a brutal soul-searing existence by a man's betrayal. Norma's career reached a high point with her marriage to MGM's production chief Irving Thalberg, leading to better roles and more publicity. Norma's life and movie roles conveyed a message that reached around the world, including the dusty small towns of the Argentine interior. Evita read all about it in *Sintonia,* a tabloid movie magazine that contained life stories and photos of stars dressed in fabulous clothes. For a lonely girl isolated from life and marooned in poverty but determined to succeed, lessons could be drawn from Norma's trajectory.[3] At fifteen Evita broke under the strain and took the train to Buenos Aires, intent on becoming a movie star.

A determined Evita moved into a cheap lodging house, then made the rounds of all the theatres, finally landing a bit part as a maid, followed by a other minor parts. On the eve of her seventeenth birthday, she signed with a touring theater group. The life of an actress carried little respect and no security and required sleeping around selectively or securing a powerful sugar daddy. Evita did what she deemed necessary, but no more. Out of her meager earnings she sent money to her family. Her big break came with radio. By 1930s, Argentina had the second largest commercial network after the United States. *Radio El Mundo,* the largest broadcaster, played popular music in the mornings and sports, news, light music, and soap operas in the evening. The first soap opera, *Chispazos de tradición* (Stories of Old), set in a rural area, milked the predictable theme of tortured love broken into half-hour segments. It became popular throughout the country. Even in areas without electricity, radio receiver sound trucks attracted avid listeners. Evita's voice conveyed suffering and intensity, all of which made her a radio success. By this time her brother Juan had moved to Buenos Aires to work with the manufacturer of Radical Soap, and he arranged for the company to sponsor his sister's radio-theatrical company. She purchased a small apartment in Barrio Norte, in keeping with her status as one of the highest paid radio performers. During her years in Buenos Aires, first as a struggling actress and then as a recognized radio personality, Evita had learned a lot; often the hard way. Acquaintances noticed the hard look that marred her beauty in unguarded moments.

Disaster threw Juan Perón and Evita together. In the distant interior an earthquake leveled the colonial city of San Juan, killing some 6,000. People across the republic responded by gathering donations to aid the victims. Disaster momentarily fused the classes together, suspending social barriers in the process. As part of the government's efforts, Colonel Perón as Secretary of Labor established a San Juan fund. He fell upon the idea of having military personal in dress uniforms, accompanied by actors and actresses, stroll through the streets collecting donations. At the end of the week an "artistic festival" concluded the fund raising effort. Perón dressed in a white tunic, black boots, and a peaked cap, promenaded down fashionable calle Florida accompanied by radio and movie actors. Evita meanwhile collected donations at another location. Finally, they met at the gala. In the early morning hours they left Luna Park together.

Evita's political education occurred slowly. She continued her acting career, uncertain how long the relationship would last. In the middle of 1944, when the broadcasting industry formed a union, Evita seemed the logical choice for president. She introduced a program called "Towards a Better Future," heard over Radio Belgrano. Evita picked up an understanding of national politics by attending discussion sessions in Perón's apartment. By the end of 1944, her political interests and duties made it impossible to continue her acting career. She had performed in over twenty-six soap operas, twenty plays, and five movies. None matched her political performances, but most certainly made them more dramatic.

PRESIDENT PERÓN

While Perón long insisted that he had no higher political aspirations, few believed him. Many hoped, and others feared, that he would claim the presidency from below. He seemed willing to flaunt his connection with those on the bottom in the most obnoxious and mocking fashion. His relationship with an all but unknown actress Eva Duarte could be tolerated, but not when he violated decorum by introducing her at official social functions. Perón aggressively mixed his private life and public role—behavior interpreted as an assault on middle-class pretensions. Many considered Evita a lower-class whore. The newly arrived American ambassador, Spruille Braden, recalled a joke told to him by General Farrell out of earshot of Perón: Evita entered an elevator with a retired general. The operator kept mumbling under his breath, "La gran P," an abbreviation for *puta* (whore). As they left the elevator an enraged Evita exclaimed, "This man must be punished! Did you hear what he said?" "Think nothing of it, Excellency," the general replied. "I have been retired from the army for five years, and people still call me general."[4] She would be wounded by cruel jokes that attacked her directly, and the real target, Perón, indirectly.

American Ambassador Spruille Braden reflected the hostility of the American State Department towards Perón. At luncheons and receptions he made his disdain of Perón obvious. His blunt diplomacy angered the general public but played well among the oligarchy and middle-class opponents. President Farrell, under pressure, relieved Perón of official responsibilities. He turned out to be letting go of the tiger's tail. Evita placed telephone calls to pro-Perón labor leaders to turn out their members in support. They responded by the thousands, crowding around the exit as Perón left his official office, chanting, "Perón for President." The radio broadcast Perón's parting comments throughout the nation, expressing his regret that he had been unable to do more for the workers. Too late, army opponents had him arrested. Workers crowded into the Plaza de Mayo in front of the Casa Rosada (the presidential palace), demanding Perón's release. A weak government unraveled in the face of the outpouring of support. October 17, 1945, became a symbolic date for Peronists, forever after known as loyalty day. Perón, released from detention, appeared on the balcony of the Casa Rosada to claim his prize.

His supporters formed a coalition party to achieve the necessary electoral legitimacy. A faction of the Radical party and Nationalist groups joined with pro-Peronist workers under the banner of the Labor Party. The new party won two-thirds of the chamber of deputies, all but two senate seats, and every provincial governor's office as well as a majority in all provincial legislatures except one—the nation appeared at his disposal. The defeated party, the Unión Democrática, made up of the Socialists, the Unión Cívica Radical, and some smaller groups, including conservatives, succeeded only in demonstrating weakness. The election of February 1946 gave Perón the most decisive mandate in the country's history. A relatively clean democratic victory forced his opponents to reach at least a temporary accommodation with President Perón. Just what he had in mind had been sketched out broadly when he served as the chairman of the National Council on Postwar Planning in 1944. Perón favored a state-directed economy; class cooperation on wages and working conditions, and the technical education needed to advance industrialization. Self-sufficiency, state ownership, an authoritarian structure, and class harmony constituted a Nationalist agenda.

The Union of Industrialists and the SRA bitterly opposed the proposed degree of state control. Opponents organized a "March of the Constitution and Liberty," attracting at least 65,000 demonstrators. Few of the marchers came from the working class or unions. The American Ambassador Spruille Braden claimed to have marched with them. Perón responded by arresting his principal enemies and detaining them for a few days. Demonstrations, lockouts, and violence polarized the population. In spite of opposition and limited discussion, a new constitution replaced the 1853 document. The Constitution of 1947 created a centralized state, expanded presidential powers, and provided stronger administrative controls. Constitutional freedoms gave way to declarations of collective social responsibilities. Property rights under the Peronist Constitution became conditional on social needs.

A PLANNED ARGENTINA

Central planning began almost as soon as Perón assumed presidential duties. A five-year plan (1947–1952) addressed the perceived needs of the country and specified steps to reach set goals. The plan emphasized technical schools, a better-trained work force, and improved nutrition and healthcare. A series of industrial priorities, each leading into the next level, promised step-by-step advances. Significantly, planned industrial modernization would be spread out evenly across the country in a effort to bring every region up to the same standard of living, closing the gap between Buenos Aires and the rest of the republic. As part of the scheme the Central Bank, previously nationalized in 1946, directed the investments of private banks. The *Instituto Argentino de Promoción del Intercambio* (IAPI), organized in 1946 as a state trading organization, replaced middlemen in the purchasing and marketing of agricultural commodities. The idea to buy directly from producers and sell to foreigners as expensively as possible would provide capital for other schemes. To reassure agricultural interests, Perón appointed a member of the SRA as his minister of agriculture and dropped talk of land expropriation. Railroads, telephones, petroleum, gas, electricity, an airline company, and other utilities operated under state ownership. A large federal workforce numbering some five and a half million, including workers in state-owned industries, functioned as a political constituency in addition to their other duties.

For all its impressive reach, central planning did not eliminate private ownership. Nevertheless, businessmen had restricted freedom of action. Employers dealt with shop stewards, worker's committees, and extremely detailed labor contracts that made decision-making a joint endeavor and wages and bonuses a matter of politics. The inability to discipline or fire workers led to shoddy work, absenteeism, drastically reduced productivity, and intimidation of managers. Perón, impatient to force industry into a corporate structure, evoked the Law of Professional Associations, making membership in an industrial association compulsory. A noncompetitive, closed economic system that protected manufacturers against both domestic and foreign competition emerged. The Central Bank manipulated foreign exchange permits to discourage potential competitors by making it difficult to import machinery.

In order to tighten political control, a new Partido Peronista replaced the Labor Party. Under the party's statutes Perón reserved the power to alter decisions and approve candidates for office. He slowly but relentlessly succeeded in imposing discipline over party members and reduced labor unions to compliant supporting agencies. A purge of the bureaucracy and the judicial establishment eliminated opposition within the government. Traditional use of constitutional power to intervene in the provinces brought them into line with little difficulty. The army and the Church presented special problem and required delicate handling. They shared certain key values that acted to re-enforce each other, but they had different objectives. Perón initially sought an apolitical military establishment that would not challenge government policies. Budget increases and encouragement to continue the modernization process set in motion by World War II kept them busy. On an individual level, expansion of the officer corps made promotions easy and timely. The number of generals doubled between 1946 and 1951, diffusing military leadership and multiplying the number of factions. Career satisfaction did not transform every officer into a Peronist, but it effectively divided military opinion. While the army did not approve of Perón's methods, it supported his emphasis on social justice, nationalism, and industrialization. Subsequently, as he gained confidence and political strength he attempted to indoctrinate the army.

The Church had to be handled gingerly. Nevertheless, the hierarchy shared the president's concern for social justice and his respect for workers and the poor. While they disliked his interference in schools and in welfare reforms, he could be tolerated. Perón, grateful for Church help during the election, did not interfere with established Church privileges, such as mandatory religious instruction in schools. The relationship between the Church and the government rested on recognition that each could damage the other, or both could profit from mutual consideration.

Dealing with other sources of indoctrination required less finesse. Openly anti-Peronist professors lost their positions, and university administrators struggled to maintain the good will of the government. Perón nationalized the three large networks of Radio El Mundo, Radio Belgrano, and Radio Splendid. The concentration of media control made censorship relatively smooth and easy. Government restrictions on foreign content and news coverage that required set percentages of international, Latin American, and domestic content, pleased Nationalists. In a similar fashion, first-run movie theaters in Buenos Aires had to devote at least 25 percent of screenings to nationally produced films, and in the provinces 40 percent. The differential supposedly took into account the more sophisticated taste of the capital. In any event, a dispute with American movie exporters over their refusal to buy Argentine films kept Hollywood productions off the country's movie screens from 1949 to 1951.

Argentina's film industry reflected the cultural aridity of the regime. The industry fell under the jurisdiction of the Sub-secretariat for Information and the Press, which also monitored radio and newspapers. A number of talented directors left the country and a blacklist effectively barred others in the industry from employment. The most popular female star, Libertad Lamarque, squabbled with the Peróns, abandoned Argentina, and went on to success in Mexican movies. Her role with Jorge Negrete in *Gran Casino* (1946), directed by Luis Buñuel, confirmed her international status. Meanwhile, state subsidies kept the domestic industry alive, but at a B-movie level.

Perón changed the print media into an advertising arm of the regime. Forced sales to trusted cronies and the creation of a Peronist media company, *Alea*, which controlled all magazines, radio stations, and newspapers, effectively silenced the critical press. Only *La Prensa*, *La Nación*, and *Clarín* theoretically remained independent. Subsequently, the expropriation of the venerable *La Prensa* and its transfer to the CGT portended the death of even the illusion of independent opinion. Small newspaper publishers and editors in the interior imposed self-censorship measures, hoping to avoid a similar fate. Opposition parties became all but invisible in the press, with only a stubborn but minor presence in congress as the government implemented the lista completa provisions of the Sáenz Peña Law.

Perón established control over the open aspects of a complex society relative easily. A number of factors favored the regime. A rare convergence of positive economic factors made Perón appear to be a genius. Agricultural export prices improved dramatically, and the value of the peso firmed, keeping imports at affordable prices. Better wages and benefits magically appeared not to dampen profits. Real wages and benefits increased by 70 percent from 1946 to 1950. The Buenos Aires stock exchange soared as many became convinced that such a fine balance and favorable economic circumstances could be maintained. Bank deposits went up, with income providing abundant credit for expansion. Taxes on the wealthy could be increased from low levels without becoming

confiscatory. Rent control and construction of low-cost housing for workers made life better in many small but important ways. Unskilled labor
gained the most, leading to an increase in consumer spending, followed
by industrial and commercial expansion. The country seemed on the
verge of creating a dynamic mass market for domestic manufacturers.
Easy credit expanded the money supply by some 35 percent annually.

Cash reserves built up during the war financed the nationalization of
public utilities. Wartime agricultural exports resulted in some 1.7 billion
dollars of credits. In the immediate aftermath of world war, demand for
food promised millions more for exporters. The IAPI exploited the market
shamelessly. Instead of the market price for wheat of the equivalent of 23
pesos a quintal in Chicago, the IAPI charge foreign purchasers 45 pesos
a quintal. Britain and other devastated countries struggling to feed their
people had little choice but to pay. All that changed with the Marshall
Plan in 1948, but for a brief period Argentina could demand high prices.

The United States' efforts to feed and rebuild Europe in 1948 required
that purchases had to be made at the lowest available price. Even when
the U.S. State Department supported purchasing Argentine foodstuffs
for diplomatic reasons, the Perón regime quoted prices far in excess of
market prices. The same year the United States began the Marshall Plan,
Perón purchased the British-owned railway and a number of American
companies. He paid much more than the actual value of the badly deteriorated track and rolling stock, concerned that a devaluation of the
British currency would reduce the buying power of the money owed
to Argentina. Although nationalization had the support of the public,
it made little economic sense and shifted the cost of railroad operations
to the state.

The government's relations with industry became counterproductive.
The importance of social justice, wages, and harmony in the workplace
pushed aside innovation, pressured productivity and profits, and ended
expansion. Businessmen and industrialists realized that the public automatically sided with the regime. Therefore, resistance appeared to be fruitless. Moving as much money out of the country as possible made more
sense. In 1948, industrial expansion fell to an annual average rate of 0.42.
Industry's contribution to the nation's GDP (24.22) remained flat from
the 1940s until 1960. At the beginning of 1949, foreign reserves declined
to minimal levels and inflation exceeded 50 percent. Britain's wartime
debt evaporated, so by the end of the year only 370 million remained of
the original 1.7 billion dollars. To complicate matters, the stock market
crashed, plunging in value from 1.2 billion to 162 million dollars by
1952. A cash-strapped government devised a tax on "eventual profits,"
imposed in 1951. The two percent tax on a company's capital assets,
not indexed to inflation, created a ballooning obligation on businesses
already in trouble.

Nevertheless, Perón had incredible political resources at his disposal, an attractive vision of what he intended to do that obscured the loss of civil liberties, and an opposition in disarray. Juan and Evita Perón's charismatic control of well-organized urban and rural workers extended Peronist influence from one end of the country to the other. Argentine appeared ready to reclaim southern cone hegemony, thrown in doubt during the war years. New communications technology provided even more effective and attractive means of getting the regime's message to the people. The government introduced television as a state monopoly in 1951 with used equipment purchased in the United States. Peron hoped to use low-band equipment (channels 2–6) but had to settle for high-band (channels 7–13) with a range of slightly over 50 miles. TV Channel 7 remained the only station until the regime ended in 1955. The first broadcast featured footage of President Perón at the Casa Rosada, the presidential palace, viewed on some 7,000 receivers. Twenty-four months later 40,000 people had purchased sets.

The completeness of Perón's consolidation of power demoralized the opposition. He controlled organized labor, a compliant industrial sector, and agricultural producers through the IAPI. The choice appeared to be cooperation with the regime or intimidation, and perhaps worse. Two companies, Masson Chemicals and Chocolates Mu-Mu, incurred his wrath by refusing to contribute to Eva Perón's foundation—Perón closed them down. His major demonstration of strength occurred in part by accident. The Bemberg Group, one of the country's major industrial conglomerates, became involved in a tax dispute over whether the 1904 inheritance tax law applied to property outside of the country. Before Otto Sebastian Bemberg died in 1932, he transferred his liquid assets to a Paris-based holding company with the obvious intention of avoiding inheritance taxes. His heirs declared a tax obligation of only 80,000 pesos based on funds on deposit in Argentina. Diversionary technicalities, coupled with less than satisfactory compromise proposals, ended with the government's seizure of property and financial records. All this occurred before Perón's presidency.

Acting on a request by the Bemberg family to review the tax case, Perón authorized an investigation that found that the family owed some 116 million pesos. With their money safely in Europe, only the Bemberg's property in Argentina remained vulnerable. Perón probably would have been open to a compromise had it not been for an incident involving his wife, then on her European tour. In Berne, Switzerland, while riding in an open car, graciously waving to onlookers, ripe tomatoes rained down on Evita, causing embarrassing confusion and some amusement among the spectators. An investigation into *el tomatazo* pointed to a Bemberg wife. Incensed, Eva demanded her husband expropriate Bemberg property. By that time, the government already managed the family's Argentine assets.

The situation of de facto expropriation would be legalized in 1954 and the enterprises then turned over to the employees.

In 1946, President Perón endorsed the creation of a large-scale steel industry and nuclear research programs, both under military supervision. Legislators authorized the formation of a mixed enterprise, with 50 percent private ownership. At General Manuel Savio's recommendation, the *Dirección General del Material del Ejército* (Army Directorate of War Materiel) incorporated the Directorate of Military Factories and the Arsenals, becoming a defense conglomerate. The plan envisioned meeting domestic needs as well competing in the international market. It appeared to be a bold step towards industrial competition, as well as a symbol of state-directed development. In the end, the government financed virtually the entire direct cost in addition to substantial indirect subsidies. Military industries paid local taxes only and had preferential access to raw materials.

Nuclear technology appeared to offer limitless low-cost energy to drive a competitive economy. Moreover, a nuclear program suggested the possibility of an atomic weapon. In one instant, Argentina's weak military position relative to Brazil could be reversed. In order to speed up development, a National Atomic Energy Commission (CNEA, 1950) under the navy's direction coordinated research and development. An overly eager Perón fell into the hands of a charlatan. Austrian nuclear scientist Ronald Richter convinced the president that he could produce a bomb. Perón made a public announcement in 1951 that the Bariloche laboratory had achieved fission. A thoroughly alarmed Brazil and international community soon learned with relief that Richter had duped the embarrassed Perón. The episode had the positive effect of calling the world's attention to Argentine efforts and the need to avert the spread of atomic weapons development. Unfortunately, the Atoms for Peace Program offered to the world by American President Dwight D. Eisenhower at the UN in 1953 did little to temper the desire for weapons technology.

THE STRUGGLE FOR PHILOSOPHICAL SUBSTANCE

The ideological decades of the 1920s and 1930s made a lasting impact on Perón. He understood the appeal of a pattern of political ideas, but as a pragmatist he avoided elaborate and rigid ideological structures. Perón saw little need to read theoretical works. In spite of his previously declared respect for history, he dismissed the past as an unnecessary distraction. As an observer rather than a philosopher, he settled for a strong emotional tone shrouded in vagueness. The name chosen to encompass such a limited structure, *Justicialismo,* implied a connection with the principle of social justice as a primary moral and social engine. Many of his notions reflected established currents of thought, providing an instant constituency. An idealized view of human behavior, along with touches of Catholic morality, made Justicialismo culturally, but indefinably, attractive. In addition, Perón used Nationalist thought to shape perceptions of the external world for his followers. He sought to shift the focus of the Nationalists away from the patria as the embodiment of the Argentine cultural spirit and attach it to Peronismo as personified by himself. He borrowed Nationalist issues as a tactical ploy and dropped them just as quickly, only to again pick them up if necessary. Prominent Nationalist Mario Amadeo complained that, Perón absorbed, "utilized, popularized, but cheapened the Nationalist agenda."[5] His decision to build a political base on the workers ignored the importance of hierarchy to the Nationalists. Perón's subsequent attempts to fuse the middle class with the masses horrified them. Justicialismo's notion of social justice implied an upward transformation of the lower classes both in status and material wellbeing to eliminate the gap between the working and the middle class. As a philosophy it had little intellectual substance to balance its emotional appeal. Justicialismo provided limited scope for intellectual elaboration and as a consequence it did not attract individuals able to provide the theoretical base needed to refine, deepen, and incorporate related philosophical principles and broaden its intellectual impact.

Efforts to insert Justicialismo into academic culture relied on anti-intellectual coercion. The *Subsecretaría de Cultura* within the Ministry of Education sought to impose rather than nurture. Persuasion became a propaganda task that closed off debate. The *Subsecretaría de Prensa y Difusión* published an estimated 2.5 million pamphlets and three million posters and produced movies and other propaganda items for the regime. The *Junta Nacional de Intelectuales* provided a learned façade but functioned with little real support. A companion organization, the *Asociación Argentina de Escritores* (AADE), created to challenge the dominance of the *Sociedad Argentina de Escritores* (SADE), failed for similar reasons. As the frustrated, semi-official *Mundo Peronista* unconvincingly declared, the "only legitimate function of intellectuals is to preach the Perón doctrine."[6]

Unity in acceptance of the leadership's directives guaranteed social harmony but required conformity at every institutional layer from kindergarten to the army. Justicialismo could be interpreted in innumerable emotional variations, always coupled with a strident sense of outrage that the poor and impoverished had been denied economic and social justice. Perón's rhetoric borrowed Catholic terminology, much to the delight of the Church. Eventually, the clergy understood that he intended to elaborate a competing doctrine. In the end, Justicialismo came down to social justice as redistributive entitlement with outraged moral principles as the energizing force and social harmony as the objective. Without an effective opposition, Perón's Justicialista philosophy officially became the national doctrine. A "philosophy of life, simple, practical, popular and fundamentally Christian and humanist."[7]

LOVE POWER

Social services remained caught in a transition stage between private charitable initiatives and modern state responsibility for the welfare of its citizens. The *Sociedad de Beneficencia* continued to play a central role in public assistance. The society reflected archaic notions of paternalism and class from another era. At Christmas, orphans with shaved heads, modestly dressed, went through the streets begging for donations. Once a year, children under the Society's care went to the Colon Opera House to be awarded prizes received from the hands of Beneficencia officials, the papal nuncio and the cardinal, a few cabinet ministers, and the wife of the president. Similar ritual acts established a line between those that received and their benefactors. The mixture of high society and charity seemed out of place in a modern country. Editorial writers and others pointed out that most of the Society's budget came from the federal and provincial budgets, as well as the national lottery. The state appeared to have recognized the need but not its administrative responsibilities.

This structure ran counter to Perón's preference for fostering emotional dependence on the state. While public opinion appeared to favor a direct welfare system, Perón had his own plan to modernize most elements of state assistance but retain useful political elements. Channeling money through unions that in turn built hospitals and operated clinics with grants from the state created an approved Peronist model. Union membership included about 42 percent of industrial workers. With more benefits to offer that number could be expected to climb. Meanwhile, union members became financial dependents. Perón intended to do the same with public assistence.

In 1948, the *Dirección Nacional de Asistencia Social* (DNAS) dispensed with the ladies. A short time before the extinction of the Society, the Eva Duarte de Perón Foundation began operations. It would not be placed under the control of the subsequently established DNAS. While not an successor organization, it borrowed some of the forms of the Society in order to maintain the personal charitable bond while reversing the social tenor of class-based charity in favor of the personal politics of social justice. It subsequently became simply the Eva Perón Foundation (FEP), indicating Evita's independent contribution to the regime's success. The FEP complemented the function of the DNAS and shared some of the same staff, including its director, Armando Méndez de San Martín, who served as the administrator of the foundation. While both organizations mobilized political support, Evita created an emotional bond.

Her organization, simple and straightforward, functioned under the sole direction of its founder with all the power of the state and constitution. The Foundation amassed assets of over 200 million dollars and employed some 14,000 workers. Annually it purchased 400,000 pairs of shoes, 500,000 sewing machines and 200,000 cooking pots. Money poured in from the national lottery; government agencies; and donations from unions, industrialists, shopkeepers, and agricultural interests—some gave willingly, others hesitated to refuse. The foundation did not account for any of the funds received. It is believed that a significant proportion ended up in numbered Swiss accounts. On occasion the foundation ordered goods but never paid for them.

A gracious and generous benefactress gave but also received. Ragged women and children crowded the Foundation's office. Evita, after listening to a heart-rendering story, turned to her brother Juan, who dispensed money from a box or handed out clothing vouchers. On occasion, she ordered the construction of a modest house along with basic furnishings. Observers remarked repeatedly on Evita's compassion for the poor and suffering. She allowed them to touch and kiss her. On more than one occasion, individuals suffering from contagious diseases received a close embrace and a kiss—such acts of spontaneous compassion elevated Evita to the level of a popular saint. Her following soon rivaled that of Perón, cutting across gender lines and possibly more powerful because of the popular religious elements associated with her. A high point came when the FEP outfitted a train as a traveling hospital with the most modern facilities and toured the interior.

THE PARTIDO PERONISTA FEMININO

Perón claimed that from the moment he met Evita he envisioned her as the person to rally female workers behind his reforms, even though at the time women could not vote. Between 1911 and 1946 fifteen attempts to pass women's suffrage legislation failed. Under President Perón, six separate bills reached the floor. Bill number 13010 passed, enfranchising women in 1947. That same year Evita bought a daily newspaper, *Democrácia,* as her own political vehicle. At a celebration in front of the Casa Rosada, Perón signed the women's suffrage bill into law and immediately handed it to Evita. Propaganda identified her as the driving force behind its success. Perón skillfully transferred credit to his wife for a struggle that began long before and that owed much to many others.

At a meeting in July 20,1949, Evita addressed women Peronistas at the first National Conference of the *Partido Peronista Feminino* (PPF) and outlined plans for a female division completely separate and independent from the men's organization. The PPF linked to the general movement only through personal loyalty to Juan Domingo Perón. Perón's re-election in 1951 by a 2 to 1 margin rested in large part on the fact that Evita rallied 63 percent of the female vote. Evita demanded fanatical loyalty from her cadres, selected candidates, and enjoyed complete political and administrative control over what in effect constituted her party. She used her position as the Peronista women's leader to establish a separate political identity. Behind traditional gender assumptions, she created a powerful constituency. By 1952, women Peronistas numbered half a million organized in 3,600 clubs.

Evita, referred by her admirers as the First Samaritan, Lady of Hope, Mother of Innocents, the Workers Plenipotentiary, and Standard-bearer of the Shirtless Ones, preferred "The Bridge of Love." The epithet allegedly captured her professed love for Perón, his programs, and her accepted gender role. As the *New York Times* reported, " love, love, love . . . makes the Peróns go around, their whole act is based on it . . . they conduct their affair with the people quite openly, they are the perfect lovers—generous, kind, and forever thoughtful in matters both great and small."

The success of the Eva Perón Foundation and the PPF unbalanced the political partnership. It became evident that Evita contemplated running for vice-president in the presidential election year of 1951. Although the constitution provided for a vice-president, few envisioned that a woman might rise to that level. The army and the upper and middle class did not support the idea; however, unions and the lower class in general favored her candidacy as a means of validating their own political importance. Posters with Perón and Evita appeared, generating intense debate over a Perón-Perón ticket. The CGT staged a mass meeting in August 1951 to proclaim their support for such a ticket, calling it a *cabildo abierto,* after the public meeting that had proclaimed the overthrow of the Spanish colonial regime. Clearly, they envisioned it as a revolutionary event.

Perón allowed things to proceed, although he kept silent. Chartered buses and trains brought in people from the provinces, with accommodations, meals and even movie tickets provided by the government. Two sixty-foot portraits of Perón and Evita graced the Avenida 9 de Julio with the slogan, "Perón–Eva Perón, la formula de la patria." Flags and banners hung from every conceivable spot, creating the impression of an unstoppable national movement. At a mass meeting, chanting crowds demanded she accept the nomination. In the end, she responded ambiguously in the absence of Perón's endorsement. Army opposition played a role in Perón's lack of support, as did concerns about her health. The day following the meeting she collapsed. An appendectomy revealed a more serious condition. American surgeon Dr. George H. Pack performed a hysterectomy and learned the extent of her cancer. As customary in the 1950s, the patient would not be told the truth. Radiation failed. The best medical care could do little. Her cervical cancer had metastasized.[8] On July 26, 1952, Evita died at age thirty-three.

THE NEW ARGENTINA IN ECONOMIC AND POLITICAL CRISIS

President Perón understood political tactics but not economics, nor the degree that luck had played in his earlier success. He viewed capitalists as individuals who lived off existing profits rather than constantly adding new sources of wealth. His static view of capital made economic justice a question of balance. It came down to the fact that one side unfairly had too much. Thus, money for reforms, social justice, and other admirable objectives required reducing the amount absorbed by one sector and moving it to other ones rather than stimulating wealth creation and competition across all sectors. Perón surrounded himself with individuals who shared his notion of economic justice, such as Miguel Miranda; a self-made man who had amassed a fortune supplying tinplate to the canning industry. As chairman of the National Economic Council, Miranda acted as an economic czar until dismissed in January 1949, as the economy went into a sharp slump.

It should not have come as a surprise that the private sector, stripped of profits, could not be intimidated into production. Rock bottom prices offered by the IAPI resulted in a drastic drop in grain and beef production. Moreover, landowners refused to rent their property under the unfavorable conditions imposed by law, preferring to leave the land fallow. The government's predatory agricultural policy alienated tenant farmers and landowners. Rising wages, falling productivity, and a growing number of holidays both formal and assumed pushed manufacturers to minimize labor and maximize machines. Nevertheless, production efficiencies failed to stay ahead of costs. A drop in productivity and rising wages inevitably led to inflation. In reality, only agricultural exports generated surplus capital, while an inefficient, protected manufacturing sector and an undisciplined labor force consumed an ever-larger proportion of the declining agricultural surplus.

Wages became a political reward rather than an exchange for time and labor. Without regard for cost trade unions declared their own holidays in honor of their contribution to the nation, held huge rallies, declared the day following a day off to permit members to rest. By the early 1950s, workers took an estimated one day off for each two days of work. Inflation reached 68 percent annually as paper money rolled off the presses to meet expenses. Perón resorted to guidelines and the threat of a freeze if producers and shopkeepers failed to hold down prices. Predictably, controls had to be put in place and easy credit ended. A sharp drop in employment forced a resumption of easy credit. The trade deficit ballooned to 455 million in 1952. A severe drought forced the importation of wheat, a totally unexpected development in a grain exporter country.

Perón blamed employers for inflation by giving in too readily to worker demands then raising prices. When employers resisted wage increases, unrest and work stoppage threats quickly forced the resumption of the inflationary process. State enterprises, ordered to set certain prices, ran huge deficits, requiring assistance from the federal treasury. The economy seemed locked in a downward spiral of declining exports, foreign exchange problems, inadequate investments, corruption, smuggling, and capital flight. The regime could not refuse labors demands, but inflation reversed the gains that presidential decrees had bestowed. Workers turned out for rallies, but they questioned whether the regime could continue to deliver.

Unexpectedly, the economy bounced back and by the next year inflation fell to an acceptable four percent. The trade balance showed a surplus in 1953 and 1954. President Perón, concerned that Argentina had insufficient investment capital to sustain the turnaround in the economy, looked to foreign investors. Standard Oil, perhaps the only company with sufficient capital to make the investments necessary to alleviate the country's energy shortfall, indicated interest. Perón negotiated a reasonably favorable contract in April of 1955. The agreement angered and alarmed Nationalists. While Perón's pragmatism alienated some supporters and galvanized the opposition, it did not bring about the regime's end. A series of political miscalculations, however, would do so before the year closed.

An explosion during a Peronist rally in the Plaza de Mayo caused an overreaction. An angry President Perón encouraged his supporters to punish those responsible. By this time his followers knew the list of enemies without being told. Thugs forced their way into the unprotected elite bastion of the Jockey Club. They destroyed priceless European cultural icons, including a painting by Goya and a handful of other irreplaceable works. The destruction of seventeenth-century French tapestries used to ignite the flames that consumed the Club and its library of some 50,000 volumes symbolized the attackers disdain for elite culture. The fire department, in the absence of orders, declined to respond. Subsequently, Perón ended the club's legal status and assumed control of its racetrack and betting facilities. The same night the Jockey Club burned, thugs attacked the headquarters of the Radical and the Socialist parties. *La Nación* newspaper barely avoided a similar fate.

Heightening tensions, Perón's relationship with the Church soured over the issue of forming a Christian Democratic party. Perón ended state subsidies to private schools as well as religious instruction and announced legal reforms, including the possibility of divorce. At the same time, the government unleashed an anticlerical campaign in the press. The campaign to canonize Eva Perón annoyed clerics. They saw it as an attempt to override papal prerogative while demonstrating the power of the regime to create rival religious icons. Militant Catholic clerics and the laity slipped out of control of their cautious bishops, making a confrontation inevitable. Middle-class opponents joined with conservative Catholics to challenge the regime. In June on the festival of Corpus Christi, a procession wended through the capital. Perón responded by deporting two clerics and charged others with flag burning. Demonstrations and a rebellion of air force and navy units suggested that the regime verged on losing control. By nightfall the rebels had been suppressed. In revenge, Peronist thugs sacked and burned churches.

Ultimately, survival of the government depended on the army and the extent that it had been indoctrinated or neutralized. While still opposed by some within the military, Peronismo had made inroads. The army appeared off balance, if not fully under control. Peronist army officers lectured at military bases on the regime's objectives and its accomplishment, while academy instructors indoctrinated cadets. After an aborted military revolt in 1951, intensified efforts to convert the military appeared to have been successful. Nevertheless, another plot resulted in the purging of the officer corps and a rearrangement of the armed forces to serve as a check on the army.

Noncommissioned officers received better pay, living conditions, and attractive uniforms. Procedures for advancement from the enlisted ranks into the officer corps became more reasonable. Officer training programs drew in more working-class candidates with the idea of changing military culture. Along with the right of military personnel to vote, formerly prohibited, came pressure to become involved in Peronist politics. Appropriate songs and banners became a staple of barracks life. Indirect pressure on noncommissioned officers to report on any disloyal behavior by their officers created tension within military units but provided a rough early warning of hostile activity. The objective to detach the ranks and their noncommissioned officers from their superiors had obvious utility. Nevertheless, although Perón entered the army while in his adolescence, he surprisingly underestimated institutional self-interest.

Plans to organize militias drawn from the CGT caused great unease even among officers sympathetic to the regime. Evita, shortly before her death, insisted that the regime needed armed detachments in case of an anti-working-class rebellion. She used foundation funds to buy and distribute small arms. Perón continued to encourage the idea. A week before the overthrow of the regime, the notion of supplying heavy weapons to the CGT had been discussed. Concern that the army would not tolerate such a move put the matter on hold. The high command understood that institutional survival could not be taken for granted if militias emerged to challenge them. Senior officers, while not yet ready to move against the government, became watchful. Others, more impatient, believed that Perón's alienation of the Church and other groups had created a sufficiently strong consensus in favor of the president's removal. A revolt, led by retired General Eduardo Lonardi, although in the end successful, did not carry the entire military establishment. Indeed, the majority of the army remained loyal. Admiral Isaac Rojas threatened a naval bombardment of Buenos Aires but did not attempt to seize the capital.

Perón resigned, then retracted, signaling supporters to battle his enemies. Shortly after calling for a defense of his regime, Perón conceded. He may have feared that a rebel defeat would turn the CGT into a force able to overwhelm its patron. The military coup ended the regime before Peronismo had been rejected at the ballot box or the economy had collapsed under the weight of corporatism. Consequently, a significant number of people hoped to restore Perón to the presidency. The coup removed him from office but prolonged his influence and political life.

CHAPTER 6

A Distant Shadow

Closing the party, jailing leaders, and placing military officers in charge of CGT unions could not exorcise Peronismo. Still, the CGT would never be the same. The CGT previously enforced discipline on its member unions and their leadership, but after the coup individual unions worked things out separately, resisting or making deals with the military government. Three factions emerged. The largest, made up of 62 CGT affiliated unions, referred to simply as the "62," claimed to represent Peronists; the second largest, the "32," expressed a wish for a less politicized union and a return to a degree of internal control. The third group of 19 unions had ties to the communists but claimed to be independent Peronists, meaning they did not automatically align with politicians. The union movement and Peronismo fragmented. To make matters more difficult, Peronist senators, deputies, and bureaucrats became reluctant collaborators or outright obstructionists when they could get away with it. Federal, provincial, and local judges also retained negative influence.

General Lonardi assumed the title of provisional president, hoping that his "Liberating Revolution" would draw Argentines together for nonpartisan reforms. He promised to reestablish the rule of law and freedom and restructure the politicized educational system. Reforms and forgiveness became his priority, not revenge. Lonardi dissolved Congress, freed political prisoners and set about restoring the old names and places of the many sites that had been used to honor Eva or Juan Perón.

To placate those who wanted blood he appointed a National Investigating Committee. Predictably, the committee came up with sensational scandals: Perón's sexual escapades with teenage girls, Evita's collection of clothes and jewels and misuse of federal funds. These scandals sold a lot of newspapers but still did not satisfy rabid anti-Peronistas. In pain, distracted and suffering from the stomach cancer that caused his death, Lonardi failed to convince opponents. They had little patience with pleas for forgiveness of those who in good faith supported Perón.

The agriculturalists wanted to reverse the emphasis on industrialization and labor. They pointed out that ignoring Argentina's natural economic advantages for an industrialization that all understood could not compete on the world market appeared to be sheer folly. Rather than insist that industry become another export pillar, agriculturalists simply wanted to eliminate its drain on their foreign exchange earnings. Nevertheless, urbanization and industrialization could not be undone, nor could Peronismo be separated from both.

Nevertheless, hard-line elements believed that they could root out Peronismo with the right president in charge. A junta drawn from all three branches of the armed forces replaced Lonardi in early November with General Pedro Aramburu. Lonardi's government lasted less than sixty days. In order to instruct the new president, the junta issued guidelines of what they expected. At the request of Lonardi, Raúl Prebisch undertook a review of the economic situation and completed it in time to instruct his replacement. Prebish advocated continued industrialization, urging that agricultural exports be encouraged in the meantime.

The government devalued the peso to stimulate exports and restrain imports and dropped direct import controls. Mixed results and contradictory economic policy reflected the inability of the government to balance agricultural and industrial interests. The government restored the Union Industrial Argentina (UIA) and allowed them to negotiate labor contracts. Meanwhile the government sought to revise labor contracts as they came up for renewal to bring productivity and wages in line. Politically, wages could not be held down drastically enough to achieve that objective.

Aramburu saw his role as one of reeducation in social responsibility. Raids on Perónist unions, seizure of offices and the arrest of labor leaders (who ended up in a prison camp in Tierra de Fuego) seemed necessary. Attempts to restart the CGT as a reformed and cleansed union umbrella failed. Union leaders continued to express Peronist principles as they interpreted them. Use of soldiers to break strikes and drafting strikers into the army proved ineffectual. In the end, both labor and employers became hostile to the government. Peronists in the army allied with workers attempted to seize control of the Campo de Mayo military compound, the home of the best-trained regiment in the army. They surrendered without a shot being fired. Nevertheless, the president ordered the execution of twenty-seven ringleaders.

Following the junta's guidelines, Aramburu called a constituent convention to update and restore the 1853 constitution, to be followed by elections in February 1958. The president sought to restore the Radicals to power, in effect a return to the 1912 compromise but monitored by the army. Aramburu ignored the reality that the Radicals had been severely damaged by the events after 1929 and 1946 and, moreover, never had a concrete philosophy or even a guiding program. Complicating matters, the Radicals split into antagonistic factions. The losing side formed the *Unión Cívica del Pueblo* (UCRP), while the winners formed the *Unión Cívica Intransigente* (UCRI). A new group, the *Grupo Tacuara de la Juventud Nacional* (National Youth Tacuara Group) appeared in 1957. Its members came from Catholic student organizations and Catholic action groups, with the original goal of reversing the ban on religious instruction and defending the status of Catholic universities, They adopted the name Tacuara (the lance used by gauchos) to indicate both their militancy and attachment to creole Argentina. At the time few realized the importance of the Tacuara.

Some military officers discussed delaying a return to civilian rule, but events had gone too far. Aramburu supported the UCRP, led by Ricardo Balbín, who had run unsuccessfully against Perón in the 1952 election. Arturo Frondizi became the candidate of the UCRI .The Perónist Party had been disqualified, as had all those who held high office under Perón. Nevertheless, mandatory voting in the election for the constituent convention demonstrated the strength of the exiled Perón. He instructed his followers to cast blank ballots; 24.3 percent of voters did so.

Arturo Frondizi of the UCRI believed he could co-opt the Peronists, but he needed Perón's help to become president. He enjoyed public respect gained as a young attorney for his defense of Argentine tobacco distributors from competition from the British American Tobacco (BAT) subsidiary. The issue became a Nationalist cause in the early 1930s. Frondizi lost the case; the courts judged the distributors, not BAT, to be in violation of the antitrust laws. Subsequently, he published *Petróleo y Politica* (1954), reaffirming his anti-imperialist credentials. Frondizi cleverly asserted that the issue went beyond a pro or anti-Peronist stance to one of industrialization or underdevelopment.

He called for a popular front embracing workers, the national bourgeoisie, the Church, and the army. Collaboration between Frondizi and Perón seemed to make some sense to the electorate and provided Perón with another opportunity to demonstrate his hold on voters. A secret pact, signed by the exiled Perón and Frondizi's representatives, cemented the agreement. Perón instructed his followers to vote for Frondizi and the entire UCRI slate in return for restoration of key elements of Perónismo. Frondizi, swept into office along with 130 UCRI deputies out of a total of 187 seats. Perón in exile had proved stronger than anyone anticipated.

THE IMPOSSIBLE BALANCING ACT

True to the spirit of the pact, Frondizi decreed a 60 percent wage increase and permitted Peronista activities, although he stopped short of legalizing the party, returned control of unions and the CGT to Peronist labor leaders, and in effect made them the stand-in for the Peronist party. An amnesty and other decrees reversed the army's anti-Peronist measures. Embracing the primacy of urban workers, he hoped to strengthen and expand industry. His objectives required energy and foreign investment. Abandoning economic nationalism, he contracted with foreign companies to explore and develop petroleum resources. Along with a new energy policy, he hoped to shift industrialization to heavy industries—steel and petrochemicals. Recasting the entire industrial sector required foreign capital, but as he insisted, directed in the interests of the nation.

The government permitted foreign companies to transfer capital in and out of the country as they pleased. In one year (1958–1959), foreign investment jumped from 8 million to over 217 million dollars. As a gesture to agricultural producers and the free market, the government abolished the IAPI in 1958. Private enterprise propaganda in slick magazines attempted to sell the policy change to the public by suggesting that the good life depended on a competitive industrial base. A flood of American and Mexican comic books did their part in the hoped-for mental transformation of the younger generation into modern consumers. A revitalized university system promised to make a social and research contributions. Frondizi permitted Catholic universities to be reestablished, gaining him some support from the Church and Nationalists to offset their hostility to foreign capital and the materialism that Frondizi's government promoted.

The president hoped to placate sufficiently both the left and the right long enough to remake the economy. In spite of initial success, he would not be able to do so. A strike of oil workers in Mendoza, although firmly put down, precipitated a 48-hour general strike. Frondizi granted wage increases, then allowed inflation to wipe them out. Inflation doubled to 80 percent, foreign currency reserves evaporated and the government faced fiscal collapse. The IMF demanded wage freezes, higher taxes, reduction in government expenditure, and other politically fatal measures. Reliance on soldiers to put down union demonstrations and support the government's policy forced Frondizi to acquiesce to army wishes. An angry Perón precipitated a crisis by publicizing the pact between Frondizi and himself.

A resourceful and unpredictable president reorganized his cabinet and brought in as his economic minister Alvaro Alsogary, one of the regime's most avid critics. A new economic program threw the country into a deep recession in1959; wages fell by 30 percent, but strikes failed to deter the government's restrictive monetary policy. Pleased foreign investors responded, pushing up the country's hard currency reserves to record levels. Labor, unwilling to wait for the economy to rebound, attacked businesses in frustration. Eventually demoralized, labor lost its disruptive power, while the army remained the only source of real authority. A shadow presidency emerged, directed by senior military officers who monitored the president. Frondizi's freedom of action fluctuated, dependent on day-to-day events. Manipulation remained the president's major tool, but it created deep suspicion about his motives.

In the 1962 midterm elections Frondizi legalized the Peronista vote but not the old party (PJ) in a calculated move to drive the upper and middle class to throw their votes to the UCRI, thereby playing out the scenario that Perón had avoided with his resignation. To the horror of the army and the surprise of the president, the Peronistas swept the election, including winning the province of Buenos Aires governor's office. An angry high command forced the president to annul the elections. Further dissatisfaction with the president resulted from his refusal to vote for expelling Cuba from the OAS, as well as a secret meeting between the president and Ché Guevara, which naval intelligence discovered. A disgruntled army removed and arrested the hapless Frondizi.

The high command, without a contingency plan, allowed the president of the senate, constitutionally next in line, to assume the office. Officers split between the hard-liners who advocated military rule and the legalists who desired a civilian regime. It required 16 months and a number of violent clashes between army factions before the legalists, lead by General Juan Carlos Onganía, won the debate. Meanwhile, the economic situation tightened under a draconian monetary policy that dried up liquidity to the point that payments had to be delayed. In the absence of paper currency, uncashed checks circulated as currency, as did government vouchers. Predictably, GDP dropped, businesses declared bankruptcy, and unemployment soared. A lucky break came with a good harvest in 1962 that brought in badly needed foreign exchange. Once the struggle within the military had been decided, an election could be scheduled. A newly organized party—the Union of the Argentine People, with Aramburu as their candidate—the UCRI, and the UCRP all faced the shadow party of blank ballots cast by Peronists. The UCRP won (1963), but only by slightly more than a fourth of the vote—a weak mandate, with Arturo Illia then in his seventies, as their candidate.

President Illia, not well known, but a seemingly respectable politician, projected an old-school provincial style that many found reassuring. A physician born in the provincial town of Peragamino in 1900, he practiced medicine in rural Córdoba, joining the Radical party in 1935. As a traditional Radical he stood for economic nationalism with its predicable anti-IMF rhetoric, rejection of foreign investors, and a more equitable distribution of wealth. Nullification of foreign oil contracts established his

Nationalist credentials in spite of the economic damage. The government saw its first priority as the stimulation of industry, then operating far below capacity with correspondingly high unemployment. An expansionist policy required an increase in money in circulation, inexpensive credit, and transfer of money to provincial governments. Resources to do so depended on earnings from agricultural exports.

The army monitored the government. General Onganía could be neutral but not supportive. Unions refused to be drawn into cooperation, even when their interests appeared to be addressed by Illia. Strikes and occupation of factories challenged the government and in the end eroded its already weak legitimacy. Nevertheless, some union leaders favored a political accommodation following their own strategies, not those of the exiled Perón.

The leader of the metal workers union, Augusto Vandor, anxious to maintain discipline in place, implied special knowledge of Perón's imminent return. He later participated in a plan to bring him back. In late 1964, Perón flew to Rio de Janeiro only to be sent back by Brazilian authorities on the next aircraft to Spain. Although an aborted attempt, it demonstrated the possibility of a return, but also the need to devise an alternative to Perón in the event that he would not be permitted to end his exile, or he died. In reality, Juan and the deceased Evita Perón had become cult figures. Perón, not quite ready to become a legend in his own time, encouraged strong-arm tactics against those that believed that Peronismo needed new, younger, and bolder leadership in place of a distant and ageing icon.

President Illia permitted Peronist participation in the congressional elections of 1965. The results indicated that Peronismo had solidified into an ideological position not dependent on orders from Madrid. By 1965 inflation reached 30 percent and another recession appeared unavoidable. To keep prices in check a government agency (*Dirección Nacional de Abastecimiento*) received authority to control production, distribution, and prices. Government agents inspected company records to ensure compliance. Mixed Advisory groups of labor and management laid out industrial objectives. Congress assumed the power to declare an economic emergency if necessary and to set limits on profits, decree mandatory production, and make management decisions. When beef supplies tightened, the National Meat Board ordered foreign packinghouses to sell 15 percent of their production at cost for domestic distribution. The National Grain Board directly purchased a million tons of grain, resold it to China, and pocketed the difference. Exchange controls provided yet another source of profit with the mandatory official rate set to produce a 15 percent premium for the state. Illia faced an industrial recession, surging unemployment, falling exports, shrinking foreign reserves, ballooning inflation, and an almost across the board decline in living standards. Illia became a ineffectual president with the public alternating between pity and anger. Discussion in the streets revolved around the timing, not the advisability, of his removal.

A military junta decided the question with an *Acta de la Revolución Argentina* that declared the end of civilian rule until such time as the obstacles to a viable, prosperous country had been overcome. Illia, escorted out of the palace by the police, simply went home. The junta dissolved congress, the Supreme Court, and provincial legislatures; banned all political parties; and appointed General Onganía as president—a clean sweep. The Night of the Long Clubs occurred the evening of Onganía's inauguration. Suspected agitators and subversives ran the gauntlet between rows of policemen who battered them with rifle butts as they passed. Over 200 individuals received such treatment.

Army frustration with the inability of civilians to devise a political solution extended to the younger generation. In the army's view, a significant number could not see beyond economic decline, a falling standard of living, and a bleak future. A drop-out youth culture emerged that revolved around rock music. Impoverished urban working-class youths, in particular, embraced lyrics that glorified their own hopeless state, slums, vagrancy, unemployment, and the empty time on their hands. Rock music stripped away respect for the bureaucracy and the state without advocating positive changes. At the time generational frustration seemed a minor problem that would disappear in the face of the renewal that the army intended to undertake.

Radicalization of the younger generation emerged out of Catholic student organizations, including the Tacuara, discussed earlier. The Tacuara's initial inspiration came from the falangismo of Spain's General Francisco Franco. In the early days, members wore a Maltese cross on their lapel. The concept of social justice provided the bridge from the right to the radical left. Members attacked Jews and synagogues, allegedly in retaliation for the Israeli abduction of the fugitive Nazi Adolf Eichmann. Almost inevitably, the Tacuara splintered into smaller groups. A break-away group, the New Argentina Movement, gained international attention in 1966 when they hijacked an aircraft and forced it to land in the Falklands, where they proclaimed Argentine sovereignty.

Full-blown radicalization came with Vatican II. Pope Paul VI in his *Populorum Progressio* (1967) condemned capitalism's profit motives, inequality, racism, and the greed of rich nations and suggested that violence might be appropriate in the event of long standing [social?] tyranny. Vatican II also began a dialogue with Marxism. Vagueness fused with strong moral principles created guilt and confusion. Individuals who started on the right ended on the left, making the case for violence as a means of achieving social justice. Many guerrilla leaders and their followers traced their roots to the Secondary Students Nationalist

Union, Young Catholic Workers, Catholic Action, the Tacuara, and other such organizations.

MILITARY INTERREGNUM

President Onganía approached the situation as a moral crisis involving the failure of the governing authorities to challenge and deal with unacceptable behavior and provide an effective political structure. He reflected his own devout Catholicism and his admiration of Spain's General Francisco Franco. Moral degeneration allegedly lay behind social and political collapse and required forthright corrective action. Censorship of indecent movies and television shows and a highly symbolic burning of books warned that the government intended to forcefully instruct society. President Onganía laid out three stages: righting the economy, distributing its fruits, and restoring a representative government. In this he copied the strategy of the Brazilian generals after their coup of 1964.

In a demonstration of force, police stormed into the University of Buenos Aires and broke radical control of student organizations. New entrance exams restricted access to universities and professional schools. In late 1966, a Law of National Defense set up a National Security Council and a companion National Council for Development. The next year, an Anti-Communist Law linked the government with the West's cold war struggle. A Civilian Defense Law (1967) expanded the concept of national security to include any behavior that complicated internal order or hindered development in any fashion. Vague language permitted the state to react as deemed expedient. The law indicated a moral direction, but not actual rules. Toleration depended on situational interpretation.

A poorly organized general strike by the CGT on March 1, 1967, failed. Onganía stripped six unions of their legal status and suspended collective bargaining until January 1969. Augusto Vandor and other union officials secretly attempted to reach an accommodation with the regime. An alarmed Perón plotted in exile to have his militant supporters head off such a tactical alliance, seeing it correctly as a step towards a negotiated Peronism without Perón. He encouraged the organization of a rival CGT to block the Vandorists. In response, former CGT unions in the provinces joined together as the *CGT de los Argentinos* (CGTA). Vandor and the old leadership eventually lost control of the original CGT, opening the way for new labor leaders, usually renegade Peronists, who challenged Perón's control and favored new tactics. Vandor's assassination by the Montoneros guerrillas provided the pretext for a state of siege that lasted until 1973 and the destruction of the CGTA.

The regime's approach to hostile public opinion made it impossible to gauge the mood of its opponents and adjust its activities accordingly. Onganía's hard-line policy ignored degrees of resistance and lumped all antigovernment elements together. Unwillingness to differentiate between opponents and ignorance of their varying objections and views, coupled with political arrogance, proved a fatal combination. The activities and opinions of intellectuals and creative artists could have provided a cautionary signal to the regime, if the government had paid attention. For example, the three-part movie of Fernando Solanas and Octavio Getino, *La hora de los hornos* (The Hour of the Furnaces), made in stages in 1966–1968, became a four-hour extravaganza of radical Peronismo shown in homes, factories, and union halls. In the battle for the hearts and minds the government failed.

THE CORDOBAZO

After an uncertain start the government settled on orthodox economic liberalism with a few twists. Adalbert Krieger Vasena, in charge of the economic ministry, emphasized controlling inflation. He took steps to modernize industry, reduced tariffs on capital goods to increase productivity, and nudged industrialists away from their attachment to noncompetitive markets. A wage freeze, voluntary price controls, and a tight rein on government expenditures brought inflation down dramatically, while industrial production increased significantly. President Onganía stood behind his minister, employing harsh measures to control and discipline workers.

In 1969, with the economy seemingly under control, the Nationalists proposed radical changes. A *Fundamental Charter* called for the establishment of national, provincial, and local advisory councils to represent the various sectors of society. The government intended to select members from a list compiled by recognized interest groups. Congress could be eliminated, allegedly because the councils directly represented the people's wishes. Córdoba Province already had councils in place and provided a model. The government sought to replace politics with administration within a corporate structure. This top-down approach insufficiently prepared public opinion for such drastic political departures. Open discussion could not take place in the environment created by the regime. Onganía, surrounded by Nationalists, believed that his small inner circle reflected national resolve.

The high level of tension created by the president's arbitrary manner and obvious disdain for those who opposed him needed only a triggering event to boil over into violence. Unexpectedly, Córdoba, the center of the automobile industry, provided that event. Foreign companies, Industrias Kaiser Argentina (IKA), Renault, and Fiat transformed rural workers into assembly line industrial workers. Its relatively new working class had little experience with impersonal and profit motivated international corporations. Retooled rural workers, while better paid, entered a world that they could not easily accept and deeply distrusted.

The city also attracted 30,000 university students. New suburbs and districts accompanied the population growth. Middle-class professionals, shopkeepers, and managers rounded out a city that had been transformed over the last twenty years. In good times employee relations remained tense but acceptable. In economic downturns employers cut costs, suspended production, and shortened hours and the work week, threatening the incomes of workers and those who depended on them, from shopkeepers to restaurants.

Two long-standing issues became symbolic of the powerlessness and resentment of automobile workers. The *quitas zonales,* a wage differential between metalworkers in Buenos Aires and those in the interior had long aggravated workers in Córdoba. Employers wanted to keep the differential to hold down costs. The other issue, the *sábado ingles* (English weekend), provided workers in several provinces (not Buenos Aires) with a full day's wage for a half day's labor on Saturday, came under attack from automobile firms.

Worker disgruntlement coincided with student anger at a regime they viewed as illegitimate. Faculty purges and restrictive policies made relations with the provincial and federal government tense. When students seized control of their district—some 20 blocks in the city—Onganía outlawed the *Federación Universitaria de Córdoba,* driving activism underground. Union halls and the churches became the remaining outlets for student meetings. Social divisions between workers and students blurred as union leaders and militant students began to see each other as mutually useful.

The Church added another element of instability. Following the bishop's conference in Medellín, Colombia, in 1968, the parish-level priesthood increasingly became radicalized. Even earlier, after a bishop's conference in Mar del Plata in 1966, clerical activists formed the *Movimiento de Sacerdotes del Tercer Mundo* (Third World Priests Movement), holding its first congress on May Day. Church militants allied themselves with Catholic students anxious to become involved in what appeared to be a religious renewal. Student unrest at the Universidad del Nordeste in Corrientes led to street violence, use of troops, the killing of a student, and the wounding of an undetermined number. Protests spread to Rosario then Córdoba, where union workers, Catholic activists, and students mounted the largest demonstration. Union leaders in Córdoba pressed for a nationwide general strike but meanwhile planned a forty-eight-hour general strike in their city beginning on May 29–30, 1969.

Separate columns of workers and students planned to march through the barrios of the city to converge in front of the CGT's offices. Nervous police fired on demonstrators, turning the strike into an insurrection that required the city's Third Army Corps to put down. Four days of street violence in the city shook the government's confidence and rattled the generals. Significant middle-class participation in the *Cordobazo* indicated that social discontent transcended ideology and student radicalism.

The possibility of a coordinated popular insurrection in other major cities worried army and police officials. A panicked Onganía dismissed his entire cabinet, including his effective economics minister. The following year, a leftist group kidnapped and murdered former president Aramburu. At the time, many thought Onganía had ordered the murder to silence one of his most vocal critics. Few realized that a new chapter in Argentine violence had opened. Alarmed military leaders demanded President Onganía's resignation. His substitute, General Roberto Levingston, faced a hostile combination of emboldened unions and a disgruntled middle class. When he appointed an undiplomatic and offensive individual to be governor of the Province of Córdoba, he precipitated a crisis and a second Cordobazo, which resulted in his removal and replacement by General Alejandro Lanusse.

General Lanusse attempted to negotiate a political truce with Perón while spending money to keep labor quiet. Consequently, by early 1973 inflation reached 100 percent. Mismanagement and doubts, not only about the viability of the current government, but the ability of anyone to govern, made Perón's return seem the lesser of evils. Years of political failure had exhausted the nation. President Lanusse attempted to engineer an acceptable political solution by galvanizing the traditional parties to form a coalition and a return of elections. The army hoped, without really believing it, that a civilian coalition could defeat the Peronists and provide a workable civilian government. Most of the country saw the return of Perón as the only hope.

In retrospect, the country engaged in a mass delusion, believing that a seventy-seven-year-old man in poor health could rescue the nation. Argentina had changed since Perón's resignation in ways that made the return an emotional fantasy rather than a practical step towards stability. The transformation of Perón from an opportunistic politician into a messianic figure testified to the degree of national distress. Many talked of the general landing in a black airplane (*avion negro*) to restore the nation. Few understood that mystical notions created an emotional state bound to collide with reality. In exile, his powers became magnified while his physical decline remained hidden from all but the occasional observant visitor.[1]

Lanusse, maintaining total secrecy, dispatched an emissary to Madrid to discuss an accommodation with Perón. The terms represented a total capitulation by the army. They included amnesty, the right to return home, early elections with all parties and individuals eligible, dropping of all court judgments, unblocking of Swiss bank accounts, and finally, the return of Evita's corpse. Digging up Evita, buried under a false name in Italy, and the delivery of the preserved corpse in Madrid, may have been the easy part of the deal. Evita played a macabre educational role in the preparation of Perón's third wife, Isabel Martínez de Perón, for the return to Argentina. She could not compete with the by now semi-mythical Evita. Inevitably, the comparisons between wives verged on insult or occurred in the context of a crude joke. A former Panama night-club dancer born in the impoverished northern Argentine province of La Rioja, she attracted Perón's interest for other than political reasons. Nevertheless, she did her best to learn. She relied upon one of Perón's personal secretaries, José López Rega, to show her the ropes. López Rega in turn relied upon astrology. Referred to by the cynical as "Rasputin" or "the sorcerer," López Rega encouraged Isabel to lie on top of Evita's coffin in order to absorb powers supposedly radiating from the preserved corpse.

ARMED OPPOSITION

The guerrillas pushed their way into public consciousness with the kidnapping and killing of ex-president General Aramburu. The different guerrilla groups and their objectives only slowly became evident. Most people assumed that they represented various forms of Peronista violence. The two principal groups, the *Montoneros* and the *Ejército Revolucionario del Pueblo* (ERP—Peoples Revolutionary Army) competed as well as cooperated when mutually advantageous.

The Montoneros, responsible for the murder of Aramburu, justified their action on the grounds that the ex-president executed twenty-seven Peronists and spirited Eva Perón's embalmed corpse off to Italy. While claiming to be Peronists, they declared that only revolutionary action could change the socioeconomic structure. In exile, Perón encouraged their violence for tactical purposes—a decision he lived to regret.[2] They drew on the Church's critical attitude towards capitalism and the support for a social revolution that came out of Vatican II, which the bishop's conference in Medellín, Colombia, re-enforced in 1968. Young idealistic Catholics such as Emilio Maza, a Córdoba University student leader, along with ex-seminarians and an ex-president of a Catholic Action youth group, formed the Montonero core. They also recruited children of military families. They vowed to destroy existing authority and construct a socialist society.

Most active guerrillas developed a taste for violence in the university politics of the 1960s. They embraced urban guerrilla warfare and sought with limited success to form alliances with labor unions. Radical priests, including Father Alberto Carbone, eventually indicted in the murder of Aramburu, helped blend the potent mixture of Peronist ideological vagueness with Marxism, Nationalist thought, and Christianity. They presented the early Church fathers as model revolutionaries in an attempt to legitimize violence and murder for a higher morality. Emphasis on social justice swept many students into political violence and subsequently into guerrilla war against the state as the social enemy.

The other major guerrilla organization, the *Ejército Revolucionario del Pueblo,* emerged out of a failed political party—the Revolutionary Party of Workers (PRT). Mario Roberto Santucho or "Robi," one of many brothers from a well-to-do family in the interior with a tradition of political involvement on all sides of the spectrum, organized the PRT and the ERP. Santucho, active in university politics and a former paratrooper—allegedly the reason for his distaste for army officers—embraced Trotskyism. During two trips to Cuba he underwent guerrilla training. The federal police succeeded in dismantling the PRT and arresting members, including Santucho, who soon made a daring escape.

The ERP began operations from a base in the Paraná river delta. The PRT theoretically served as the governing body of the ERP and, assuming victory, would reemerge as the state party. A handful of other groups formed to coordinate with Ché Guevara's Bolivian foco or the guerrilla movement in Chile. The FAP, *Fuerzas Armadas Peronistas* (1970), briefly functioned as an urban group. With the capture and death of Ché in 1967 and other setbacks, most of the surviving members of defunct organizations joined the Montoneros or the ERP.

Both organizations dismissed the idea of revolution from below. The workers might be organized in support, but the leadership had to come from the intellectuals to have any hope of success. Revolutionary experience in Russia, China, and Cuba provided the model. Networks in universities became very important, although terrorist groups also recruited among high school students. Workers, allegedly unable to create a revolution, became wards of radical intellectuals. Elitism made it difficult to form a reliable socio-revolutionary connection downward to the workers or the slum dwellers.

AN ABORTED RESCUE

President Lanusse intended to meet Perón's conditions but hoped to preserve the army's dignity in the process. He failed. Perón understood that he had the upper hand and had no interest in saving the army's face or making any concessions. A one-day general strike forced the pace of negotiations. When President Lanusse indicated that Perón could be a candidate if he returned by August 25, 1972, he ignored the deadline and returned unexpectedly on November 14. The government lost the ability to manage the transition. General Lanusse pleaded with his fellow officers to accept the reality that a return to civilian rule meant Perón. Meanwhile, General Perón promised national unity and suggested he would meet the social and political needs of his people. Rhetoric, flatly contradictory, soothed many anxious for a respite from political chaos. Perón appeared to be all they had left. Before some substance could be given to the public's exaggerated expectations, the rescue took an unexpected turn back to chaos and uncertainty. Suddenly, on December 14, 1972, Perón flew to Paraguay, then on to Madrid, leaving behind his selection for president and vice-president. His stay lasted only four weeks. A stunned country and uneasy army wondered what Perón had in mind.

In reality, health, not plotting, motivated Perón's departure, but at the time few knew the real reason. He covered up the medical emergency by explaining that his election would be too provocative for the military to accept. His excuse adroitly blamed the army for his truncated rescue mission. Perón's stand-in candidate in the election of March 1973, Héctor Cámpora, duly won the office with 49 percent of the vote. A former dentist with few political skills, he had the limited legitimacy of a caretaker. The disjunction between the requirements of office, which presumed independent presidential authority, and the actual situation made for a fragile regime unable to maintain order. His administration became a combination of farce and chaos, while behind the scenes various Peronista factions jockeyed for power. The radical left seized the advantage from off-balance right-wing Peronistas.

Immediately after the swearing in of the new president, the Peronist youth converged on the main prison, forcing the release and pardoning of captured guerrillas. The next day congress approved an amnesty for the Montoneros and other terrorist groups, repealed antiterrorist legislation, and abolished the Federal Criminal Court of the Nation. Freed guerrillas and their associates seized control of government offices and other state enterprises, hospitals, schools, airports, train stations, communications, banks, and anything that seemed useful. Intimidation and violence, characterized by the powerless president and his cabinet as mere exuberance, included dangling the Thoracic Surgery Institute's director wrapped in the Montonero flag, by his feet in an elevator shaft. Cámpora could only take the paternal high ground, referring to the radicals as our "marvelous youth." President Cámpora, referred to as "uncle," might be technically in charge, but young radicals intended to exercise actual power. The universities fell under thinly veiled guerrilla control. Constant denunciation of enemies, demonstrations, and loud meetings maintained a level of excitement. Replacement of administrators by unqualified radicals leveled authority, as all became *compañeros.* Elimination of academic requirements transformed universities into convenient recruitment and mobilization points.[3]

The left talked of replacing the army with revolutionary militias. Right-wing Peronistas, initially taken off-guard by the excesses of the left, counter attacked to regain control of the factories and offices from the radicals. Both sides used violent methods to defend what they saw as political assets. Meanwhile, President Cámpora established diplomatic relations with East Germany, North Korea, and Vietnam, posturing in a vain effort to appear to be in charge. Aghast, Perón in Madrid saw all his plotting on the verge of irrelevancy as order deteriorated. At what point the army would intervene, or an alarmed public would demand that they do so, remained the question. A return could not be delayed.

When Cámpora arrived in Spain to accompany his general back to Argentina, an angry Perón, ignoring his own encouragement of violence, gave him a dressing-down for jeopardizing years of planning and struggle. Perón understood that the guerrillas had to be suppressed, the Peronista youth brought up sharply, and some semblance of discipline reestablished in order to have a viable government. Cámpora had added significantly, perhaps fatally, to the problem. Perón's safe reception in Buenos Aires could not be guaranteed. Anti-Perónist military elements might seize the opportunity to end the perceived problem in a burst of machine gunfire. Left wing Peronists, anxious to construct a regime without Perón, might be tempted to do the same. Even some right-wing Peronists might prefer a martyred Perón as an excuse to liquidate the Peronist left. Moreover, the army and police could withdraw their protective forces and allow events to take a fatal course.

A RESTORED REGIME

Even before the aircraft carrying Perón landed, the extent of the task became evident. Peronistas on the right and left gathered along the route from Ezeiza airport to the city to greet their returning leader. Free train passage, make-shift tents and other facilities, rallies, and marches catered to and entertained the expectant crowds. A national holiday proclaimed by the government added to the sense of a major historic event. Three thousand armed men, mostly from various unions, provided security. Helicopters and bulletproof facilities stood ready to transport and protect the returnees. The left viewed the gathering as a crucial last-minute opportunity to prevail over those still attached to the physical being of their leader. If the right-wing could be decisively weakened or destroyed, Perón would be an honored icon but a political captive while a new leadership directed the movement. They almost succeeded.

The right understood that their survival also hung in the balance and are generally believed to have started shooting. Photographs of right-wing Peronists firing into the crowd appear to support the charge. The two sides, both heavily armed, fought throughout the day. The police stood by awaiting orders from the interior minister, never given. Eventually, the left retreated, many to be shot by their pursuers and others to be tortured and beaten. Meanwhile, air traffic controllers diverted the general's aircraft to the Morón airforce base. After nineteen hours at the airport's Hotel International, ensconced in the presidential suite waiting to formally enter the country, he proceeded to a heavily guarded residence. A prudent Perón, well aware of the dangers, successfully made his reentry.

Army commander General Jorge Carcagno met with Perón; both agreed that the country had to be pulled back from the brink of uncontrollable chaos. Perón, moving swiftly, dispatched José Rucci of the CGT to instruct President Cámpora to resign or face a general strike. Cámpora resigned after a little over a month and a half in power. New elections provided Perón with 62 percent of the vote, with his wife Isabel as vice-president. It might have been a convincing mandate if the electorate had voted for a clearly laid out program. Instead, the election represented a messianic acclamation and a desire for national salvation.

Perón wrestled with a Peronista leadership accustomed to functioning on its own and a dangerous and disrespectful left, still claiming to be Peronistas, but in reality with their own ambitions. The president reordered the military hierarchy to put an apolitical command structure in control. A social pact with the unions suspended their power to collectively bargain with employers for the next two years and provided an inadequate 20 percent raise, but froze prices. Encouraged by Perón, the traditional union leadership led the fight against the radicalized wing of the movement. Inflation came under control by the middle of the year, only to be thrown in doubt by the oil crisis of 1973 that drove up the price of imports, which made the wage and price freeze difficult to sustain. Meanwhile, Perón hoped to purge the left of extremists while holding both the moderate left and right to together—a Herculean task for even a master politician. For the Peronist left something had gone terribly wrong with the general. They found it almost beyond comprehension that President Perón accorded state honors (May, 1974) to visiting General Augusto Pinochet, leader of the Chilean coup.

Montonero and ERP violence, including attacks on military facilities, assassinations, and reprisals made every day a crisis. Perón appeared on television in uniform to announce increased efforts to apprehend the guerrillas. He also demanded that congress reinstate counter terrorism legislation and removed provincial governors sympathetic to the Montoneros. The destruction of proguerrilla newspapers, firebombed or closed by the police, eliminated a powerful propaganda and recruitment tool. Conservative newspapers considered too critical of the government closed in a burst of a submachine gunfire. When a show of support became necessary he relied on the CGT. In a calculated move, Perón spoke from the balcony of the Casa Rosada, threatening to resign, hoping to regain the control that appeared to be slipping away. A month later on July 1, 1974, a little over a year after his return and with success or failure still in the balance, Juan Perón died. Isabel succeeded to the impossible presidency.

LABOR'S DECLINE

Perón artificially elevated workers as the dominant political force. Without government support labor could not sustain that role. Consequently, the worker's share of the nation's income receded along with official support from a high of 50.8 percent in 1954 to 35.9 percent in 1972. Employment in fields where unions had been traditionally strong declined as a service economy began to emerge. Moreover, employers preferred investing in modern machinery rather than in reluctant, low-productivity workers. Strikes did little to reverse the decline. Fighting between unions for a shrinking membership pool and attempts to control workshops undercut their legitimacy. A number of unions broke with the Peronists to become part of the so-called anti-Peronist 32 Democratic Majority. Subsequently, an independent group emerged claiming to be neither pro- nor anti-Peronist. Continuous fragmentation destroyed alliances before they could exert any influence. The CGT, once broad-based, now relied upon a narrow membership.

Many union officials became predators. Surcharges on dues, special levies, and assessment of a one-month fee on any wage increase on the assumption that they should be rewarded for a successful negotiating effort became common practice. The large amounts of money handled by unions, supposedly for the benefit of the members, often proved irresistible. The Power and Light Federation managed an investment account of slightly under 15 million dollars, and operated resort hotels, a golf course, country clubs, a chain of department stores, day care centers, clinics, retirement homes and more—in short a financial empire. The railway union managed just slightly less. Unions owned an estimated fifty percent of the luxury hotels in the beach resort of Mar del Plata. Corrupt officials set up dummy companies to do business with their unions and provided services at inflated costs. Armando March of the Commercial Employees Union diverted some 64.3 million pesos from union housing construction to his use. While his official salary of 657 pesos seemed inadequate, he nevertheless stretched it to cover a mansion, expensive artwork, prize dogs, and silk suits. A political misstep ruined his prospects, but others managed to prosper into retirement, such as Rogelio Coria, the General Secretary of the Construction Workers. Union boss Coria had his own company that provided construction material. He lived in a luxury apartment and eventually retired to a large estancia in Paraguay prudently out of reach—or so he thought—only to be assassinated.[4] A leadership position provided a better life and a magnificent legacy for heirs. Competition for such posts could be fierce. Honest union elections became a rarity.

The government, well aware of fraud and rigged union elections, chose to overlook illegalities. More of a restraint on corrupt union officials, the

Montoneros cut down those they claimed to be working-class traitors. Perón had little patience with labor leaders. The decline of unions, already well advanced when Perón returned in 1973, could not be reversed, although he attempted to do so by forcing unions to join the Peronist CGT. With his death the rank and file lost their last psychological and emotional link with the union ideal.

PRESIDENT ISABEL PERÓN

President Isabel Perón, ill prepared, lacking the instinct for politics but a stubborn survivor, had few positive supporters. Nevertheless, the army believed that constitutional procedures should be followed. Others saw some advantage in the name and the fact that she had been selected by Perón to be vice-president. She intended to govern and did so with the help of López Rega, who knew all the right people and fully understood the violent nature of politics. He used a convenient militia, the AAA (Argentine Anti-Communist Alliance), which General Perón had allowed to operate to intimidate and kill the regime's enemies. The Triple A, recruited from the Federal Police, collaborated with that organization, although AAA thugs did most of the dirty work. Victims received an anonymous warning to flee the country. Those who ignored the warning died, gunned down and left to bleed to death. In several instances, police guards withdrew just prior to an assassination. A known 248 died between July 1974 and September the following year. López Rega's use of the AAA represented a calculated move to assure the army that the unrewarding task of dealing with the violent left could be entrusted, at least in part, to the regime.

A University Law of March 1974 prohibited politics on campus and restricted the functions of Student Unions. The appointment of Oscar Ivanissevitch as minister of education signaled an all-out assault on what came to be called the "rear-guard guerrillas," meaning the student left and potential recruits for the Montoneros and other groups. Fifteen universities fell under federal control, resulting in the dismissal of some 4,000 lecturers and the arrest of 1,600 students. The government closed the Montonero's daily newspaper, *Noticias*, as well as the weekly *La Causa Peronista* and banned rallies. Along with the AAA's murderous activities, the regime came close to crippling the organization. By September the Montoneros went underground. They anticipated that urban terror would demoralize and exhaust the population, undermine the economy and the will of the state to resist, or goad the army into such harsh repression that they would lose all public support.

The Montoneros demonstrated their disregard for Isabel, referred to as Isabelita, by raiding the grave of General Aramburu. They announced that they would return the body only when Evita's corpse, still in Spain, returned to Argentina. The Montoneros made it clear that they did not accept her as the legitimate political heir of Perón and considered her a tool of López Rega and the radical right. Messages scrawled on walls that, "Isabel is not Perón" and "there is only one Evita," attempted to extinguish the last remaining connection between Peronismo and a living symbol and complete its transformation into an ideology.

Strategic and tactical differences separated the Montoneros from the ERP. The ERP, studying past guerrilla successes in China and Vietnam, believed that urban terror alone could not over turn the state. "Robi" Santucho, leader of the ERP, emphasized that the final stage required the establishment of control over territory, eventually leading to a decisive battle between armies. He chose the distant province of Tucumán as the logical place to start preparations for the final stage. A region of mountains and tropical jungles, with an economy devastated by the collapse of the sugar industry, it appeared to offer safety, supplies, and potential recruits. Small contingents of ERP guerrillas established camps in 1974. Police organizations failed to root out the ERP, who soon controlled at least 30 percent of the province, collected taxes and highway tolls, and increasingly acted as a state. Isabel, pressed by the army, placed the province's police under military command.

In early 1975, the army launched Operation Independence. General Acdel Vila read the same guerilla manuals as Santucho and understood the tactics. After a slow start, the army cut off ERP supplies and supporting contact with the population. Helicopters and infrared technology ended the Tucumán threat. Confiscated papers led to the ERP urban headquarters and its destruction. Torture, followed by disappearance, elicited information and leads. The guerrillas sustained heavy losses but remained capable of inflicting crippling blows. On Christmas Eve 1975, a combined Montonero and ERP force of some 1,000 heavily armed guerrillas attacked the Monte Chingolo arsenal on the outskirts of Buenos Aires. The army, tipped off by an informer, lay in wait. After a five-hour battle lasting well into the night the attackers withdrew, leaving 100 guerrillas dead. In spite of the successful defense of the arsenal, the prolonged battle shocked the nation. Few realized that the attack marked the high point of the guerrilla campaign and would never again be matched.

Isabel faced an impossible situation on virtually all fronts. An important challenge came from labor. The CGT, justifiably worried that their control over workers had weakened, intended to play a larger role in formulating economic policy. While soaring inflation had to be brought under control in order to receive IMF credits, the CGT demanded wage increases to relieve the desperate plight of workers and, perhaps more important, bolster their eroding control. Meanwhile, the government saw an opportunity to reduce wage pressures by discrediting the already weakened union leadership. Officials ignored customary negotiations with unions

over new contracts and wage levels, as well as the extent of price adjustments needed to compensate for increases. When union contracts lapsed,
exasperated workers took to the streets and occupied factories.

Union leaders struggled to regain control, demanding free bargaining
with employers. Subsequently, the government overruled wage increases
of 160 percent with a counter offer of much less. Workers again refused
to wait for their leaders and shut down factories. Union bosses had no
choice but to order a general strike, shutting down much of country and
costing the economy an estimated 66 million dollars a day. The government capitulated; the entire cabinet resigned, and López Rega withdrew
from all official positions, although he continued to advise the president.
Isabel Perón could not force labor to take less than they wanted. Her
already weak administration lost even more credibility. Nevertheless,
the regime lingered on for another eight months as authority and power
drained away.

The army could have struck a deal, perhaps for the appointment of
a civilian provisional president followed by elections, but decided on a
coup. The decision to establish a military regime came down to the fear
that a weak government would allow the guerrillas to gather strength,
resulting in a prolonged indecisive contest. Under such circumstances,
demoralization and exhaustion, two major objectives of guerrilla groups,
could not be avoided. Some cautioned that the army should wait until
things became absolutely desperate, forcing the public to demand military
intervention. Others believed a delay risked plunging the country into
third-world status, with unrecoverable economic and political damage.
Industrial production fell as inflation rose to new levels, as did unemployment in the two major industrial centers of Buenos Aires and Córdoba.
Antonio Cafiero, suggested by the unions as an acceptable minister of the
economy, tried a gradual indexing of prices, wages, and exchange rates.
Perhaps a sensible strategy had it been implemented earlier, it now failed.
Yet another minister instituted drastic measures, resulting in a final wave
of strikes. Those in favor of intervention prevailed.

After attending a festive party the president boarded a helicopter to
return to her residence only to have the pilot land at another location,
inform her of her removal, and place her under arrest. Her ousting on
March 24, 1976, marked the end of any physical link with General Perón.
Her regime survived much longer than anyone expected. Before it ended
she suffered several breakdowns.

A junta representing the various military services assumed authority
under the direction of army General Jorge Rafael Videla. Orders, by now
almost formulaic, dissolved congress, suspended financial transactions,
and intervened to take control of all provincial governments, major
municipalities, and unions. Sweeping arrests of Peronista leaders and
officials and decrees to ensure order completed the transfer of authority.

"Councils of War" to summarily try subversives promised to punish only those guilty of criminal acts. Few could imagine how broadly subversion would be defined or the consequences of that definition. The coup triumphed without resistance and had the support of the Radical party, business groups, and even some unions, while the public readily accepted the end of a dysfunctional regime. Although the immediate goal of the army remained to complete the destruction of the ERP and the Montoneros, the military government could not ignore severe economic problems.

Videla abruptly changed economic policy, adopting neo-liberal principles that favored private ownership and market forces. State enterprises preferred by many, including union workers, military technocrats, noncompetitive industrialists, and some Nationalists, became privatization possibilities. The president believed he could override entrenched interests and radically restructure the entire economy along the lines of the Chilean experience. Nevertheless, the army did not favor allowing unemployment to purge the system. Inflation seemed a less provocative way to reduced salaries. In the first three months of military rule, public employees' wages declined by 40 percent.

EL PROCESO: ELABORATION OF THE DIRTY WAR

The army approached the crisis in the manner of a desperate cancer surgeon. Argentina's "diseased tissue" allegedly needed to be cut away aggressively and completely, until no trace remained to re-infect the body politic. The *Proceso de Reorganización Nacional* (The National Reorganization Process) envisioned an all-out, unrestrained effort to exterminate the guerrillas, punish those that supported them, and convince the country that a continuation of the violent cycle of instability would not be tolerated. The division between military interventionists and professionals, who believed that the army should focus on the profession of arms and not politics or the suppression of violence, eroded under repeated acts of guerrilla cruelty. Moderates within the officer corps stood aside. A conscious decision to broaden the use of counter-terror, brushing way judicial procedures, reflected the army's loss of faith in the judiciary. In any event, they did not want to create vast numbers of political prisoners or risk escapes such as the one in 1972 in which Santucho and others fled, or a future mass release ordered by opportunistic politicians. Sorting out the moderates from the violent left seemed a fruitless and unnecessary endeavor. Suspicion would be sufficient and judgment summary—a decision that broadened the reach of state terror. Ironically, terrorism peaked in 1975 at Monte Chingolo, but at the time many believed that the outcome remained dangerously uncertain.

The army's counter terrorism doctrine relied on the experience of others, but with adjustments for Argentine uniqueness. The American experience in Vietnam seemed too much of an emphasis on conventional force to be useful—besides, it failed. On the other hand, the French experience in Vietnam and Algeria appeared more useful as a model in spite of its ultimate failure. For some time the Superior War College (ESG) had studied counter terrorism methods and concluded that the French model made more sense. French veterans lectured at the ESG, published articles in its journal, and laid out the pros and cons of their tactics. The army understood that it faced a struggle over control of the state, uncomplicated by a colonial independence movement, cultural and racial issues.

The structure of the counter terrorism effort partially explains the sadistic cruelty and the large number of individuals it engulfed. A maze of security zones and sub-zones blanketed the nation, resulting in a highly decentralized process. Pressure for results from the top, but without supervision, prompted junior officers and NCOs to go about the task as they saw fit. As all understood, terrorism relied upon a network of supporters not directly involved in the struggle. An estimated 25,000 Montoneros bore arms, while some 250,000 noncombatants supported the group out of conviction or fear.

Guerrilla supporters operated arms repair and manufacturing workshops, printing facilities, safe houses, and underground prisons, as well as collected information. The ERP operated along similar lines. Financing came from many sources, including kidnapping and bank robbery. Guerrillas abducted the heirs to the Bunge and Born conglomerate and pocketed 60 million. Foreign companies also provided substantial ransom amounts. Fearful individuals paid protection money or sent as many family members as possible out of the country. Eventually, foreign companies pared down their resident staff and in some cases withdrew from the country completely.

To the army, coercion appeared central. Rapid information gathering, before others became aware of a capture and took evasive action, depended on speedy extraction of information. French lecturers stressed the need to supervise and control those involved in order to minimize atrocities. As they knew, torture could backfire, becoming a propaganda disaster, and victims might attract international attention. To Argentine officers, the situation seemed too desperate to worry about theoretical notions.

Removal and killing of a suspect who disappeared without a trace appeared to provide the solution. Moral objections could be minimized by secret operations and compartmentalization. Unfortunately, it made any ongoing evaluation of effectiveness relative to the number of victims of the Proceso impossible and may have prolonged the use of state terror. Nor did it allow for the emergence of restraining devices limiting the extent of executions and torture. The Church lamented but supported the need for repression. When absolutely necessary to protest, the Church did so in a mildly disapproving manner. Only four Bishops denounced human rights violations. Clerics that failed to follow the Church's lead could not expect much help or protection. The assassination of three priests and several seminarians (1976), probably by the government, prompted a letter of concern. While the return to civilian rule became obvious, the Church made it clear that it preferred reconciliation not condemnation and warned of the dangers of demagoguery.

Not all individuals swept up in the counter terror simply disappeared, but many did—the number can only be estimated. Amnesty International came up with figure of 20,000 victims; others gave much lower estimates. The Proceso encouraged the belief that virtually every sector of society and the economy had been infiltrated. Paranoia fed on the numbers of victims, innocent or guilty, that went through the system. Union activity and workers' demands immediately became suspect. Pressure on organized labor also offered an opportunity to reverse the balance between management and labor. In the case of the National Power and Light Union, when a work slowdown in response to wage and work hour changes went into its fourth month, union boss Oscar Smith "disappeared," ending the work action. Strike-prone factories often experienced raids and arrests of shop committees by military personnel. An arrest could be followed by a release within hours, days of interrogation, or perhaps by torture and disappearance. Uncertainty created an atmosphere of intimidation that made any type or degree of resistance potentially fatal.

On occasion, innocent family members became hostages in order to force relatives to cooperate. State terror broke the guerrillas by killing or intimidating noncombatant supporters and sympathizers. The use of torture to obtain information rapidly made it possible to root out cells, isolate leaders, and eventually capture or kill them. As General Luciano Benjamín Menéndez predicted at the beginning of the Proceso, "We are going to have to kill . . . 25,000 subversives, 20,000 sympathizers, and we will make 5,000 mistakes."[5] The damage went far beyond numbers.

As the military learned, physical disappearance could not counter the psychological power of memory and unverified loss. Life became grindingly stressful, particularly if the family included university students or young adults. The kidnapping of family members, relatives, or friends and the impossibility of discovering what happened when, why, and where produced a sense of powerlessness and despair. The organization of Mothers of Disappeared Persons, known internationally as the *Madres de la Plaza de Mayo*, made the point that uncertain loss prolonged hope. In their criticism of the published report of an investigative commission, they objected to treating disappeared persons as dead without producing bodies. Closure needed more than presumptive death, no matter how rational the assumption. The adoption of newborn babies of disappeared suspects by military and police families created another emotional issue, with the potential for traumatic revelations years later.

Control of news and information became an important aspect of the Proceso. Invention of an official reality became as important as the armed battle for dominance. Control of the media relied upon large carrots and harsh sticks. After taking over, the military dropped the tax on ad revenues and increased official advertising by 60 percent. Those that could not be bought paid dearly. A graduated harshness went from death threats, to imprisonment and torture, to property seizures, to assassinations. The government expropriated *La opinion* and detained and tortured one of its owners, Jacobo Timerman, in what became an international incident. Some 72 journalists disappeared during the Proceso, hundreds remained in detention, and many experienced torture. The prudent fled into exile. Sudden disappearance of an entire edition of a magazine from the kiosks became commonplace. The military banned a number of domestic and foreign magazines. Book production fell from 31.5 million in 1976 to 8.7 million in 1979.

Newspaper circulation dropped 50 percent and many magazines folded. Only the English-language *Buenos Aires Herald* had some leeway to report on sensitive issues and carefully voiced opinions. Newspapers, more than other media, struggled with the traditional obligation to report events as objectively as possible. Heavy censorship coupled with coercive advertising policies brought most into line. The regime, along with three major newspapers, formed Papel Prensa to control all newsprint sales in the country, selling to its owners at a discount and manipulating paper prices to gain cooperation or punish other publishers.

Television required a similar approach. Selected individuals bought up air time and resold it for approved programs. On occasion, the government directly allotted prime-time slots. Enticing advertisers to continue business as usual constituted a propaganda objective made possible in most cases by adjusting fees and handing out thinly disguised kickbacks. Combined newspaper, radio, and TV ad revenues rose sharply, according to the Argentine Chamber of Advertisers—by 60 percent in 1975–1976.[6] Official propaganda merged with news reporting that supported the regime to create an official reality difficult to challenge. News of guerrilla attacks or criticism of the armed services, including incidents of human rights abuses, fell under the censorship restrictions. Violations of national security carried stiff penalties. Minor infractions brought a stern warning.

Television and radio had the least difficulty adjusting to the non-news format, accelerating the already established tilt towards entertainment. Almost total dependency on advertising revenue had long before created an accommodating attitude to the wishes of sponsors. Expansion or contraction, life and death, depended on commercials. Pay TV began in 1962 with live programming from Buenos Aires, until videotape became readily available in the middle 1960s. Pay TV offered entertainment almost exclusively. The military regime introduced color

TV in 1978 to televise the America's Cup and show the world a normal Argentina. Color became the standard by 1980 with 191,000 receivers. Entertainment buried both social responsibility and guerrilla activity in light programming. The dreary, sometimes fatal, touch of politics occurred against an unreal backdrop of a TV fantasy life. People and the government endured by pretending to be normal.

CHAPTER 7

The Proceso's Dark Shadow, Menem, and Neoliberalism

THE END OF MILITARY RULE

Many officers understood that the Proceso damaged the army's moral position in spite of the claim that it saved the country. Moreover, the armed forces failed to govern effectively, quite apart from its conduct of the Dirty War. The question of what other options might be implemented could not be easily answered. A fatigued regime without a clear objective and convincing rational for holding power could not broker a return to civilian rule under favorable terms. A renewal of their presumptive mandate or a favorable withdrawal from government appeared to require a defining moment. The perfect event seemed to lie just of the coast in the form of the Falkland Islands. Forcing the British to relinquish control appeared to be a low-risk operation that would reemphasize the army's traditional role as guarantor of the nation's territorial integrity. In one glorious moment, establishment of Argentine sovereignty over the disputed islands would restore military prestige.

President (General) Leopoldo Galtieri, like many of his predecessors, pressed Britain to withdraw from the Falkland Islands (Malvinas). The islands, well within the continental shelf, seemed a natural extension of the mainland. Argentina's historic claim to sovereignty rested on proximity and Spanish claims that antedated the initial British occupation of the islands in the early nineteenth century. Nevertheless, Britain had continuously occupied the islands from the 1830s, a reality ignored by Buenos Aires. Shepherds, sheep, and the Falkland Islands Company turned the colony into a reasonably viable dependency. After World War II, as various European Empires began to spin off colonies, some voluntarily, some violently, the timing seemed favorable for a return of the islands. Subsequently, a United Nations resolution in 1965 supported negotiations between the two powers, indicating that it expected a transfer of sovereignty. Diplomatic talks began, but the Falkland Islanders insisted they would not accept transference to Argentina. Britain preferred to put the whole issue on a back burner, much to the irritation of Buenos Aires.

Nevertheless, the discrediting of colonialism and its worldwide retreat emboldened the Argentines. Navy Captain (soon to be admiral) Jorge Anaya, the Naval representative on the military junta when Galtieri assumed office in 1981, had long admired India's seizure (1961) of Portuguese Goa. In one bold stroke India ended the problem of a colonial enclave. In the case of Goa, Portugal did not offer a defense. Most, including Captain Anaya, believed that Britain would not go to war over the Falklands. Galtieri saw a similar seizure of the Falklands as a way of restoring the government's popularity and agreed on the improbability of war over the islands.

The invasion began in the South Georgia islands to the south of the Falklands. When a contractor raised the Argentine flag and refused to cooperate with British authorities, the warship HMS *Endurance,* with a contingent of marines, left Port Stanley for the South Georgias. In response, Argentina dispatched three warships, forcing the Endurance to withdraw. Now, planners in Buenos Aires believed they had to strike the Falklands well in advance of a British defensive build-up. The decision to invade on April 2, even through they had yet to complete their military plans, rested on the belief that in the end, Britain would negotiate rather than respond militarily.

The government failed to consider national pride, or the possibility giving up the Falklands without a fight might jeopardize their hold on other British territories. The generals also misunderstood, and certainly underestimated, British Prime Minister Margaret Thatcher, the Iron Lady. Misplaced confidence led them to believe that the United States would stand aside and, after Britain conceded, would resume its friendly relations with Buenos Aires. After the seizure of the South Georgias, Galtieri received a call from American President Ronald Reagan who bluntly warned him that Britain would respond militarily and that Argentina's relationship with the United States could be jeopardized. A weak president and a policy-making junta made it impossible to change course. After the British put their counter strike in motion, a panicked Galtieri called Reagan and reportedly babbled that "the British are coming." Reagan responded in effect with a "no kidding." By that time, the die had been cast.

Eighty British marines and a militia of 120 resisted the invasion force briefly. Unexpectedly, a United Nation resolution demanded immediate withdrawal of all troops, and the third world failed to offer support. The Organization of American States voted only to support the United Nations.

Within days, Argentina found itself isolated diplomatically. The British fleet moved south, refueling and taking on supplies provided by the United States at Ascension Island. The submarine *Spartan* arrived off Port Stanley on April 12 to set up a zone around the islands to prevent resupply. British commandos landed at the South Georgia Islands and quickly resumed control. Naval gunfire and carrier-based jets began to attack military targets. On May 2, the nuclear submarine *Conqueror* torpedoed the Argentine cruiser *General Belgrano* just as it turned back to its homeport—368 Argentine sailors died in the freezing waters. Meanwhile, the Argentine air force sank four British ships but lost 70 jets to heat-seeking missiles.

A British force landed on the opposite end of the island from the capital, Port Stanley, advancing over 65 miles on foot after a missile attack sank the ship carrying their helicopters. A series of mountain defenses blocked their approach to Port Stanley. Fighting became hand-to-hand on more than one occasion. Argentine commandos fought well, providing one of the few demonstrations of the nation's military expertise. The stubborn belief that Britain would make only a token effort to resist and would soon concede became an operational obstacle, explaining in part the ineffective strategy that guided the operation. Platoon and company-level officers and their soldiers lacked communications, had little ammunition, and had no idea of the constantly changing battlefield because of the reluctance of the high command to share information. Ill-trained draftees fought well under the circumstances, but fruitlessly. Ironically, better-trained and equipped troops remained deployed along the border with Chile under the assumption the Chileans might take advantage of the situation to invade. Within twenty-four days, 11,313 disarmed and dispirited Argentine soldiers returned home. The war cost 746 Argentine and 252 British dead, and many more injuries.

The shock of defeat, made worse by unrestrained radio and newspaper propaganda rather than accurate reporting, discredited the military. The army command proved incompetent, while the navy prudently kept its ships in port. Only the air force performed well. Recriminations and attempts by the military branches to shift blame to each other indicated that the military itself had little prospect of pulling together to hold onto political power. In defense, Admiral Anaya's attorney asserted that Britain might well have been defeated except for the betrayal of the United States. Few accepted that notion. Army commander General Mario Menéndez faced a court-martial. The armed forces lost self-confidence and public respect. The bitter mood left only one option—a quick transition to civilian rule. The high command replaced Galtieri with retired General Reynaldo Bignone to manage the transition.

A major objective, the protection of officers from prosecution for Dirty-War activities, required a call for national reconciliation and a blanket amnesty for all those on both sides of the conflict. Public disapproval could have been predicted, but not the intense level of anger. That became clear with a mass 24-hour march of protest around the Plaza de Mayo. Nevertheless, the army proceeded to grant themselves the protection they sought with the self-amnesty law. On October 30, 1983, citizens voted for the first time in ten years when the army returned to the barracks in a state of political and military disgrace. They left the country deeply divided, alienated, demoralized, and angry. A huge debt that ballooned from 18.8 billion in 1978 to 46 billion in 1983 continued to mount as unpaid interested accumulated.

THE RADICAL PARTY RETURNS

Raúl Alfonsín had precious little charisma, but he appeared to be a decent man committed to democracy. While most political observers predicted a Peronist victory, Alfonsín unexpectedly won with 52 percent of the popular vote. The Radicals had broad support for the first time since 1928. Many Peronist voters, upset with their party's involvement in the Dirty War, cast their ballot for the UCR or left it blank. Optimists suggested that the Justicialista Party could no longer count on winning every democratic election as it had since 1946. Rather than the country's natural ruling party, it appeared that the PJ would have to earn the support of the voters or face disintegration. Meanwhile, the victory represented a new democratic beginning for the Radical leadership, confident that they could shape a new era. A majority, albeit slim, in the Chamber of Deputies, and the crucial governorship of Buenos Aires Province and five other governorships provided the core elements of a major political victory. In the Senate the Radicals had 18 seats to 21 for the Peronists, but the opposition's poor showing at the polls weakened their position.

Voters wanted concrete action to deal with the economic crisis and the legacy of the Dirty War, not just democratic consolidation. Radical political leaders and citizens had different opinions as to what issues should be addressed first and how quickly. Pressure for decisive actions made normal democratic deliberations and consensus building difficult. The military regime had left an interconnected mess that touched on virtually every facet of national existence.

One of the president's first acts ordered the arrest of all former junta members as well as criminal proceedings against former guerrilla leaders. Alfonsín strengthened the Ministry of Defense, transforming it into an agency that actually controlled defense policy and planning and supervised the three services. The president attempted to punish the highest ranks for the excesses of the Proceso while avoiding any appearance of revenge that could lead to military unrest. Nevertheless, the public insisted on a cathartic examination of the Dirty War and punishment of all the guilty, not just junta members. Yet, how far down the ranks investigations should go remained unclear. Defeat in the Falklands and resentment of the Dirty War left the military vulnerable and unable to make suggestions to resolve the issue. Consequently, the entire burden rested on the political authorities under pressure from an angry electorate

The president authorized a civilian commission and a separate council of twenty retired officers to investigate and court-marshal those responsible. The commission eventually submitted a 350-page report documenting thousands of cases of disappearance and the existence of secret prisons and named 1,200 military and police officials as directly involved. In sharp contrast, the military council found no one guilty. Their explanation, that the military had saved the nation and only did what had to be done, outraged the public. Former presidents Videla, Viola, Galtieri, and six others stood trial on 711 counts of torture and murder. The court acquitted Galtieri and his junta. General Videla received a life sentence, as did Admiral Massera, but not before he made an impassioned defense that laid out some unpalatable views.[1]

Opponents claimed that criminal terrorist activities should have been left to the police and the courts. They insisted that, rather than saving the nation, the military had turned on it and its people. Torture and disappearance on a scale that dwarfed that of the guerrillas had to be punished. The new president faced both moral and political challenges of enormous proportion. Pulling apart the armed forces and police organizations with arrests and trials posed many risks, including revolts, rebellion, or worse. To delay dealing with the moral outrage on one side and the resentment and fear on the other created dangerous tensions. Attempting to strike a balance failed.

Establishment of a statute of limitations (*punto final*) did just the reverse. The Punto Final Law, passed on December 24, allowed charges to be filed against alleged Dirty War participants for the next 60 days. Judges took their vacations in January, so the government expected that only a limited number of charges would be filed. The scheme backfired when judges postponed their holidays to accept filings against 300 senior officers. In April 1987 a revolt, "Operation Dignity," by army commandos (the *carapintadas*, the camouflaged faces) led by Lt. Colonel Aldo Rico, twice decorated for valor during the Falklands war, signaled that the entire army verged on rebellion. Alfonsín negotiated personally with Colonel Rico when it became evident that military units would not move against the carapintadas. A 40 percent military wage increase and changes in the high command bought a respite.

The army existed in a state of resentment and demoralization. Reduced budgets made it impossible to maintain units at anything close to strength. In 1988, only 28,000 draftees entered the army, down sharply from the previous years. Equipment shortages and lack of funds made field training impossible. Some 90 percent of the tanks of armored regiments awaited repairs. Military pay scales provided so little at the lower levels that junior officers worked on the side to support their families. The president's attempt to establish a balance between accountability and integration of the army into civil society floundered. Both the navy and the air force sent cadets to civilian universities to take courses, attempting to establish a bridge of sorts, but with little effect.

A Due Obedience Law to shield the junior officer corps, amnesty, the trial and conviction of the juntas' top officers—all failed to put an end to the national agony. Constitutional procedures, measures passed by congress only to be undone, release of prisoners followed by re-arrest, and an amnesty revoked indicated a destructive stalemate between evenly divided factions, with the Dirty War's victims and their putative victimizers taking up sides. Polarization resulted in a hardening of positions. Both sides rejected reconciliation, a willingness to forgive, forget, and move on.

Meanwhile the economic foundations of the country continued to erode, with little room to maneuver. Inflation went from 626 percent in the last months of 1983 to 1,080 percent a year later. The foreign debt of some 46 billion dollars depleted hard currency reserves and, along with inflation, high unemployment, and a declining standard of living, made for an unsustainable situation. Some 60 percent of the country's export earnings went to service the foreign debt. A standby IMF loan came with demands for the usual shock treatments. Technocrats agreed that the problem required holding wages below inflation, forcing state industries to earn a profit, cutting subsidies and a reduction in military spending. A new currency also seemed in order, for both technical and psychological reasons.

In June 1985, the president announced his Austral Plan, which imposed wage and price controls, budgetary restrictions, and a new currency—the Austral. The plan's ambitions far exceeded the government's resolve. After initial success and another electoral victory in midterm congressional elections in 1985, fiscal discipline collapsed. New taxes raised federal revenues substantially, but government spending could not be controlled, nor could wages and prices. By early 1987 inflation again threatened the nation. Tax evasion for survival, hard currency kept under the bed because banks seemed too risky, and arrangements to send money out of the country all acted to limit resources.

Newspapers and magazines became unexpected casualties in an era of democratic revival as inflation forced many out of business. *El Heraldo* increased its price almost daily in a vain effort to meet costs that went up 430 percent between April and May. An alarmed Argentine Newspaper Association warned that newspaper and magazine failures imperiled democracy. The number of movie theaters dropped to 410 (at the high point in 1960, 2,228 cinemas operated) as high-ticket prices and cheaper alternatives such as video and cable television absorbed a shrinking entertainment budget in hard times. Elections in late 1987 drained away the fruits of previous Radical victories, with the PJ winning by 41 percent to 37 percent for the UCR. With two years remaining in office, President Alfonsín had become the caretaker of a deteriorating situation.

Attempts at democratic reforms of union electoral practices to end lifetime office holding failed, but unified the leadership in opposition to the government. A hostile environment made strikes and wage negotiations difficult to resolve. In December of 1988 the president faced another army revolt. Colonel Mohammed Ali Seinaldín (nicknamed, *Khomeini sin barba*—Beardless Khomeini), a very conservative Catholic in spite of his name, unsuccessfully challenged the government. Although Alfonsín survived, it became evident that the military problem still threatened democratic stability.

To make matters worse, the *Movimiento Todos por la Patria* (All for the Fatherland Movement-MTP) professed fear of another coup led by army commandos and drifted into violence. Former guerrillas appeared to have infiltrated the MTP, suggesting an attempt to restart an armed movement under the pretext of protecting an endangered democracy. Provocatively, they styled themselves the New Argentine Army. An attack on the La Tablada army base (January 23, 1989) resulted in the deaths of 28 guerrillas and 11 defenders. Army and police units managed to seal the base and trap the intruders inside, although the battle continued for almost 30 hours. The MTP's defeat, the large number of casualties, and widespread public condemnation ended its ambitions.

The high hopes of 1983 for a broad Radical political revival and disintegration of the Peronist party dimmed when a reform movement swept the opposition. During the Radical party's interregnum the Peronists completed a long delayed renewal. Their 1983 political debacle strengthened the reform faction, which wanted a more open party that did not fluctuate between anarchy and rigidity, and one not so closely identified with labor unions. Respecting constituencies within an actual party structure allowed for new ideas and leadership as well as the inclusion of other interest groups.

The Radical's political supremacy, seemingly in hand in 1983, evaporated with demoralizing rapidity. To complete the rout, IMF reluctance to continue a high level of support, a disastrous foreign exchange rate, hyperinflation that reached 4,924 percent, and a tottering banking system indicated that the government had lost economic control. The economic minister and his assistants resigned en mass, leaving the public wondering if anyone remained to deal with the crisis. Food riots and looting of supermarkets and shops in poor districts set a depressing tone for the last months of the besieged government. A desperate president declared a state of siege as the nation verged on chaos. The extent of the failure and its financial, physical, and emotional toll resulted in an exhausted president turning over the office to his elected successor four months before the end of his term.

Assessments of Alfonsín's presidency tend to be negative. Nevertheless, it provided an interlude of democratic decompression that reduced tension significantly in the region. In 1986, with both Argentina and Brazil under civilian rule, Alfonsín signed the Program for Integration and Economic Cooperation (PICE) with Brazil, followed by the Argentine-Brazilian Economic Integration Program (ABIP), side stepping old trade differences and paving the way for the subsequent Common Market of the South (*Mercosur*), established in 1991 during his successor's term. The PICE and ABIP may well be remembered as his most important economic and regional achievements. They made possible the subsequent end of nuclear competition between the two South American powers as they developed cooperative trade ties and a degree of mutual trust. A long overdue law legalizing divorce cost Alfonsín Church support but brought domestic relations law into the modern era. Unfortunately, his positive accomplishments did not compensate for a failed presidency.

PERONISMO WITH A FRIENDLY, FLEXIBLE FACE

The Peronista front-runner for the presidential election of 1989, Antonio Cafiero, leader of the *Renovación* (Renewal) faction, supported the democratization of the party. Widely seen as the man who had awakened *"el elefante dormido"* (the sleeping elephant), he provided the party with a new sense of direction and legitimacy. Cafiero, rewarded by being elected governor of Buenos Aires Province, positioned himself as the most likely Peronist presidential candidate. Ironically, the new party system, which opened the primary election to select the party's nominee, presented an unexpected challenge. Carlos Saúl Menem campaigned tirelessly for the primary vote, playing on the fears of old labor leaders who opposed reform and attracting others with his plucky outsider stance. To everyone's surprise, Menem won his party's nomination. Menem won by cutting deals and adopting whatever vague notions potential supporters appeared to hold. Menem's selection in an open process constituted a victory for the Renewal faction and, ironically, a defeat for their candidate.

Candidate Menem concentrated on grassroots support by traveling around the countryside in the Menem-mobile, calling for vague changes, national unity, social justice, and most importantly although not fully appreciated at the time, higher productivity. Menem realized that redistributive politics had far exceeded sustainable limits. The only solution appeared to be economic growth and wealth creation sufficient to reverse an already deteriorating standard of living.[2] The myth of an Argentine cornucopia had run it course. Most citizens wanted some semblance of stability, but also change. Menem, the outsider, offered the hope of both; consequently, he received 49 percent of the vote, while the hapless UCR candidate (Eduardo Angeloz) received 37 percent.

The Peronista victory arose as much from desperation as Menem's personality. What Carlos Menem intended to do remained unclear. For some time, just what constituted a Peronista had been impossible to determine. In the absence of the General, various groups and factions claimed to represent true Peronismo. Menem's activities as governor in La Rioja Province had been Peronista in the traditional sense of easy (depreciating) money, wage increases, and generous support for social services. His background seemed to rule out major political innovations.

Carlos Saúl Menem, *El Turco* (the Turk) to his friends as well as detractors, twice governor of La Rioja Province, joined the Peronistas as a university student in Córdoba. A Syrian-Argentine, he first met Perón when the ex-president lived in exile in Spain. Perón recognized Menem's energy and potential usefulness. When Perón returned to Argentina for the first time, he requested Menem to accompany him on the airplane when he made the emotionally charged journey home. As Menem told the story, he confided to the General that he intended to be the next elected Peronist president after Perón. His general only smiled. Menem seemed an unlikely crown prince. In fact he achieved his wish, albeit as the result of a long interlude of a military regime and the democratic uncertainty of Alfonsín's truncated term.

The son of Syrian immigrants who arrived in 1912 to join the Middle Eastern community in the impoverished northwest province of La Rioja, Menem grew up understanding poverty, hard work, and the importance of politics. The family's success enabled him to pursue a law degree and enter local and provincial politics. A natural athlete, he excelled in competition, developing a special fondness for fast cars. He appeared to move easily between several cultures, going to Syria at his family's request to arrange for a Muslim wife, but then becoming a Catholic. He liked people, showering them with warm and natural congeniality. He avoided large meetings as much as possible and disliked committees and events that separated him from one-on-one personal and physical contact. He understood what motivated people and approached everyone with respect, regardless of social position. A natural populist, more emotional than intellectual, Menem developed an effective style.

After Isabel Perón's removal in 1976, Menem spent five years under military detention. His Peronista credentials could not be challenged. Nevertheless, Menem seemed hopelessly provincial to Buenos Aires sophisticates. His clothing, shoes, long hair, and exaggerated sideburns reeked of rustic La Rioja. Few considered him a serious national politician, certainly not a potential president. Most underestimated his political skills, carefully calculated opportunism, and ability to bond with people.

The new president let it be known that he played an entire soccer match with Diego Maradona, the reigning sports figure. Menem's identification with the soccer star had an interesting psychological aspect. Maradona scored a goal with his hands, not observed by the referee, to knock England out of the 1986 World Cup that Argentina then went on to win. A demoralized nation accepted any boost to its self-esteem, even if it resulted from a flawed play. Menem, then fifty-nine, signaled that he could in a similar fashion rescue Argentina.

President Menem faced a daunting situation. In the previous decade the country's economy experienced little growth. The percentage of the population classified as middle class sank from half in the 1960s, to one-third of the population as he took office. Per capita income declined, plunging many into the lower classes and poverty. Runaway inflation made investments almost impossible. Prudent individuals shifted some 40 billion dollars into foreign bank accounts with no intention of bringing them back. Debts could not be paid—Argentina appeared to be dead broke. Corruption, tax evasion, crime—all the options of the desperate—provided only individual relief. Widespread public understanding of just how serious a situation Menem faced gave him some breathing room, but he had to demonstrate positive steps—results seemed too much to hope for, at least in the early period of his presidency, yet hope remained the only option.

To complicate matters and distract the president's attention from the critical economic situation, the Dirty War's aftermath showed no sign of playing out. Personally, he had no desire to exact revenge for his own five years of detention or antagonizing a dangerous opponent. Moreover, President Menem wanted all the support that he could get to carry out his proposed economic program, which he expected to encounter popular opposition. Once elected, Menem gave more substance to a rumored amnesty plan that had circulated during the election campaign. He proposed a pardon or amnesty for both guerrillas and the army. He cautiously awaited public reaction. Predictably, all sides disagreed, opening the way for action. An amnesty in October 1989 excluded the most sensitive figures. Menem pardoned a number of officers and civilians, allowing them to return from exile, and promised to review more cases.

The carapintada problem surfaced, again under the leadership of Mohammed Ali Seineldín. It required a bloody encounter before government soldiers ended what appeared to be an attempted coup. The Supreme Military Council took action, sentencing the leaders to life imprisonment. On the positive side, the encounter indicated that professional officers who believed the army should avoid politics dominated the military and that with care the entire institution could be removed from the political arena. The economic crisis provided the opportunity to reduce the size of the military without seeming to attack the armed forces.

Clearly, the desperate situation required all, including the armed services, to make sacrifices.

A smaller military budget required a reduced draft and a cut in the number of men in arms by 50 percent, to 100,000. Menem included military factories in his privatization scheme, reduced training budgets, and virtually eliminated equipment purchases. Protests did not deter the president; however, he took the edge off military anxiety by raising salaries and occasionally mixing socially with senior officers. His willingness to commit military forces to UN foreign peace missions restored a degree of professional pride. The Dirty War issue, however, continued to pull the army back into politics. In spite of protests, a pragmatic Menem pardoned the remaining junta members. The issue appeared to have become a matter for history to judge. It soon became evident that a moral question could not be so easily dispensed with no matter how politically convenient.

Some of those pardoned wanted to be declared innocent, instead of quietly accepting their release. Others published books relating their involvement, some with contrition, others with pride, and all in grisly detail. Captain de Corbeta Adolfo Francisco Scilingo, at the time a junior officer, provided details and documentation to an investigative journalist providing the basis for a shocking bestseller. *El Vuelo,* published in 1995, described the Dirty War activities of the Intelligence unit of the Navy's Mechanics School. Drugged and stripped victims disappeared in the icy waters of the South Atlantic, dropped from an aircraft far from shore to prevent bodies from washing ashore in any recognizable form.[3] Public outrage cooled, only to be re-ignited with every new revelation. Menem's attempt to put an end to the constant state of recrimination unraveled. Congress repealed barriers to further criminal proceedings; the president had little choice but to accept. The struggle to determine guilt and punishment outlasted Menem's two-term presidency; passing into the next century. The involvement of Spanish courts in the disappearance of that country's citizens provided an international element.

Appealing to different levels of morality created insurmountable moral conflicts. The Montoneros, ERP, radical priests and their supporters, and the army and its defenders all evoked a higher morality. To both the guerrillas and the army the overriding importance of their goals justified any means. The Madres de la Plaza de Mayo and others concerned with individual human rights rejected the validity of such claims and the morality of torture and disappearance.

RESCUING ARGENTINA

Before assuming the presidency, Menem contacted businessmen and industrialists to help fashion an economic program. The large, privately held conglomerate Bunge and Born, had previously attempted without success to provide useful economic data and forecasts to the Alfonsín government. Menem now courted their help. Bunge and Born executives gave his government credibility in an emergency situation. A comprehensive economic review indicated continuing decline and suggested what needed to be done to reverse the situation. Bringing inflation under control, stimulating foreign investment, radically reducing government subsidies, privatizing state industries, reducing public social expenditures, cutting the number of public employees, cutting the military budget, ending tax evasion, and attacking corruption all seemed politically overwhelming yet necessary.

Menem appointed a series of Bunge and Born executives as economics ministers in what appeared to be a united front to save the country. The government convinced major companies to freeze prices for ninety days, sharply raised utility prices, and devalued the currency by 53 percent. An accountant, Antonio Erman González, assumed the economic task. In January 1990 the government surprised the financial system by freezing high-yield short-term austral accounts and converted them to medium-term (10-year) government bonds payable in US dollars. The action to remove money from circulation pushed interest rates down and relieved the pressure of high interest rates on government operations, suggesting that Menem intended to stabilize the economy. Pegging the currency to the dollar seemed a strong probability, promising future stability.

The economics minister announced the intention of establishing a free-market economy. Privatization began with the telephone company, sorely in need of new equipment investments, and the state airline, Aerolineas Argentina, both high-profile enterprises sure to attract buyers as well as publicity. Menem repeatedly declared that all government industries, including most of those controlled by the military, awaited buyers. During the military government, the army's factories absorbed resources financed in part by a huge expansion in debt. The three services (the air force became a separate service in 1944) controlled military industries, although the army directed the largest percentage. The three services employed an estimated 32,000 workers. Emphasis on development resulted in a strategic mindset that made the national objective more important than costs, inefficiencies, and wasted resources. Profit, although not disdained, remained secondary. After the return of civilians to power and the beginning of privatizing state assets, it became evident that useful balance sheets and exact financial information did not exist. What constituted a profitable military enterprise relied upon guesswork, complicating the sale of assets.

Inflation came down with such speed that the economy went into a deep recession, which posed new problems. The first year extracted a heavy cost as income fell, unemployment surged, and consumption dropped, alarming union leaders and industrialists. Menem's crucial

SOCCER

Soccer in Argentina is as popular as it is in Brazil but does not attract as much international attention. The country won a gold medal in soccer at the 2004 Olympic games, the first gold medal since 1952, and Argentina's only gold in the Athens's competition. Clearly, Argentina is a world-class soccer power. To fans, the connection between clubs and the barrios they are associated with appears to be more important than regional or national recognition, although Argentines are overjoyed to win the World Cup and other major trophies.

Soccer arrived in Argentina in 1867, twenty-seven years before the game arrived in Brazil. At the time the rules of the game had not been codified. Two Englishmen, the brothers Thomas and James Hogg, established the Buenos Aires Football Club, playing the first match in Argentine history in 1867 in Palermo. It remained a minor pastime of the British community until 1885, when Englishman Alexander W. Hutton introduced the game into private schools. Eight years later, the clubs formed the Argentine Football League Association.

Isaac Newell, who immigrated from England in the early 1880s, founded a secondary school, the Colegio Anglo-Argentino, in Rosario in 1884. The curriculum included football. Alumni (old boys in British public school parlance) founded a club in 1903. To honor their old headmaster they called it the Club Atlético Newell's Old Boys. They carried the Nob's colors, white and sky blue with the Union Jack in the center, to victory in the first championship game (1905) of the Liga Rosario de Fútbol. Today Newell's Old Boys are in the Argentine National League under Red and Black colors.

The spread of soccer may be traced in part to its simplicity. As a sport it did not require elaborate field preparation or expensive equipment. Fabrication of serviceable leather ball posed little difficulty in a society more than familiar with leather working. Argentina made it to the finals in the first World Cup in the 1930s but lost to Uruguay. Finally in 1978 Argentina won the World Cup, a victory marred by the military regime's manipulation of credit for the triumph.

Buenos Aires supports eight first-division teams; of those the Club Atlético Boca Junior and its traditional rival the Club Atlético River Plate are the most popular. Both emerged in the early twentieth century. Boca Junior began in the lower-class barrio of La Boca in 1905. Adolescents formed a club with little expectation that it would attract attention. Rather than argue over club colors, they decided that they would adopt the colors of the flag of the first ship that entered the harbor. The 4,146 ton Swedish freighter, the *Drottning Sophia,* supplied the vivid blue and yellow colors of the Boca Juniors. Their home stadium, the Bombonera (the Chocolate box), a concrete utilitarian structure built in 1944, holds some 65,000 fans and is often sold out.

The River Plate (the name in English is used) grew out of two smaller groups that merged into an athletic club in 1901. Unable to afford imported uniforms, the team wore white polo shirts, until a member picked up an unattended red silk sash and draped it across his chest. A diagonal red stripe on white became the team colors. The club's name originated when Pedro Martínez, one of the founders, observed British sailors playing amidst gigantic crates marked "The River Plate." The club is associated with the barrio of Palermo and is called simply, "river."

Fans organized in groups called *barras bravas* attend games as units. Attendance at the stadium is not for the faint hearted. Women, children, and the elderly watch the game on TV, while the fans engage in verbal and at times physical battle along with their team.

Boca Junior appears to be the club that captures the spirit of Argentine soccer. The country's most revered player, Diego Maradona, known with affection as El Pelusa (fluffy [hair]), joined the Boca Juniors in 1981 and in 1986 led Argentina to the World Cup in Mexico. He moved to Barcelona, then to Italy as globalization swept the soccer world. At the Olympic games in 2004, Carlos Tevez, a twenty-year-old Boca Junior player, scored eight goals, including the winning goal and the gold medal for Argentina. Boca is owned by Franco Marci, an Italian immigrant with a fortune in real estate, mining, frozen foods and an assortment of enterprises, including garbage, predictably one of the insults thrown at Boca fans in the heat of a match.

Soccer provides a base for politics; in the 2003 race for mayor of Buenos Aires Mauricio Marci, son of the owner and president of Boca, ran against Aníbal Ibarra, a fan of River Plate, which tore fans between club loyalty and civic duty.

---

test came in September 1990. The telephone worker's union in Buenos Aires hammered out a new contract providing for a wage increase. The Economics Ministry refused to ratify the agreement, setting off a strike that made an already inefficient phone system impossible.[4]

The president moved rapidly to pressure the National Telephone Workers Union to oppose the Buenos Aires strike and dismissed strike leaders. Telephone workers enjoyed little public support, so after a bitter stand-off Menem broke the strike. The president's victory appeared to be a turning point in establishing control over union demands. Editorials compared it to Ronald Reagan's crushing of the air traffic controllers and Margaret Thatcher's taming of British coal miners. In fact, union strength had weakened long before the incident. Nevertheless, breaking the strike demonstrated Menem's willingness to fight. As the president observed, "Argentina had only one bullet to kill the tiger of inflation," and as prudence suggested, "one should not wake the tiger before the gunshot."[5]

In spite of the sacrifices already demanded of the public, inflation returned. The economy marked time in the expectation of replacing the currency with the dollar. The old currency (the austral) rapidly lost value. *Swiftgate,* an unexpected scandal at the beginning of 1991, led to the resignation of the entire cabinet, including González. Meatpacker Swift complained to the American ambassador that high officials demanded illegal payments. Consequently, yet another Economic Minister (the fourth), Domingo Cavallo, readied the hoped-for long-term solution to monetary instability. Menem and Cavallo worked well together, one a skilled politician and the other a first-rate economist who understood the technical aspects of the economic situation.

The Convertibility Law (March 1991) dropped the austral in favor of a peso and backed it one to the dollar. In order to give the peso a reason to be in circulation, all tax bills and official accounts required settlement in the national currency. Nationalists would be somewhat mollified by the continuing existence of a national note. The inflation-depleted austral converted to the peso at 10,000 to one. While the law specified foreign reserves or gold, it in effect constituted a partial *dolarización* that appeared to shift monetary discipline to the Federal Reserve in Washington. The Convertibility Law required that government expenditures not exceed the total amount of dollar reserves, theoretically imposing fiscal restraint. The plan envisioned a two-step process: first dual circulation of dollars and pesos, then a move to back the currency with a trade-weighted basket, including European currencies. The peso presumably would become the main legal tender. Success could not be assumed. As the president of Telefónica de Argentina nicely put it, "In the 1950s Argentina fell into a profound sleep, in 1990 it was not clear whether it was sleeping or dead."[6]

Confidence returned and the economy stabilized. The fundamental problem, the lack of fiscal restraint that underpinned everything, remained dependent on political resolve. How to keep the provinces from overspending relied more on political will than effective law. In addition, corruption continued to drain the treasury. Cavallo finally left the government over the issue.[7] The new monetary arrangement had the unanticipated effect of forcing "reality pricing" on state services that could no longer be covered by printing more money. Moreover, the old problem that had forced Argentina on and off the gold standard (finally dropped in 1914) still remained. Tying money in circulation to a fixed source in good times worked well, but it ignored the normal rise and fall of prices of agricultural commodities. In hard times, the fall of hard currency earnings restricted the money supply, made money more expensive, restricted credit, and made economic recovery much more difficult and slow. In the short run it seemed a bold but necessary step.

Righting the economy also meant stimulating foreign trade and direct investments. The obstacles to good relations with other Latin American countries, Europe, and the United States had to be dissolved as rapidly as possible. On a visit to Chile at the end of 1990, Menem bluntly confessed that Argentina's grand illusion that it could flourish in "privileged solitude" had damaged the nation and poisoned relations with its neighbors. He said that one of his aims involved destroying the idea that "we are Europeans in exile [convincing] the Argentines [and others] that we are unmistakably and inevitably Americans."[8] Menem ended the trade embargo against Britain, subsequently reestablished diplomatic relations, and temporarily closed the open wound of the Falkland war. He directed the foreign minister to develop closer relations with London. Menem suggested an imaginative array of solutions to the problem of contested sovereignty over the British dependencies in the South Atlantic—from rental, to special status along the lines of Puerto Rico with the United States, to a special trade zone and arbitration. Coolness in London and the prospects of offshore petroleum production in waters around the islands made agreement impossible, but Menem did not allow the lack of resolution to poison relations.

Pragmatism seemingly governed all decisions. Menem's boldness stunned many, although a poll indicated reasonable if not complete approval of his approach. Nevertheless, perhaps only a Peronist could have made such an about face. Throwing open the economy to international capital, privatizing state industries, tightening finances, cutting subsidies, reducing social services, and breaking and discouraging strikes all seemed to take place at once. Impelled by a crisis mentality, the government, moved before it considered how to regulate neo-liberalism and the marketplace to allow for an orderly transition and healthy competition. Corruption accompanied the privatization process both at the sale and disposal of the proceeds. Bell Atlantic (Verizon), initially interested in bidding for a portion of the telephone network, allegedly withdrew rather than contend with payoffs. An open, transparent, and honest process perhaps could not be expected after years of corruption.

The president used informal methods to preserve a degree of control over public opinion. He made it obvious that he viewed unfavorable editorial comment and embarrassing news reporting as a hostile act.

Selective violence intimidated the media and, on an individual basis, forced journalists to make a choice between personal safety and honest reporting. When asked about physical attacks on journalists, the president responded, "Its part of their job."[9] Withholding advertising silently punished without the necessity of making demands to temper opinions. The government's hostility towards journalists increased as Menem's domestic life became a tabloid event. His estranged wife, Zulema Yoma, provided soap-opera glimpses of presidential life that few editors and their audiences could resist. Photos of Menem in his underwear sitting on an unmade bed made their way into the sensational press. His estranged wife divulged details, and the press expanded upon the scandalous morsels. The divorce must have been a relief. Their daughter, Zulemita, acted as the president's official hostess until the end of his term.

Menem changed the tone of Peronismo, projecting a modern democratic openness. He connected his actions to the momentous changes that took place in world affairs. In his opinion the fall of the Berlin Wall, the end of the Cold War and the rigidity of Marxist-Leninism, and a new age—the information age—changed everything. Peronism had to reinvent itself in response to events he compared to the world's transition from agricultural to manufacturing economies.[10] Menem's interpretation of world events and his responsive role stripped the renewal faction of Peronismo of any credit and shifted the focus to what would be called *Menemismo*.

The reversal of economic policy coupled with an energetic decisive president created hope, but not optimism. An increase in direct foreign investment seemed an international endorsement. Spanish and American banks opened subsidiaries, creating a sense of trust long absent from domestic banking. Nevertheless, the transition had costs. Problematic public utilities, newly privatized, promised technological upgrading to the latest standard, but at prices not many could afford. Rail companies, no longer subsidized, cut services in marginal provinces and raised rates to provide a reasonable return to potential investors. Inadequate planning for privatization pushed some provinces even deeper into recession. An unexpected setback, the Mexican default in late 1994, staggered Latin America and almost overturned the Argentine economy. Depositors rushed to withdraw their money, causing concern that the banking system might fail. The peso came under extreme speculative pressure, but the financial system survived, although a bit battered and bruised. The Buenos Aires stock exchange recovered, reflecting renewed confidence in the future.

Menem's pragmatism appeared unpredictable to a public accustomed to an ideological approach. Critics on the left and right had a rigid notion of Peronismo that the president constantly violated. An impatient and dismissive President Menem lectured his critics about the evolutionary unfolding of Justicialista's living philosophy. Its objectives remained the same, but its practitioners made tactical adjustments. While to many Peronismo appeared to be evolving into Menemismo, the president insisted that it continued to be Justicialismo—not populist or neo-liberal.[11] In an inspired political move designed to emphasize the nationalistic, organic continuity of Peronismo, he arranged for the return of Juan Manuel de Rosas' mortal remains from England. A statue of Rosas on horseback just off Avenida Sarmiento, which the president dedicated and his image printed on banknotes distanced Menem from neo-liberalism and glossed over his own liberal reforms. The makeover of Peronismo legitimized the president's opportunistically pragmatic, unpredictably creative methods. Many found his approach acceptable and became Menemist-Peronistas. Voters gave his policies their midterm blessing and did not object strenuously to changing the constitution to permit him to run successfully for reelection in 1995.

EXTENDING MENEMISMO

Menem's first presidency represented "an [attempted] escape into the future," while his second term appeared to be a resurgence of reality with a few new twists.[12] Privatized companies did not employ the same number of workers as politicized state industries. It came down to either profit or employment in return for political support, but not both at the same time. Eventually, as the economy expanded jobs might follow. Meanwhile, redundant workers could not be reemployed rapidly. Proposed labor-code reforms to make it easier for companies to shed unneeded workers promised hard times ahead. Unemployment and reduced social services pushed people into the informal economy. The lack of transitional employment schemes risked the impoverishment of a large number of workers, with political consequences that might well be unacceptable. Whether the government could muster the will to ride out a difficult economic transition remained to be seen.

By 1998 recession set in, unnerving politicians, who backed away from painful reforms. In its second term the regime had arrived at the point of political exhaustion with no fresh ideas and little capital to throw into the struggle for reform. Moreover, Menem contemplated running for a third term in 1999. To do so he would need political support. Fiscal restraint at all levels of government collapsed. Almost nonexistent accountability, particularly in state social services, facilitated corruption. Money evaporated without a trace, in part because of the easily portable US dollar. Ordinary citizens turned away from the peso almost entirely, preferring dollars, which had a global value beyond the ability of Argentine politicians to destroy it. The amount of pesos in circulation, initially about the same as the number of dollars, fell as consumers avoided their acceptance. The number of dollars also declined as prudent people held them out of circulation. Lack of legal tender had a further negative impact on economic activity. Cautious savers opened accounts across the estuary in Uruguay, inadvertently spreading Argentina's distortions to their neighbor.

The cause of the drift towards default is not easy to pinpoint. In the 1970s, surplus capital generated by OPEC spread throughout the world, including Argentina. During this period the military regime ran up debts. Between 1993 and 1998 debt went from 29 percent of GDP to 41 percent. Bankers competed to underwrite Argentine government bonds, earning lavish commissions and bonuses in the process—an estimated one billion dollars in fees between 1991 and 2001. Brokerage firms sold the bonds to pension and mutual fund managers as high yield but acceptable risks. Investors, reassured that Argentina would maintain convertibility of pesos into dollars and would not default on sovereign debt, continued to buy bonds. In the United States, brokerage houses, including Solomon Smith Barney, J.P. Morgan, Goldman Sachs, and Merrill Lynch put out glowing reports on the Argentine economy. Optimistic views caused the Argentina stock market to soar to record levels. Rogelio Frigerio, in charge of economic policy in 1998, subsequently mused: "If you get the money so easily as we did, it's very tough to tell politicians, 'Don't spend more, be more prudent, 'because the money was there, and they knew it."[13] The IMF warned the government that it courted disaster and should cut its budget deficit drastically. In fact, the deficit ran at a manageable percentage of GDP. Moreover, if the cost of privatizing social security, recommended by the IMF, had been added back into the budget, it would have been in surplus. Nevertheless, the monetary agency ignored the reality that their recommendation had unbalanced the budget and insisted on tightening. Between 1999 and 2001 the government cut federal expenditures by 10 percent.

The actual problem had little to do with the budget and more to do with a fixed exchange rate that tied the country to the fortunes of the American dollar. When the Euro dropped to a record low against the dollar, Argentine exports could not compete in the European market. Argentina slipped into recession in the middle of 1999. Tax revenues dropped, increasing the budget deficit. Tied to a fixed exchange rate, the government could not manipulate the value of the currency to make its exports affordable. Eventually the dollar would fall against the Euro, but it would be too late to help Argentine exports.

Investors began to have doubts about the country's ability to service its debt. The belief that the country would eventually be forced to abandon a fixed exchange rate led many to shun the peso in favor of the dollar. Currency exchange uncertainty pushed up interest rates. A vicious circle began that developed momentum over the next three years, leading to default. A certain surreal quality about events made the Argentine situation into a Greek tragedy of sorts, with the audience on the verge of tears (but still hopeful) well before the final event. Argentina's slow-motion slide towards default at least had the virtue of avoiding a sudden catastrophic shock to the global financial system. The role of the IMF in the debacle is subject to debate. Columbia University professor of finance and economics Joseph Stiglitz observed that the collapse occurred because Argentina followed the advice of the monetary fund and not solely because of government irresponsibility.[14]

Meanwhile, diverting attention away from the unfolding crisis, the unresolved question of responsibility for the bombing of the Israeli Embassy (1992) and the Jewish Community Center (1994) in Buenos Aires that killed 85 and injured some 300 people continued to fuel speculation about the president's involvement in a cover-up. Rumors that police and Argentine intelligence services served a Middle Eastern regime circulated. The known presence of radical Islamic groups in the isolated Province of Misiones and across the border in Paraguay where Brazil, Paraguay, and Argentina come together, made such speculation plausible. Menem appeared to have been drawn into Middle Eastern politics and profitable but illegal weapons sales to Croatia and Ecuador. Many believed that he had responded to terrorist threats to his family. In 1995 his son Carlos Jr. died in a suspicious helicopter crash linked by many, including the boy's ,mother, to shadowy interests. Whatever the case, the focus on the country's economic problems had been lost and little if any vision remained.

An assessment of President Menem's ten years in office must be mixed at best. Menem entered office a pragmatist determined to do what he deemed necessary. His realism attracted those who wanted things fixed, not debated endlessly. His flexibility seemed a political virtue in a nation that had suffered from excess rigidity during the Proceso. Those that questioned his pragmatism received a chiding about the evolving nature of Justicialista philosophy.[15] Menem did not take advantage of the good times, when the economy grew by 5.8 (1996–1998), to establish a healthy fiscal situation and reduce the debt load. In an era of controlled inflation and growing prosperity, debt could have been reduced to a less daunting level. For all his daring, he feared to follow through with fundamental fiscal and bureaucratic structural reforms, and as a result his program stalled.[16]

Memen's willingness to override democratic norms to rule by decree weakened the institutional structure but could not conceal the loss of direction. In his own defense, Menem asserted that during his presidency the vote had been scrupulously respected, and his administration responded to the will of the majority. He proudly observed that he had never resorted to a state of siege (suspending constitutional guarantees) or deployed the army to deal with civil society, a record matched only by President Marcelo T. Alvear (1922–1928) in the twentieth century. Some of the smaller reforms may prove important over the long term. Menem cut employer's social benefit cost by half. Although it remained relatively high the reduction encouraged hiring. He also transformed the Internet into a useful tool for the public and for commercial interests. The government reduced the price of leased lines and created a dialup category for Internet calls at a favorable price. He ignored those who complained that the dominance of the English language on the Internet made it an objectionable tool of the United States.

THE ROAD TO RUIN ENDS BADLY

The presidential election of 1999 attracted several candidates, including the Governor of Buenos Aires Province and former vice president (1989–1991) under Menem, Eduardo Duhalde. Considered to be the most powerful man in Argentina with the exception of Menem, he had a shady reputation. Duhalde contended with a bestselling, unauthorized biography authored by investigative reporter Hernán López Echague, titled *El Otra Eduardo Duhalde: una biografia politica*, that questioned the source of his wealth, including extensive land holdings and questionable business partnerships. Even more devastating, the exposé claimed that the American Drug Enforcement Agency maintained a file of his drug-related activities. The book sold 60,000 copies in six weeks[17] and contributed to the perception that the country had been engulfed by corruption.

Not surprisingly, the Radical party candidate, Fernando de la Rua, won the presidency in 1999. Many, remembering Alfonsín's hasty exit from the presidency, had doubts about the Radicals, but they took comfort in their alliance with FREPASO, composed of an assortment of outsiders, including Socialists, Communists, alienated Peronists, Christian Democrats, and other disgruntled elements. FREPASO had energy and ideas, even if the UCR did not. Few anticipated that within months the banking system and the presidency would be in turmoil. In March of 2001 Domingo Cavallo, the father of Menem's currency plan, again assumed the post of economic minister. Credit Suisse First Boston came up with a scheme to swap debt to avoid bunching up the repayment schedule. A voluntary swap of old bonds for new ones at higher interest rates bought time to get their house in order. Some 30 billion dollars in bonds switched to the higher rate, further adding to the debt. Credit Suisse First Boston made a commission of $100 million on the exchange. Interest at 10.5 percent over US treasury bonds attracted the unwary. Even concerned bankers believed that somehow Argentina would muddle through. A lot depended on the IMF and the confidence of investors.

The progressive failure of the de la Rua presidency tracked the sinking economy. Eventually, the IMF refused to extend more credit. Consequently, the government forced domestic banks and pension funds to buy unbacked government bonds. In December 2001, the president imposed a partial freeze on all bank deposits, including those held by foreign banks. The *corralito* (round up) indicated the government's intention to "pen in" deposits and prevent a run on the banks. Desperate depositors crowded in front of banks, demanding their money. Foreign banks, which many preferred because of the ill-founded notion that their deposits had some sort of extra-territorial sovereign protection, received bitter condemnation. Those with accounts in Uruguay crossed the estuary to withdraw funds in order to survive. Random violence and graffiti soon escalated to more organized protests just before Christmas. Police moved into the streets to head off what some feared would become a popular rebellion. Besieged and frightened, President de la Rua resigned; a helicopter lifted him off the roof of the palace in what appeared to be an escape from a fallen city. Domingo Cavallo resigned at the same time.

Following the president's resignation, a series of four different individuals occupied the presidential office in less than a two-week period. Dangerous political paralysis at the federal level threatened a state implosion. Eventually, congress elected Eduardo Duhalde, a Peronist politician then serving in the senate, as president. Duhalde ran unsuccessfully against Fernando de la Rua in the presidential election of 1999. President Duhalde formally declared a default and ended the peso's connection with the dollar in January 2002.

He succeeded in calming the public by announcing that all frozen deposits would be eventually paid in the original currency of deposit—pesos or dollars. Several days later, the government devalued the peso, and then in February ruled that dollar accounts would be paid in pesos at the new lower value. A long string of half measures ended with the decision to turn deposits into long-term certificates of deposit payable in several years or in government bonds. Few believed they would ever receive their money, and congress refused to consider such a bill, claiming that it favored foreign banks.

Finding anyone to accept the position of economic minister proved almost impossible. The financial newspaper *El Cronista* warned that the country teetered on the edge of disaster. After an all-day emergency session, Duhalde and provincial governors announced a fourteen-point plan to get the country back on its feet in 90 days. Their plan, short on details, pledged to establish a "solid and trustworthy" financial system and make fiscal and political reforms. Subsequently, President Duhalde admitted that the government did not have a plan. Moment-by-moment decisions kept the government from collapse. Meanwhile, provincial governors took temporary measures, including issuing paper scrip to keep their imploding economies afloat. Default on the nation's $141 billion debt and suspension of debt servicing lifted a major burden off the economy and moved the issue into the political sphere.

Internal rebuilding, however, could not wait. In an attempt to cope with rising homelessness, the government suspended mortgage foreclosures. *Cacerlolazo* demonstrations (banging saucepans) with people shouting "all must go" relieved some pressure but brought scant results. Well-known politicians and judges thought to be corrupt hesitated to walk in the streets without a bodyguard. Assaults, vitriolic shouting matches, and the small but loud groups that picketed politicians' houses and apartments made life unpleasant. More important, the situation indicated the public's lack of respect and trust in their representatives. Many wondered if the army should assume a role in what constituted a grave national emergency.

Daily survival could not wait for authorities to act. The collapse broke what a psychologist called "the chain of payments. I also only pay my bills when I can."[18] People organized neighborhood groups (*asambleas vecinales*) to purchase food and necessities collectively and provide mutual support. *Clubs de Trueque* (barter-exchange clubs) sprang up to trade goods and services. The desperate newly poor had to dispose of treasured family possessions in order to eat. Clubs issued vouchers and worked out agreements with other organizations, thus creating a type of currency. Paper scrip (*créditos*), bar-coded to avoid counterfeiting, fused the latest technology with a primitive economic system. Clubs met basic needs for food, clothing, and services such as beauty care and dentistry. Yahoo! Argentina posted a list of the clubs by city and towns, with information on meeting times and locations and links to other useful Web sites. Within weeks most clubs had their own Web sites, complete with personal columns to facilitate dating between economically stricken couples. An embarrassed government offered little assistance, although eventually the economics ministry began a program to train trueque traders in basic marketing and bookkeeping.

The clubs made it possible for employers to pay employees in kind with the expectation that they would barter such goods for services and items they formerly paid for in cash. Workers took over factories on the verge of liquidating and kept them in production, with or without the owner's permission. Some 10,000 workers paid themselves in cash and kind. Within six months the *Movimiento Nacional de Empresas Recuperadas por los Trabajadores* (MNERT, National Movement of Businesses Reestablished by Workers) had members throughout the country. State incapacity pushed responsibility downward to the social bedrock of individuals organized within a community. As to why more violence did not occur under such dire circumstances, an explanation can be found in the per capita food supply (2004) that held at a reasonable level, even above that of Brazil and the oil-rich Venezuela.

The crisis forced the nation into what game theorist Robert Sugden called "brave reciprocity," an implicit bargain based on trust, not enforceable by a third party but subject to moral penalties, reputation damage, social exclusion, or ostracism. Everyone had to accept third-party assurance that individuals could be trusted. Acceptance of exchanges based on trust alone represented an important step in strengthening social capital. Virtuous circles of trust and reciprocity lead to increased civic participation—the fodder of a functioning democracy.

Meanwhile, the federal government struggled to restore its legitimacy. Ideally, a presidential election campaign would turn up possible solutions to the nation's problems. Duhalde, charged with organizing the presidential election, could not run for the office. He could not have won anyway. His past electoral ventures did not impress many voters. He lost to Fernando de la Rua in 1999, a piece of luck as it turned out. When he ran for a senate seat (October 2001) his winning total just barely exceeded the number of blank ballots cast, in what appeared to be a "none of the above tally." Violent clashes between demonstrators and the police and large crowds demonstrating in front of the presidential palace demanding acting President Duhalde's resignation created a sense of insecurity. In response, Duhalde moved up the presidential elections to March 2002. At the time, few expected him to hold on to power. The fact that he survived gave him some creditability, at least in the eyes of other politicians. As the Peronista boss of Buenos Aires' provincial faction and provisional president, he retained some power. Although few of his fellow citizens gave him much credit, he could claim to have halted the disintegration of the state.

Virtually all Peronista factions understood that Duhalde functioned as the kingpin. He dominated the party apparatus with virtually no voter support. In spite of his wife's patronage of slum dwellers and his own public works projects when he served as governor of Buenos Aires Province, he remained profoundly unpopular. Three Peronist candidates ran for the office, making it unlikely that anyone would receive an overwhelming mandate. Carlos Menem, fresh from Chile, received a mixed reception. His new bride, Cecilia Bolocco, a Chilean beauty queen and former Miss Universe and a much younger, attractive blonde, got most of the attention. An avalanche of jokes about the couple's age difference (35 years), love life, and newborn son undercut his credibility. Moreover, Menem's lifestyle grated on individuals newly caught in poverty, and on those who feared they would be drawn downward. While the ex-president could escape in his red Ferrari, saved from the impact of unemployment by a rumored Swiss bank account, most Argentines faced hardship and poverty.

While out of office, Menem had kept his political oar in the water with blistering attacks on President de la Rua. He had rescued the country after Alfonsín and promised to do so again. Menem advocated close ties with the United States as the only alternative to continued decline. Many however, blamed neo-liberalism for their problems and rejected that option.

Duhalde had broken with Menem when he served as his vice-president and now put forward his own candidate. His preferred selection, Néstor Carlos Kirchner, seemed a long shot, "the man nobody knows."[19] A slightly awkward, gangly individual with a slight but noticeable lisp, he seemed mismatched against the flashy ex-president. Kirchner, born in Río Gallegos, the capital of Santa Cruz Province in distant Patagonia, appeared colorless, a bit rustic, and not ready for the sophisticated world of the northern littoral provinces and bruising Buenos Aires politics. Nevertheless, he had been mayor of Río Gallegos and twice governor of Santa Cruz Province, with its small population of 200,000, much less than many secondary cities in the north. During the Proceso he seemed to have some sort of ties to the Montoneros, although he denied it. The authorities detained him briefly two separate times. During the election campaign, Kirchner promised to reverse the policy of not extraditing ex-military officers accused of Dirty War crimes.

A split Peronist vote resulted in a run-off election between Menem and Kirchner. When the polls showed that Menem would lose, he chose to withdraw rather than risk embarrassment. Kirchner automatically won, taking office with only 22 percent of the vote. Menem's unexpected action denied the president the final electoral victory but failed to tarnish his legitimacy. More problematic, President Kirchner headed the nation but not the party. Duhalde held on to his dominant party role along with its patronage. Complicating Kirchner's reform agenda, Supreme Court judges owed their jobs and allegiance to ex-president Carlos Menem. Moreover, the president's choices for congressional elections and for the capital's mayor did not receive party backing. To many observers Kirchner appeared to be a pawn in a game that others intended to play. Kirchner had to win control or risk becoming a figurehead president. The option, to appeal directly to the public as a populist, complicated relations with the international community, but it appeared to be the only way.

Almost predictably, the Proceso became one of the first issues that faced the president. Spanish Judge Baltasar Garzón requested the extradition of prominent individuals on human-rights charges.[20] An Argentine court then issued provisional arrest warrants for General and former president Jorge Videla and Admiral Emilio Massera, in all detaining some 40 individuals. The complicity of the guerrillas also came under scrutiny. An Argentine judge ordered the arrest of two former Montonero leaders and requested the extradition from Spain of Mario Firmenich, an important Montonero leader. The president announced that Argentina would sign the UN convention that eliminated the statute of limitations on war and human-rights crimes. Under pressure, Congress repealed the amnesty laws, potentially reopening proceedings involving at least 400 individuals. Jurists worried that Kirchner's actions violated constitutional prohibitions and usurped the role of the Supreme Court. High court judges, charged with corruption, had little moral authority to protest. Many Peronist politicians saw little to be gained by reopening the issue. Significantly, the public supported reopening the issue. A growing number of Argentines objected to allowing Spain to try such cases. Judge Garzón withdrew the request for extradition after the repeal of the amnesty law on the assumption that the Supreme Court would not raise constitutional objections.

The army viewed the reopening of Dirty War cases as an attack on institutional integrity and honor. Nevertheless, antagonizing the army appeared a low-risk endeavor. Under-funding and unpopularity made any military threat unlikely. President Kirchner attempted unsuccessfully to reassure the army that his action had a moral basis, not the goal of revenge. When the president addressed officers at a "camaraderie dinner" early in his administration, they greeted him in silence. His still-unspecified connection with the guerrillas remained an issue that fueled resentment. The fact that Kirchner forced out many senior officers did little to endear the president to the army. While some 90 percent of army's soldiers joined after the return to civilian rule, the upper ranks included many Dirty War veterans. Formerly junior officers at the time of the Dirty War who now occupied senior positions worried that they would be targeted. Many officers believed that the focus on the Dirty War diverted attention from other problems.[21]

Another pending issue involved the capture of those responsible for the attacks on the Israeli Embassy in 1992 and the Jewish Community Center two years later. The reinvigorated investigation may have been a way of discrediting ex-president Menem. Many believed the rumors that the ex-president had protected the guilty in exchange for a $10 million bribe. Equally as plausible, the government may have sought to placate the United States, which had expressed dissatisfaction with the lack progress in solving the case. Murky politics served to keep the international community busy attempting to find some rational explanation of events. Argentina officially requested the arrest and extradition of the Iranian ambassador, then in Britain, who had been present in Argentina at the time of the attacks.. Tehran protested the arrest, breaking off cultural and economic ties with Buenos Aires. The Iranian ban on imports cost the Argentine economy some $475 million in lost exports as of 2002. In early 2004, Swiss authorities placed Menem's name on a list of foreign leaders suspected of corruption, with a bank account of at least $500,000. A federal judge ordered a freeze on all of the ex-president's personal assets. Meanwhile, the bombings remained unsolved.

RIGHTING THE ECONOMY

The billions owed to international agencies continued as the main economic hurdle. A default threatened to damage them more than

Argentina. The old saw that if you borrow enough you own the bank verged on becoming a reality. The IMF lent Argentina $14.3 billion, soon to be $16 billion, far in excess of the amount authorized by the bank's governors. In addition, the World Bank lent 8 percent of its assets, and the Inter-American Development Bank risked 20 percent of its portfolio in Argentina. All three institutions had a lot to lose. The only way out required lending more money to forestall a default on their portion of the debt—in effect, using IMF money to pay the IMF and associated institutions' debt services. It appeared to be a bookkeeping bailout of the IMF, not of Argentina. Private bondholders faced the reality of default with little expectations of payments resuming. European investors made up the majority of small individual investors. Italians, who bought bonds from a variety of institutions, would be hard-hit, just as in the Baring crisis of the 1890s. Individual claims by Europeans totaled $24 billion.

No longer servicing loans, the economy, rebounded, and unemployment came down from an estimated high of over 50 percent to a still-difficult, but at least better, 17 percent. A government program offered selective individuals a monthly allotment of 150 pesos to stay off the unemployment roles, artificially driving down the figures to 14.3 percent by year's end. Although it undermined the usefulness of statistics, the program pumped money into the economy and helped a select group. The *Piqueteros* (derived from the tactics of blocking downtown streets in Buenos Aires and in provincial capitals), organized groups to disrupt traffic as a means of gaining political leverage. The government funneled funds through the Piquetero leadership, which then doled it out and pocketed a percentage, presumably in exchange for some sort of restraint.

Additional money went to local Peronist leaders to distribute to their grassroots constituency. The president's discretionary spending competed with that of Duhalde's jobs for votes scheme. Handouts and other forms of informal relief made it impossible to calculate real unemployment or determine how many employees went on the political payroll. The absence of an apolitical unemployment scheme to provide financial relief to all the unemployed angered those without the right connections. Rival Piqueteros groups, allied with the president or with his rival Eduardo Duhalde, at times clashed violently, contributing to the tension in the streets.

Ironically, economic globalization, never very popular in Argentina, responded to the weak peso to help put people back to work. Suddenly, exports, made inexpensive by currency devaluation, resulted in a trade surplus. A budget surplus also materialized, adding substance to the popular belief that bondholders, the IMF, and others had been parasitically draining the country. As President Kirchner reportedly told IMF Director Horst Köhler, "You are greatly responsible for what happened in Argentina."[22] He might have added that a large part of the debt had been taken on during the military regime from 1976 to 1983.

By the end of 2003 the economy began to reclaim lost ground as idle factories resumed production. The GDP expanded by seven percent, while inflation held at three percent. The economy with its debts unpaid continued to recover. To reassure the IMF that the government intended to restrain borrowing the president pressed for a Fiscal Responsibility Law (2004) limiting the ability of provinces to contract debt. At the same time the IMF suggested that the amount of money shared with the provinces (*coparticipación*) be raised to a reasonable level, thereby restraining federal government spending.

Tourism emerged as one bright spot, although it could be viewed as taking advantage of the economic misfortune of the nation. Foreign tourists attracted by rock-bottom prices flooded into the country. Three million tourists from Europe, the United States, and Brazil visited in 2003, double the previous year's number, to enjoy what a weak peso could buy. By 2004 a new record of 5.25 million tourists passed though Buenos Aires. Hotel renovations to meet tourist demands drew on Buenos Aires' well-established sense of nostalgia to create an ambiance that tourists found irresistibly charming. Tourism's glitter and success obscured a grim reality. At the beginning of 2004, over half of all Argentines lived in poverty and another 25–30 percent lived in extreme poverty. Only one fifth of the population had a reasonably secure economic base, a reality that acted to kept wages low and labor plentiful.

Economists estimated that putting idle factories back to work would add 10 to 15 percent to the GDP, but in order to grow beyond that point direct foreign investment would be required, as well as the return of money deposited off shore, estimated at $100 billion with another the $20 billion safe-guarded under the mattress.

IN THE SHADOW OF DEFAULT

President Kirchner ignored the default's long-range impact to deal with the immediate wolf at the door. The decline in the peso's value made it even more difficult to repay foreign currency debt. Just how much bondholders holding high-yield bonds could expect to salvage out of the collapse became an international issue. Italian dealers had marketed Argentine bonds to some 400,000 small investors who claimed to have been unaware of the risk involved. Large-scale bond holders, while unable to make such excuses, nevertheless expressed outrage at Kirchner's proposal to return pennies on the dollar with an implied take it or leave attitude. The federal government retained a European firm (Lazard Freres) to advise the government. Buenos Aires Province hired Citibank to help resolve its default on the province's $2.6 billion foreign debt. Hardening opinion in the international financial community forced the government to meet with groups representing foreign bondholders. The government's hard line with creditors forced them to accept 30 cents on the dollar. With some 80 percent of creditors accepting the government's harsh conditions, the country's credit rating improved dramatically. The settlement appeared to be a political and economic victory for the president. Private companies, such as the Mastellone Hermanos, restructured their debt of $329.1 million in May 2004, as did the dairy products company San Cor ($167 million). A growing number of companies took steps to assure future access to credit markets—an indication that they expected to survive and grow.

The president made a political virtue out of truculence and hostility. People referred to the president and his minister of planning, Julio de Vito, as the penguins because both came from the Patagonian province of Santa Cruz, known for its frontier feistiness. The president added to his popularity by walking around the capital, exchanging greetings and pleasantries with citizens without the normal formalities of the presidential office. Less admirable, he developed what people called the K style, a mixture of Patagonian provincialism, eccentricity, and rudeness. When President Hu Jintao of China arrived for a state visit to announce plans to invest some $20 billion in Argentina, Kirchner sent a low-ranking aide to welcome him. In a similar dismissive fashion, when the then CEO of Hewlett-Packard, Carla Fiorina, arrived to meet with Kirchner, he kept her waiting; eventually she left without seeing him. Regional heads of state, accustomed to social niceties and diplomatic norm's had to endue rudeness. President Kirchner, dependent on populist rhetoric to rally the people, appeared unable to pass up an opportunity to score points even when it had a negative economic impact. When Shell raised gasoline prices in early 2005 in response to inflation, the president called for a boycott. Sale of Shell petroleum products dropped 70 percent. The president's populist behavior ignored the problem in favor of punishing the messenger. Nevertheless, to Argentines his attacks and lack of respect for foriegn dignitaries demonstrated that they had not been humbled by the crisis.

Meanwhile, as an economist ironically noted, but for the default Argentina would be a miracle economy. Short-term tactical moves that avoided adding to the suffering pushed problems off into the future. Controlling utility costs alleviated suffering but suddenly jeopardized economic recovery in early 2004. Failure to adjust prices following devaluation and a rate freeze shifted the cost of artificially low electricity rates to producers and distributors. Power companies, already in default on dollar loans, could not recover their costs or service demand and eventually could not produce electricity. A severe energy crisis reduced power to factories, threatening production and wages. The government cut gas exports to Chile by 15 percent and stopped the sale of electricity to Uruguay, all without notice. Ironically, energy privatization under Memen made power companies efficient, resulting in an over 50 percent rate reduction and the exporting of electricity, gas, and oil. The days of plentiful supply at reasonable prices had gone. The Kirchner government unconvincingly blamed the producers, not official policy, for the crisis. Argentina had to buy electricity from Brazil and gas from Bolivia and confront the true cost of forcing others to bear the financial burden of populist measures, no matter how well intended.

President Kirchner's decision to concentrate on reviving domestic employment before addressing the demands of creditors slowly stabilized the economy. After a rocky first year, the economy grew by eight percent in 2003 and 2004. Even more amazing, the peso remained stable. An estimated two million new jobs cut the numbers of people living in poverty from over 50 percent to slightly over 40 percent by January2005— still high, but with a downward trend that offered hope. High single-digit gains, while welcome, came from a low base. Two important factors, a high Euro exchange rate relative to the American dollar and the Argentine peso and low interests rates helped lift the economy. Moreover, soybean prices in 2003–2004 continued to be strong. Both these factors resulted from lucky breaks rather than government actions.

Nevertheless, President Kirchner's economic policy challenged the wisdom of the traditional IMF method of imposing harsh measures to shock a country into recovery, no matter what the immediate social and economic cost. Insistence on tight budgets, increased tax revenues, and a budget surplus before a country restarted its economy weakened the government's ability to perform. Argentina turned the IMF formula on its head. As Economics Minister Roberto Lavagna observed, "It's very simple, nobody can collect from a country that is not growing."[23] In 2005, the economy regained its 1998 peak, and in July 2005 the government issued dollar bonds—the first issuance of government bonds since the default. A budget surplus and strong exports underpinned the renewed willingness to invest in Argentina.

The country's successful passage through default obscured the reality that Argentina had stabilized at a lower socioeconomic level than in 1998. Real wages fell 30 percent and many lived below the poverty line. The formal economy, with its social safety-net benefits, fell to its 1980 level, Meanwhile, the informal economy, including the estimated 8,000 rag pickers that recycle items from the garbage, doubled. Those lucky enough to have good-paying jobs, some 10 percent of workers, made 33 times more that the lowest 10 percent.

Economic and political mismanagement plunged many citizens to a level almost impossible to reverse. Social and economic assets disappeared. Argentina, once known for its high educational level, accepted the reality that only 60 percent of students completed secondary schooling in 2004. University graduates made up only 5 percent of the workforce compared to the 15–20 percent that marks a first world country. A formerly educated and skilled workforce appeared to be in the process of degradation.

Conclusion: Who or What Is to Blame?

What constitutes a faltering nation is harder to define than an obviously failed or a successful one. Success has many contributing factors, and the need to pinpoint them or show how they interact is useful, but not vital. In contrast, understanding failure is important not only for those directly effected, but also for other nations anxious to avoid whatever traps can be identified. Unraveling the weak and broken strands to find the sequence of a progressive failure is difficult and speculative. In the case of a faltering nation, like a ship taking on water and listing but not yet sinking, finding the right explanation is crucial if it is to be righted before it slides to the bottom.

THE DIAGNOSTIC INFLUENCE OF NATIONALISM

The Nationalists first raised doubts about the socioemotional and political state of Argentina. While they constantly lamented the country's inability to crystallize into a national community, their chronic pessimism suggested that the lost past made positive change in the present impossible. Their reactionary attacks on alleged villains, and conspiratorial mindset favored revenge and authoritarian regimes. Nationalist resentment indicated that the fusion between Creole Argentina and Argentina Atlantica remains incomplete.

Ricardo Rojas' *La restauración nacionalista* (The Nationalist Restoration) attacked Buenos Aires' imposition of a foreign civilization that smothered the country's true spirit. Nationalist Carlos Ibarguren accused liberalism of destroying the native aristocracy, and with it religion, honor, and tradition, while poet Leopoldo Lugones questioned liberalism's ability to create a nation because it ignored tradition, a central element of nationality in his view. Gustavo Martínez Zuviría (aka Hugo Wast) occupied an extreme position on the Nationalist spectrum that went from mild resentment to unrelenting hostility. Martínez Zuviría employed emotional nostalgia to portray the simple but honest values of the interior as objects of amusement by cynical, uncaring Porteños, smugly confident that only they mattered. As Hugo Wast, he churned out cheap novels that drew on anti-Semitism for a variety of plots. His books portrayed Argentines as victims of an international conspiracy ignored or abetted by liberalism. His cultural and intellectual influence rested on both his official position as the director of the National Library (1931–1955) and the popularity of his books.

Nationalism's solution to the ills that they identified with liberalism amounted to an impossible antimodern return to the past. Religious values and a dominant Church role in education directly conflicted with modern trends. Opposition to liberal democracy and a desire to replace it with social harmony within a traditional, ordered society followed Catholic doctrine but suggested the need for an authoritarian government. They believed that social justice could not be achieved through compromise. Their attraction to power and authoritarian governments reflected the desire to imposed a past on those who had tried to exterminate it after the fall of Rosas. Nevertheless, their inability to articulate practical action plans made Nationalists ineffective, even when they occupied government positions. Nationalist influence in the army and among out-of-power political groups, faded when these groups achieved political power. Perón and others, used Nationalists but soon removed them from authority.

The Nationalist movement depended on a sense of victimization, and frustration—characteristics evident in the works of Raúl Scalabrini Ortiz and others. Victims, drained and bloodless, without direction, await an unknown force to rescue them. Enemies are clear, but not friends. One of Scalabrini Ortiz's most popular works captures the impotence in its title, *The Man that Is Alone and Waits*. Old wounds remained fresh and constantly reopened.

A resentful and angry mindset that looked for and found enemies domestically as well as internationally influenced public discussion. Anger focused on forces that could not be controlled. Political and economic failures generated abundant emotional material that paralyzed, rather than galvanized. The myth of a flourishing middle-class nation left many disappointed—socially and economically insecure individuals susceptible to varying degrees of Nationalist rhetoric. Their message, often mixed with Marxists terminology after the 1920s, framed public discourse and provided scapegoats. The oligarchy's acceptance of British imperialism and their appropriation of the lion's share of export wealth appeared to underpin the Nationalists' economic complaints and fueled their resentment.

Ezequiel Martínez Estrada and Eduardo Mallea, among others, accepted many Nationalist complaints but saw the social divisions encouraged by Nationalists' beliefs as part of the problem. In 1933, Martínez Estrada (1895–1964) published his *Radiografía de la Pampa* (X-Ray of the Pampas), winning the National Literature Prize for that year. He explained the title as his recognition that the problem had become deeply embedded and structural; therefore, one should consult a radiologist, not a photographer. Negatively influenced by the turmoil following 1929, he cast Argentina's history in a negative light. Martínez Estrada rooted the problem in the elite's failure to consider Argentina as a whole. The failure to contemplate the complete historical reality made it impossible to address the country's needs. Acceptance of a European illusion, magnified the oligarchy's status but diminished that of others. Perhaps more to the point, he observed that the inability to accept negative aspects of the nation's history made it impossible to absorb its positive lessons. He saw the nation as caught in a static situation of an unabsorbed past mixed with a defeatist present that made fixing the future impossible.

Subsequently, collective resentment, an attraction to power, and suspicion of individual motives became vices that burdened Argentina. Martínez Estrada traced the failure to the social-economic configuration of the pampas in the 1870s and 1880s and the refusal to integrate the urban and rural experience into one composite. The son of Spanish parents, he nevertheless decried Europeanization and the discarding of native virtues that led to what he saw as a denatured people.

Martínez Estrada called for a recasting of Argentine history and hence the nation itself, but had little faith that it could be done. The influence of Nietzsche's philosophical-psychological approach is evident in his search for a reality behind a false façade. In his *La Cabeza de Goliat* (Goliath's Head, 1940) he portrayed Buenos Aires as a capital detached from its provincial body. The country's rural Creole population remained disconnected from the urban immigrant experience. Consequently, a disjointed people followed sterile formulas without conviction or faith while the fissures that split the country remained unattended. Such divisions hardened into physical restraints that hobbled the nation. Little joy, pleasure, or hope attended his views.[1] Nevertheless, a redemptive compromise can be identified but buried beneath layers of pessimism.

In a similar fashion Eduardo Mallea's (1903–1982) *Historia de una passion Argentina* (1937) suggested the existence of two nations, one repugnant, materialistic, and false overlying the true Argentina. The genuine soul of the country existed out of sight, suggesting both its existence and the possibility of resurrection. Both Mallea and Martínez Estrada recognized the damage inflicted on the country by a materially seduced republican elite that continued to employ liberal rhetoric, while in reality it had long since become a calcified oligarchy. Monopolizing the nation's wealth, with firm options on future prospects, they divided the nation and put the middle and lower classes under chronic pressure. The gap between rhetoric and reality and the use of a fraudulent democracy as their vehicle to protect their greed acted to undermine trust. That both men wrote in the 1930s perhaps explains their veiled hope for a future social and economic balance. That they addressed the complaints of the Nationalists and linked them to an objective reality separated them from those that preferred only to react.

Martínez Estrada and Mallea raised important and valid issues. In contrast, much of Nationalist thought craved a fight more than a solution. Nationalists sought revenge for a betrayed past. Emotion, rejection, and fear led to an exaggerated desire for control and a taste for rigidity in moral and sociopolitical conduct. Paranoia emerged to do battle in what appeared to be an impending apocalypse. Nationalists, profoundly antidemocratic and antiforeign and infused with hierarchical notions derived from Catholic doctrine, pitted Creole Argentina against liberalism. They constantly recreated and updated the destructive divide that polarized the nation before 1853. The elevation of class harmony and social justice over the form of politics and the structure of the state and the economy opened the way for violence in the name of a higher good.

In the 1970s, V.S. Naipaul observed that the country exhibited the symptoms of a decadent imperialism.[2] Abandoned and left to shift unsuccessfully for itself, with few ideas and tarnished ideals, its people became individually rapacious and collectively diminished. That the governing elites imposed British economic imperialism upon the country discredited them, while the politicians that followed became parasitically corrupt. A demoralized country that appeared to prefer to flagellate itself drives its citizens into exile.

Novelist Tomás Eloy Martínez wrote of a culture of exile, detachment, and lies. Embracing myths as truth in the end destroys what should be used to create. A long list of exiles, some who fled violence or chased material success and others who fled to preserve their mental health, drained away the energy needed to rally the nation. Even heroes seemed to flee. José de San Martín, instrumental in the South American independence movement, left for Europe in 1823 to reside in Paris. San Martín visited Uruguay in 1829 for several months but never made the short journey (admittedly uncomfortable at the time) across the estuary to step once again in the country that claimed his grandeur. After 1881, Alberti lived in Paris. Rosas died in English exile, although not by choice. Literary figures found inspiration abroad. Although not unusual in any society, it seemed in Argentina that all must leave or struggle against creative sterility. Julio Cortázar wrote most of his work in exile, returning just before his death, as did Martínez Estrada. Manuel Puig, best known for his *Kiss of the Spider Woman*, fled during the Perón era, eventually settling in Mexico. Borges went to Geneva to die, and so on. Those exiles that returned after the Dirty War found that "history is on the run… last week's 'eternal values' are interred tomorrow. Even cultural and historical truths are overtaken."[3] Pessimism, a form of counter-nationalism, became ingrained and served as a partial replacement for the myth of a soon-to-be-great country. The Nationalists have not served their country well. Nevertheless, Nationalist thought influenced all social levels and is symptomatic of the nation's malaise but cannot provide a rescuing diagnosis.

THE ECONOMIC EXPLANATION

Noble Prize laureate Paul Samuelson's much-quoted comment that four economic systems exist: capitalism, communism, Japan without resources but everything works, and Argentina with resources and nothing works obscures in humor the notion that more than just economic factors are in play. Economic factors are part of a system that goes beyond production and consumption and other basic functions. Civic attitudes, political structures, history, perceptions, and psychology are also part of the system, with regional, class, and other variables that complicate matters. The idea that Argentina is a naturally wealthy country is a powerful economic fallacy. Although embraced by Argentines and foreigners alike, this fallacy became an obstacle on the road to sustainable prosperity.

Similarly, the export elite believed that agricultural innovation ensured the future. Their agro-centric approach resulted in innovations that maximized productivity but did not spread prosperity across the nation. New and improved breeds of sheep, cattle, grains, and grasses, as well as the latest techniques along with wire fencing, refrigeration, and other processing facilities received their full backing. The state stepped in to float loans for ports and guarantee loans and profits for railways. Foreign investors saw a profitable opportunity to share in what appeared to be a cornucopia.

Britain's investments in Latin America constituted 20 percent of its exported capital, most of it going to Argentina and Brazil. The rush to prosperity reached its height in 1913, just prior to World War I when Argentina received £650 million of the approximately £3 billion pounds of British wealth invested in all of Latin America. Some 80 percent of Argentina's stock of foreign capital came from London. The fragility of a narrow agro-export economy coupled with over-reliance on surplus British capital could be brushed aside until the bottom fell out.

Britain generated too much surplus capital that searched the world for higher rates of return than could be secured in its own developed economy. Large investment banks took risks that reflected cheap money, while pensioners and small shopkeepers naively accepted guarantees that the higher rates available in Argentina had the solid backing of a sovereign government. Too much capital encouraged speculation and the floating of loans, often to restructure previous debts and make room for more borrowing. In addition, European financial institutions manipulated the gold premium, the spread between gold-backed currencies and Argentine paper money. They did so in order to encourage imports that in turn balanced the cost of Argentine exports. Equally as important, purchase of paper money securities at higher rates of return required a moderate gold spread as paper money payments purchased gold-backed currencies. A transatlantic game made banking profitable by manipulating an inherently unstable situation.

A prolonged addiction to inconvertible paper money for domestic use and excessively loose emission of paper discouraged savings while encouraging speculation in land purchased with depreciating paper. Although a rational choice, land speculation appeared to be more rent seeking than creative investment. Agricultural earnings in gold provided a core foundation, but one that also required debt in order to finance imports and development. With the exception of maintaining meat distribution centers in Britain, little money went into vertical investments that could maximize hard currency profits, such as transatlantic shipping. Mineral exploration and development within the country or across borders in Bolivia or Brazil could have cut the cost of imported energy and metals and stimulated manufacturing.

The oligarchy's entrepreneurship did not extend, beyond their admirable management of commercial agriculture. Land served to safeguard the value of their assets, and export agriculture provided a return on their holdings. The rapidity with which the land generated wealth for the few saddled Argentina with a crushing oligarchic burden that cut short the development of a more energetically creative society able to broadly develop the economy.

Many recognized the role of industrialization in the modernization process in England, Europe, and the United States, but they did not believe that Argentina could follow those models. They feared that in order to sell in foreign markets, they had to buy overseas. The tariff of 1877 protected the nascent flour, sugar, and wine industries, all processors of raw agricultural production and inexpensive manufactured goods. Meatpacking and beverages, closely connected with agricultural export, made up a large percentage of industrial operations. Repair facilities and public utilities grew along with the development of the country's electricity, gas, and water systems. Nevertheless, industrial concerns appeared to be "orphans of every national tradition," in the words of Eusebio E. Garcia in the 1913 industrial census.[4] The "mother industry" remained agropastoral activity.

Industrial development continued to be secondary, in spite of the shock of World War I. Import substitution could only be cautiously implemented because of the fear of jeopardizing the export market. The Roca-Runciman Agreement confirmed those fears. Even those individuals willing to assume the risk of developing a new enterprise faced a daunting environment that increased the likelihood of failure. Lack of reliable sources of energy, transportation bottlenecks, and the small domestic market made investment in industrialization less attractive than in the profitable agro-export sector. Despite these obstacles, import substitution did take place. World War I, the Depression, and World War II forced Argentina to develop an industrial base, but one that produced poor quality goods at high prices. Industrialization remained shallow. Importation of machinery and technology rather than generation of more advanced industrial products and methods, restrained what should have been a dynamic buildup of an industrial base. The absence of significant industrial exports to pay for importation of needed inputs mattered little as long as the country's efficient agriculture earned sufficient export revenues. Industry developed a parasitic grasp on a captive domestic market and a dependent relationship with an efficient agro-export sector. In the post-1945 period, Perón's corporatism discouraged expansion by limiting industrial competition. Controlling the ability of new enterprises to import machinery allowed the state to maintain what it perceived to be the appropriate corporate balance. Until the 1950s, Argentina had the largest industrial economy in the region, but it appeared to be a reactive survival response, not an attempt to move into the competitive international market.

Structural and perceptual obstacles also retarded development. The poor distribution of wealth and insufficient domestic investment restricted the size of the domestic market and depressed urban wages. Individuals had little incentive to develop entrepreneurial skills or invest in innovative activities. In the absence of self-sustaining industrial momentum, the government made investments as needed in areas considered crucial. The army, concerned with national security, responded to the neglect of industrial development by creating military factories owned directly or with mixed ownership. In spite of positive intentions and lots of money, military industrialization absorbed more capital than it generated. State economic intervention politicized decision making and shifted the focus away from profits and competitiveness. The country dissipated its advantages and lost the opportunity to develop an industrial economy. Argentina fell short of overtaking the United States or Australia in the nineteenth century and lost out to Brazil and Mexico in the twentieth.

The urban middle class, faced with a discouraging environment, sought refuge in the professions and bureaucracy while the working class looked to the state.

The notion that the country functioned as an informal member of the British Empire may be only a slight exaggeration, but one that has a hidden significance. Had Argentina been a full member of the empire they could have at least taken advantage of imperial paternalism. As the relationship with Britain evolved, Argentina experienced many of the negative restrictions of colonialism without counterbalancing positive aspects. Insecure semi-colonial status hobbled the nation's leaders and created a colonial mentality that shaped Argentina's self image. While Britain flourished so did Argentina; when its fortunes declined, so did those of its imperial stepchild.

Britain emerged from the Great War (World War I) a bankrupt power dependent on the liquidation of overseas assets and American money. The war diverted international capital from previous channels, leaving Argentina with only a reduced amount of foreign resources compared to prewar days. Following on the heels of World War I, with only a short respite, came the Great Depression, then another war in Europe. International capital's percentage of investment in Argentine went from 47.7 in 1913 to 20.4 by 1940. Domestic accumulation could not sustain development, quite apart from historic risk aversion. Even during the boom years domestic investors shied away from direct participation in stocks and bonds, preferring to allow foreign investors to take the risks, losses, and profits.

Although post World War I realities made Wall Street the financial center of the world, New York markets had little interest in replacing London as a source of capital for Argentina. Investments went into projects directly useful to the needs of American industry, with a preference for direct investments in subsidiaries. A wide range of companies invested in overseas operations in the post World War I period. In spite of an impressive list of American companies with subsidiaries in Argentina, other countries—Mexico, Central America, and the Caribbean—had the advantage of proximity. Mexico supplied a significant amount of minerals and raw materials that flowed northward on a rail system linked to that of the United States. Tropical fruit from Central America and Ecuador, coffee and cotton from Brazil, and Cuban sugar and tobacco may have been the only agricultural imports of great interest. With the opening of the Panama Canal in 1914, investors turned their attention to Asia, further isolating the Southern Cone. The dependent food chain that linked Argentina to Britain had no American equivalent.

Argentine remained tied to Britain in a narrowly profitable arrangement. While export profits lavishly supported the landed elite, they did not provide sufficient income to balance imports or generate capital to replace foreign loans. Argentina consistently avoided the bold steps necessary to broaden its manufacturing economy. During periods of economic difficulty, Argentina reverted to inconvertible paper to assure continued economic activity and to buy a degree of social peace by mandating wage increases in inflated currency.

Perón made the most ambitious effort to redirect existing wealth, but not in a sustainable fashion. From 1946 to 1955, he drew on the cornucopia fallacy to restructure wealth, but ignored the need to create it. He did so through wage and prices controls that turned basic elements of an economic system into political tools. Perón did not create an innovative fluid economic environment able to develop momentum. State-directed development became inflexible as political considerations made it impossible to shift resources around as economic needs changed. Any substantial redeployment of resources became a political decision. Insufficient investment in wealth creation failed to create new pools of resources available for economic expansion and social needs. What little surplus emerged often had been politically committed already.

Perón sought a social balance that made industry subordinate to society's needs. His labor policies, while negatively impacting productivity, served social and political ends. Perón and the CGT damaged the work ethic on the shop floor and distorted the union movement in general.[5] Paternalism and political manipulation undermined factory discipline and the basic economic underpinnings that rested on the work ethic. Economic bonds, cooperative work, a sense of fair treatment, and just wages are elements that engender productivity and social connectivity. Corruption, resentment, and survival strategies as discussed below damage the psychological resources of the workforce. Under Perón, the cost of demonstrations, unauthorized holidays, and even riots shifted to the employer, the consumer, and the economy in general. Perón created a static factory layer, rather than a dynamic, independent, and expansive industrial sector. Union labor became a key, but dysfunctional, component of Peronismo.

In the post Perón era inflation and hyperinflation became a recurring problem. Argentina's political instability discouraged foreign investment, but not loans. Beginning in the 1970s petro-dollars flooded international market as OPEC sought to recycle the cartel's profits. The need to invest capital that could not be employed in the developed countries took precedent over the actual ability of borrowers to use the money. Argentina, like other Latin American countries and a number of African and Asian nations, fell into a debt trap characterized by out-of-control budgets, poor debt servicing practices, corruption, off-shore bank accounts, and political instability. The availability of money encouraged reckless borrowing. International institutions, the World Bank, Inter-American Development Bank, large multinational banks, and governments encouraged development schemes in the "undeveloped world," while the IMF unintentionally provided a false sense of security. Flush times in the hemisphere encouraged the floating of bonds. Governments ignored the danger that changes in demand or lower prices for the region's products might make debt servicing difficult in the future.

In 2001 the inevitable default occurred. The rush of international investment banks to float bonds and the willingness of brokerage houses to sell them to institutional investors played a major role in the default. The other part of the equation, the acceptance by politicians of hard currency debt at market rates with insufficient attention to debt repayment, created a debt bubble that eventually burst. Uncritical boosting of the Argentine stock market by foreign brokerage houses fueled what became a feeding frenzy. Loose talk about Argentina's commitment to convertible currency, allegedly because they had finally conquered the old economic problems, convinced many investors that they would receive generous returns on their money in safety. Rollover loans, new short-term loans, and other devices became a deepening quagmire with few possibilities of painless escape. Lender mismanagement compounded Argentine failures in both the Baring Brothers crisis in 1890 and the collapse of 2001. When an overextended IMF balked and insisted on austerity measures, the dominos fell. Argentina tested all the limits of the international financial system. The world's largest (to date) default of $141 billion in 2001–2002 ended the fantasy.

Postmortem analysis stripped away the euphoria and identified obvious mistakes and the irresponsibility of banks, international financial institutions, brokerage houses, pension and mutual fund managers, and Argentine politicians. Of more significance, after examining appropriate data, a number of economists concluded that the five most successful periods of Argentina's macro economic history are all associated with the "establishment or convergence towards a convertible monetary regime."[6] Argentina may have been on the right track with the 1991 convertibility plan but did not make the comprehensive reforms that could have supported the plan in both good times and bad. Menem's partial reforms engendered optimism that soon became euphoric speculation that the country had finally found the key to fiscal and monetary stability. Letting go of optimism, even when the signs turned mixed, occurred reluctantly and over a considerable period. In the slow-motion economic collapse and its dreadful finale in 2001, the government failed to take proactive measures, other than pressing the IMF for more loans and, in the process, setting up the bank of last resort to take the blame. Political considerations added to the paralysis.

A sense of entitlement encouraged by Peronismo and a resentful nationalism nurtured over decades by the Nationalists created an emotional and powerful mindset that made acceptance of an objective analysis impossible. Silvia Bleichmar's popular explanation, *Dolor País* (Painful Country), predictably blamed neo-liberalism imposed by corrupt politicians allied with the IMF and international capital for the collapse.[7] The book went through a number of editions. The IMF is not without blame; its insistence on immediate measures ignored reality and precipitated default, but the agency is not the root problem . Nevertheless, Silvia Bleichmar is correct, there are villains, but it is more important to understand the problem and the process than finger the culprits. The demands of the IMF for basic structural reforms, including a higher income-tax rate (Argentines pay less than comparable Latin American countries), to provide the revenue for entitlements cannot be dismissed as fiscal imperialism. It is systematic of a problem that has prompted Argentina to petition the institution for help time after time over the course of the last half- century. If anything, the IMF has been too quick to help when a type of fiscal tough love might have been more appropriate. Repeated promises to restrain deficits had been broken, suggesting that governments have been unwilling to tell the nation that the system is broken. Moreover, to fix it will require all groups to make sacrifices. Misidentification of the problem complicates remedial action.

Moreover, politics subordinates economic issues, including budget deficits and debts, to social ones. Argentina employs opportunistic financing instead of structural reforms to generate the funds for social expenditures. Actual social costs are concealed in a progressively inflated currency, while international borrowing meets hard-currency needs and covers trade imbalances when they occur. In Argentina, economics is much more than what it appears to be to foreigner observers. The centrality of social justice in Peronista thought reinforces the sense of outrage when things go wrong. When resources are perceived to be abundant, lavish distribution is expected. During a fiscal crisis, however, politicians divide the remainders among themselves. Those without political connections face hard times when favors and services are withdrawn, increasing their anger. Meanwhile, IMF bashing is popular with those who have been impoverished by domestic and international fiscal mismanagement. President Kirchner used his opposition to the monetary agency to fan nationalism to levels equivalent to those just prior to the disastrous Falkland War.

Perhaps the solution lies in Paul Samuelson's reference to Japan. An island nation without resources became an industrial power even before it ventured into war in China and the Pacific. As two journalists and admiring supporters of Menem noted, Japan made scarcity into virtue, while Argentina made abundance into scarcity.[8] Japan created a regional market, unfortunately by force, before it moved to a global one. Regional economic zones serve to eliminate the economic obstacles of borders without the negative consequences of annexation or wars over resources. The collapse of the Spanish American empire in the early nineteenth century eliminated a unified market for goods and labor, but the market lingered on in the shadowy world of contraband and illegal migration across South America's borders. The need to recreate that unity is a driving force in the push for economic zones. Mercosur has a positive potential for unifying the region. It will not be smooth or without friction, as President Kirchner's recent loud complaints demonstrate. On the eve of the Mercosur Summit meeting (July2004), Buenos Aires threatened to impose a 21 percent tariff on Brazilian refrigerators and stoves, with a similar tax on textiles. A planned arbitration court to be based in Paraguay to resolve differences without going before the World Trade Organization appears stalled by distrust of Brazil. President Kirchner, after relinquishing the six-month rotating Mercosur presidency, admonished Brazil that, "it is important to promote industrial development in all Mercosur nations, not just Brazil."[9] Mercosur's tenth anniversary, celebrated in Belo Horizonte, Brazil, on December 17, 2004, could not gloss over tension between the two major members. In spite of provisions for a common external tariff, member countries impose additional taxes as goods cross their borders. Some 800 exemptions to the common external tariff impede cross-border trade. In addition, quotas limit access to each member's domestic market. Regional economic cooperation is important to Argentina if it is to develop a balanced economy with a competitive industrial base.

Argentina's viability as a functioning nation may be best assured in a regional context in spite of antagonisms within the region, particularly with Brazil. We know that active industrialization draws in commodities and raw materials from other regions. Britain, the United States, and most recently China, with initial start-up resources, eventually outstripped domestic supplies and created multinational supply networks. Brazil already is pulling in Bolivian natural gas and oil as well as labor to feed its industrial demand. Transnational hydroelectric energy is another indicator of a regional process that only Brazil has taken full advantage of to power its exports. In contrast, the extent of Argentina's industrial lag is underscored by the paucity of multinational companies. Although in the end, the American Free Trade Area of the Americas may draw the country out of it relative industrial isolation, forcing it to engage in the world market, a high degree of regional economic integration remains crucial.

The export agricultural sector remains subject to boom and burst cycles. In the current century, basic food resources worldwide are in surplus supply. Critical shortages as a result of civil wars, politics, and distribution problems occur but do not offer long-term or dependable markets. All that may change. Rising living standards in Asia may outstrip food technology and recreate the demand that grew in the late 1800s as a consequence of rising European living standards. Other unforeseen events could stimulate the market. Use of organic sources of energy or bio-technological advances, including organic chemicals—already a growing segment of the industry—may provide a resurgence of agricultural prosperity. Negative possibilities must also be considered. Perhaps the failure of global trade to distribute its benefits in an acceptable fashion could end with the formation of trading blocks in which Argentina could only be a subordinate member.

THE ROLE OF DYSFUNCTIONAL DEMOCRACY

The republican ideal collapsed as an oligarchy emerged on the heels of escalating land prices and agricultural demand. Form with limited substance replaced the republican promise with a democratic illusion that enabled Argentina to claim to be a liberal democracy. By 1880, the oligarchy seemingly had displaced all possible contenders for power. The Partido Autonomista Nacional, founded in 1881, marked the moment that the oligarchy replaced the republican elite. Nevertheless, the PAN came into existence at the moment when one party could not accommodate the varying and complex interests of the elite. Earlier objectives, such as the preferential acquisition of land as the Indian frontier receded, no longer unified the elite. Provincial camarillas fragmented the party at its inception. Consequently, PAN presidents struggled to control congresses and provincial governors, theoretically supporters of the governing party. Deal making within the PAN became progressively more difficult and at times acrimonious. Federal intervention to overturn governors in the provinces reflected conflict within the oligarchy. That they could not agree on how to deal with urban issues, let alone the pressure for change coming from the middle class, is not surprising. Nor could the government impose dictatorial rule. Within a generation (31 years) the elite had to devise a scheme to share power to avoid revolutionary violence.

The Sáenz Peña reforms of 1912 constituted explicit recognition that the complex and varying economic interests of the oligarchy could only be protected to a degree and not within one party. In a calibrated distribution of assets, they turned over tangible government resources (jobs, contracts, and concessions) to the Union Civica Radical (UCR). They continued to control land and the lion's share of wealth. Only their collective desire to retain wealth unified them. Looser associations, such as the SRA and the Jockey Club, suited the changed circumstances of the elite more than a political party.

The UCR took power at the height of reactionary violence often caused by its own members as well as radicals. Fear that violence would continue indefinitely, jeopardizing agricultural exports unless the oligarchy conceded resources, lay behind the transfer of political power. Members of the elite scattered across the political spectrum, including membership and leadership positions in the UCR and various splinter groups.

The UCR's congressional ticket in 1916 included three members of the SRA who earlier would have belonged to the PAN. The party's presidential candidate's affiliation with elite organizations reassured them. Yrigoyen's first cabinet drew heavily on members of the Jockey Club and the SRA. Significantly, it did not include working-class candidates. It represented a change in style and an important shift to accommodate the rising middle class and acknowledge divisions in the oligarchy.

The rapidity of Argentina's development in the nineteenth century outstripped the nation's ability to make adjustments in a timely fashion. Economic change came with the speed of technology, leaving viable politics dangerously behind. After 1876, immigrants entered an already socially solidified society that remained so well into the twentieth century.[10] As a consequence, the new governing party, the UCR, did not incorporate the working-class. Nor, did it reach out to the large segment of the population made up of noncitizen male immigrants through reforms of the naturalization process. The failure to draw in the working class left them with only the option of radicalism until Perón emerged in 1943. Meanwhile, workers resented the UCR favoring of the middle class and the continued protection of the interests of the agricultural elite.

The post-1912 arrangement slowly but surely failed. Lack of vision in the face of change and unaddressed social stresses made for a fragile regime. The Great Depression, beginning in 1929, impelled elements of the oligarchy in alliance with disillusioned Radicals and Nationalists to support an authoritarian solution. The new regime represented a national unity government of the disgruntled as much as a response to economic conditions. Although the 1912 compromise could not be undone, the army could be used to manage the crisis. The leader of the coup (General Uriburu) made adjustments to the 1912 agreement, and the *Concordancia* refined them to preserve a democratic facade that everyone knew to be false. The problem of how to balance class interests in an effective but acceptable manner remained. The hodgepodge of supporters of the *Concordancia* represented the inability of a weak party system to offer alternatives.

The military assumed a political role in the absence of strong parties. A succession of major economic shocks and world events brought the army directly into politics. World War I and the subsequent surge of nationalism, the collapse of world trade after 1929, and the humiliation of the Roca Runciman agreement with Britain appeared to threaten the nation's economic survival. Even more troubling, the predatory nationalism of Germany, Italy, and Japan of the 1930s made the weak vulnerable. Nationalism legitimized military involvement in politics and other civilian spheres. The army had an administrative structure, a separate national vision and force that together provided a crude but effective political arsenal. It became a political actor in its own right from 1930 until the 1980s. Its vision, objectives ,and interpretation of the historical context diverged from that of the civilian politicians, who were more concerned with immediate issues. Nevertheless, civilian politicians frequently but opportunistically endorsed army objectives. A stronger degree of external validation of the army's vision came from the Nationalists, but in reality the army had started down its own road.

General Perón refined and reinforced the Concordancia's early corporatism but tilted the balance to the working class. Unlike European fascists, he relied on the working class more than on the middle class. Although he had middle-class supporters, many opposed him. Workers' advances often came at the expense of the middle class. The unbalanced tilt in labor's favor destroyed productivity and ,along with other predatory fiscal and monetary measures, weakened the economy. Perón polarized the nation, although he did not intend to do so. He believed that social justice created social harmony, not conflict. Peronisimo represented the other half of the political and social compromise of the Saeñz Pena Law of 1912, but the halves could not be brought together within a responsive party system, Perón could not allow enough philosophical flexibility to draw the classes into a cooperative and mutually sympathetic arrangement to create a cohesive party, society, and nation.

Interim regimes between the coup of 1955 and the General's definitive return in 1973 staggered under the economic problems and the impossible burden of Perón's transformation into an antidemocratic (in spite of his ability to win democratic elections) messianic figure. Peron's paternalism became a personality cult, useful in the short term but an obstacle in the long run. The belief that he would set things right could be used by others with their own agenda. Armed guerrilla groups could not be reined in by their alleged leader. Perón's death (1974), the coup (1976), and the Proceso (1974–1979), followed by the Falkland War debacle (1982) left little time for the country to regain its footing and recover politically, economically, and psychologically. The army's legacy, deep social wounds, and a large debt burdened the nation after its retreat from power in 1983. Unexpectedly, it all fell to civilian politicians to deal with as best they could.

The political counter balance, the UCR, has not served well. Each time the party has been elected to the presidency after World War II, it has ridden a strong reactionary current The party won the presidency in 1916, 1922, and 1928, sat out the 1930s and 1940s, returned in 1983 and 1999, and now seems played out. UCR failed to consolidate its initial hold on the broader middle class and attract the working class. It became the party to elect when all else fails. Low expectations that the Radicals can or will perform seems to suggest that the electorate's objective is to punish the Peronistas by ejecting them from the presidency and barring their access to the resources they cherish.

The methods employed by both parties, including corruption and patronage, differ only in small details. When Fernando de la Rua won the office at the end of Menem's second term, defeating the Peronist candidate Eduardo Duhalde, he portrayed himself as a family man, honest and reassuringly boring, who could steady a sinking ship. He bought legislative support as needed, although he channeled it through cabinet ministers who then passed it on to recalcitrant senators. He got into trouble when it became evident that some got more and some less than they thought their votes deserved.

Argentine political parties meet the criteria of failed parties.[11] A nonresponsive party structure allows individual politicians to pursue their own interests unrestrained by party principles. The failure to emphasize party differences results in individual agendas and personal machine politics. Ineffectual political parties cannot create a consensus to deal with concrete issues and provide actual solutions. Rallying to meet an immediate crisis must contend with debilitating factionalism, as those charged with responsibility maneuver as individuals rather than as candidates of a party. Perón attempted to create a party and a supporting philosophical structure but failed. Only the residue of rhetoric and social expectations remain, although individual Peronistas create sub parties. Long after General Perón's dream became untenable, the government and the treasury buy their people off, if funds are available, rather than respond to principles embedded in a strong party system.

One dominant source of wealth controlled by a relatively small group results in a political impulse to redistribute the wealth, but not necessarily usefully. Reallocating resources by raising wages to increase demand and stimulate more production and jobs has been tried repeatedly. It fails because it all depends on agricultural export earnings, while inefficient industry and labor fight over an inadequate surplus. The shortage is bridged by debt and fiscal and monitory policies that stimulate inflation and distort social attitudes, but do not solve the recurrent economic problem. Mandated wages, subsidies, social services, and personal patronage create dependency on politicians rather than on economic activity.

The extent to which Argentines developed civic values is another consideration. Civic values are reflected in social and political behavior. They constitute a functional part of the operational underpinnings of any society. Such values may be more directly pertinent to an explanation of how a society actually works than any other element. As Niccolò Machiavelli observed, everything depends on the civic virtue of the citizenry. In Argentina, the rapid commercialization of land skipped over the yeoman farmer stage of development. The small farmer stage tends to create an involved citizenry and a positive civic attitude that remains even after large scale commercial agriculture has pushed them off the land and into the cities. In Argentina, an oligarchy crystallized before a strong tradition of civic virtue had a chance to emerge. Beyond the degree to which civic values have emerged the context within which they function is also relevant. The belief that all have a stake in the proper functioning of society is crucial. This involves trust and the perception of equal responsibility, as well as an acceptable distribution of the benefits of the society served by the civic minded. In Argentina, few would make the case for equality or trust. Suspicion that others are taking advantage of the situation to gain an unfair advantage converts it into a self-serving system and, consequently, civic virtue becomes naiveté.

If wealth cannot be achieved through hard work and merit, then it must be wrested from those who have it. A sense that one has been shortchanged sets off a "grab what you can" mentality, outright theft, systemic corruption, and totally self-serving political and union careers. A negative approach to the law further undermines predictability and trust and sets off a race at every level of society to get what one can before the opportunity passes. It negatively colors social relations, politics, economic activity, and ethics.

Argentina has never had a fully democratic system in place. A façade bolstered by the accoutrements of democracy obscured a fatal lack of substance. Historic deformities have left their mark on the people and the society. *Incivisme* (uncivil) characteristics, in contrast to those that identify a civic society, provide a measure of Argentina's civic crisis.[12] The most important are those that pertain to a citizen's relationship with authority and the degree of assumed responsibility. An intense focus on personal survival subordinates collective issues not directly connected with an individual's well being. Understandably, the direct personal impact on individuals and their families pushes all else aside and it becomes a situation in which it is "*sálvese quien pueda*" (everyone for themselves). An implosion of empathy results in "amoral familist" behavior that strives to maximize advantage for the individual family unit, and overrides guilt with the assumption that everyone is doing the same.[13] People contact their representatives, not over broad public issues, but to ask for favors, jobs, permits, tax matters and other specific personal needs. The understanding that their political representatives will exchange favors in return for personal loyalty creates clients rather than citizens. Currying favors and personal advantage is the extent of their interest in government, very distinct from the issues that drive mass politics. Payoffs, bribes, and other forms of corruption become an everyday matter.

Transparency International's corruption index (2003) placed Argentina number 92—in the same range as Ethiopia, Pakistan, and Zambia. The World Bank estimated that corruption at the middle range reduces a nation's GDP by 20 percent. Argentina's corruption, far beyond the middle range, reduces GDP by significantly more. Uruguay's President Jorge Batlle exploded with anger when Argentina's economic crisis of 2001 spilled over into his country, as depositors from Buenos Aires withdrew their dollar savings to meet living expenses. Batlle called Argentine politicians "a bunch of thieves, from top to bottom . . . Argentina would be all right, if only its politicians stopped stealing for a couple of years."[14] In the same vein a senator and union leader declared that the "country's problems could be solved if the politicians stopped robbing for two years."[15] Unfortunately, politicians are the least likely to be able to objectively examine the issue, given their high level of culpable irresponsibility. Time-limited corruption is unlikely to make a difference in the absence of more comprehensive steps, even in the unlikely event its criminal practitioners accepted the notion. Corruption is a question of degree, not necessarily any particular act, and exists in any society. When it exceeds certain bounds corruption becomes symptomatic of structural and social failures. Politicians, even if personally honest, cannot avoid using or tolerating corrupt practices when they have become a governing tool as appears to be the case in Argentina.

Office holding is believed by many to be motivated by greed and personal ambition rather than a sense of public responsibility. Politicians and those they govern, regard corruption as the norm. Even those that do not engage in corruption are assumed to do so. Nevertheless, individuals feel that they are victimized by those with better contacts or manipulative skills and thus feel exploited by their fellows. Laws are perceived to be obstacles that can be suspended by the powerful when approached properly for a favor. In any case, it is foolish to obey laws and regulations because no one else will except self destructive, naïve individuals. Tax evasion becomes an admired skill rather than a criminal vice. The slow-motion collapse of the economy set off individual efforts to avoid the evitable disaster of 2001. They saw it coming and chose to open foreign bank accounts well in advance rather than demanding an effective response to save the community. Casting blank ballots appears to be self-indulgent, while not solving the problem of poor political accountability. Citizens in effect are victims as well as collaborators with their victimizers.

People voting with their feet may be both an indication of the problem as well as a causal factor. Those immigrants that returned to their European home countries made only a temporary commitment conditioned on their success. The swallows that went back and forth between Argentina and Europe until the outbreak of world war in 1914 suggested both a psychological and actual option for descendents of immigrants. Many governments recognize citizenship back several generations. An Italian or Spanish ancestor provided an option to return to the old country and enter the European Union's transnational labor market. Meanwhile, it is not clear whether the crew is abandoning a sinking ship, or the ship is pulling away from the crew. Satirical commentator Enrique Pinti mused (1993) that while the country had many great individuals, they only can succeed abroad. A joke, now grown stale, captures the notion: Father to son, "What do you want to be when you grow up?" Son, "A foreigner."

Such attitudes reflect the nagging fear that survival is the best that can be hoped for because the good times will never return. It is impossible to determine the degree to which every Argentine shares such pessimism. Nor is it necessarily permanent. Nevertheless, pessimism makes it difficult to rally the energy to change. Out of the ruins of 2001, perhaps a different set of variables will come into play. Citizen self-help organizations and the social capital that they engender may provide a new beginning. Solidarity in bitter times can be both socially and politically empowering.[16]

Predicting the future of Argentina is not fruitful. It continues to confound Cassandra, Pollyanna, and realists. The signals remain mixed. Nevertheless, a 2002 poll taken at the height of the distress following the default indicated that 65 percent rated democracy the best form of governance, while 90 percent express dissatisfaction with how it works, and zero percent voiced confidence in political parties.[17] It is generally believed that institutional reform can change political behavior. So far demands for reform have had little support. To be effective, a reform movement requires a high level of moral outrage directed at the proper target, and operationally it must result in the formation of a strong party able to govern in response to the people. It is not clear that citizens have reached that level of frustration and anger, or that they ever will. The leadership for such an effort has yet to emerge. Meanwhile, a sense of chronic, perhaps fatal malaise, acts to demoralize and emotionally drain the nation, a feeling expressed in words of the rock song "*San Jauretche*":

> We missed the right time
> to be a great nation
> today, being a small country hurts
> in our souls and our ambitions
> there was a day when history
> gave us the opportunity
> to be a country with glory
> or a colonial granary.

. . .
"klepocracy" is what there is
raiders of this land
please leave right away
I ask San Jauretche
Let the good vibes come.[18]

Argentina's third century of independent existence that begins in 2010 will be interesting but decidedly different from the 1910 celebration when Argentines still clung to the illusion. Nevertheless, let us hope "the good vibes come."

Glossary

AAA: *Alianza Argentina Anticomunista:* Argentine Anticommunist Alliance. A militia and vigilante group used during the presidency of Isabel Perón.

Camarilla: Political grouping often based around one individual or an extended family.

Caudillo: A strongman who exercises political authority by force as well as the consent.

CGT: *Confederación General del Trabajo:*

General Confederation of Labor, used by Perón as an umbrella organization for organized labor.

Concordancia: A pact between the National Democratic Party, dissident Radicals, and the Independent Socialists to govern the country from 1932 to 1943.

Creole: In modern Argentina, a person of old stock and Hispanic culture, as opposed to the culture of nineteenth and twentieth century immigrants.

Descamisados: Shirtless ones. Term used by Juan Perón and Evita to refer to the poor and marginal working class they sought to incorporate into their constituency.

DGFM: *Directorio General de Fabricas Militares:* The General Directorate of Military Factories, eventually the largest conglomerate in the country.

Estancia; Estanciero: A cattle ranch; later a mixed agricultural estate. The owner.

Gaucho: Originally a frontiersman. Subsequently, a cowboy or estancia worker.

Justicialismo: Political philosophy elaborated by Juan D. Perón.

Lista Completa: Complete List. The Constitution of 1853 included a provision to discourage political fragmentation—the party that won a simple plurality in an electoral district took all the seats

Littoral: The Paraná River provinces of Santa Fé, Entre Rios, and Corrientes.

Nationalists: Individuals dedicated to preserving Hispanic culture, initially anti-immigrant but then economically and culturally anti-imperialistic.

PAN: *Partido Autonomista Nacional*: National Autonomist Party formally founded in 1881. It served as the governing party until 1912.

PJ: *Partido Justicialista*: Party created by Juan D. Perón, simply referred to as the Peronist Party.

Porteño: Native or resident of the city of Buenos Aires.

Proceso: Proceso de Reorganización Nacional: Military regime's plan to restructure politics and society in 1976. Became associated with the strong-arm tactics employed by the government until 1983.

Radicals: See UCR

Saeñz Peña Law of 1912: Opened the electoral system to the middle and lower classes, elevating the UCR and its leader Hipólito Yrigoyen to the presidency in 1916.

SRA: *Sociedad Rural Argentina*: Argentine Rural Society represented large scale agriculturalists.

UCR: Unión Cívica Radical: Radical Civic Union formed in 1890 representing middle-class elements opposed to the corrupt dominance of the oligarchy.

UCRI: *Unión Cívica Radical Anti-Personalista*: A splinter party of the UCR opposed to the Hipólito Yrigoyen's personal hold on the party leadership.

UIA: *Unión Industrial Argentina*: Argentine Industrial Union formed as a association of businessmen and manufacturers to represent urban industrial interests.

Unitario: A proponent of a centralized political structure.

yerba mate: Paraguayan tea. Popular caffeine stimulant in the Southern cone region.

Notes

INTRODUCTION

1. Economist Paul Samuelson's International Economic Association presidential address in 1982 speculated whether other nations would begin to suffers "their own version of the Argentine sickness."

FRINGE OF EMPIRE

1. An earlier plan called for crowning Princess Carlota Joaquina, sister of Spain's monarch Fernando VII and wife of the Portuguese regent in Brazil, soon to be King João, under the title of the Queen of La Plata. Searches turned up various possibilities, including the Prince of Lucia, Fernando's nephew, and a handful of French princes.

2. Quoted in C. Galvan Moreno, *Rivadavia, el estadista genial* (Buenos Aires: Claridad, 1940), p. 326.

3. See the findings of Ricardo D. Salvatore, "Heights and Welfare in Late Colonial and Post-independence Argentina," in J. Komlos and J Baten, eds. *The Biological Standard of Living in Comparative Perspective* (Stuttgart: Franz Steiner,1998).

4. Rosas died at the age of 84 on his farm in Southampton on March 14, 1877.

THE COMPROMISE

1. Quoted in John Lynch, *Argentine Caudillo: Juan Manuel de Rosas*, p,158.

2. Quoted in Julia E. Rodriguez, "Sexual Aberration, Degeneration, and Psychiatry in Late Nineteen Century Buenos Aires," in *Argentina on the Couch: Psychiatry, State, and Society, 1880 to the Present*, ed. Mariano Plotkin (Albuquerque: University of New

Mexico Press, 2003), p. 35. Psychiatry associated hysteria with modern women and change.

3. Mann supplied the model that Sarmiento applied in Argentina. A central figure in the Common School Movement in the United States, Mann asserted that universal education led to civic virtue. He believed that public education could transform the masses into citizens and avert class warfare. Jonathan Messerli, *Horace Mann: A Biography* (New York: Knopf, 1972).

4. The Río de la Plata forms at the confluence of the Uruguay and Paraná rivers. The estuary, initially 25 miles wide, rapidly broadens to 217 miles as its waters empty into the South Atlantic. The Paraná flows some 2980 miles, about half in Argentine territory, carrying water equivalent to one-and-a-half the volume of the Mississippi.

5. Conceived in an informal setting in Paris after a day at the races in Chantilly, the club's origins are described in Jorge and Lily Newton, *Historia del Jockey Club de Buenos Aires* (Buenos Aires: Ediciones L.N., 1966). In a similar fashion, the consolidation of the Mexican elite revolved around Mexico City's Jockey Club, also founded in 1882.

6. The Constitution of 1853, art. 25, charged the federal government with stimulating European immigration free of entry taxes or other restrictions.

7. In 1889 the average weight of a South American sheep carcass was 45 lb., much lighter than those from New Zealand and even Australia. English sheep at the time averaged 70 lb. The price differential in the 1880s ran from 3 to 4d. a pound, compared to 4.5 to 5d. of the New Zealand product. Perren, *The Meat Trade*, p.194.

8. Ingrid E. Fey, "Peddling the Pampas: Argentina at the Paris Universal Exposition of 1889," in *Latin American Popular Culture: An Introduction,* eds. William H. Beezley and Linda A. Curcio-Nagy (Wilmington: Scholarly Resources, 2000), pp. 61–85. Quoted in Fey, p. 78.

9. Minted from 1881 to 1896.

10. Quoted in Paula Alonso, *Between Revolution and the Ballot Box: The Origins of the Argentine Radical Party in the 1890s* (Cambridge: Cambridge University Press, 2000), p.50.

11. See the table in Albert B. Martinez and Maurice Lewandowski, *The Argentine in the Twentieth Century* (London: T Fisher Unwin, 1911), p. 213.

12. Martinez and Lewandowski, *The Argentine in the Twentieth Century*, pp. 162–173.

13. See the discussion of profitability in Samuel Amaral, *The Rise of Capitalism on the Pampas: The Estancias of Buenos Aires, 1785–1870* (Cambridge: Cambridge University Press, 1998), pp. 211–229.

URBAN REALITY

1. Quoted in Paul W. Lewis, *The Crisis of Argentine Capitalism* (Chapel Hill: The University of North Carolina Press), p.109.

2. Household budget figures are from Lewis, *Argentine Capitalism*, p. 105.

3. Quoted in Carl E. Solberg, *Immigration and Nationalism, Argentina and Chile, 1890–1914* (Austin: University of Texas Press, 1970), p.98.

4. Solberg, p. 84.

5. Dr. Veyga defined degenerates to include stock market speculators, political bosses, and lawyers who defended degenerates, among others. Mariano Plotkin, "Psychiatrists and the Reception of Psychoanalysis, 1910s–1970," in *Argentina on the Couch: Psychiatry, State, and Society, 1800 to the Present*, ed. Mariano Plotkin (Albuquerque: University of New Mexico Press, 2003), pp.177–178.

6. Quoted in Donna J. Guy, *Sex and Danger in Buenos Aires: Prostitution, Family, and Nation in Argentina* (Lincoln: University of Nebraska Press, 1995), p.67. An account of the trade in women is presented by Albert Londres, *The Road to Buenos Aires* (New York: Boni and Liveright, 1928).

7. Marta E. Savigliano, *Tango: the Political Economy of Passion* (Boulder, Col.: Westview,1995), pp. 139–144.

8. Raúl Scalabrini Ortiz, *El Hombre Que Esta Solo y Espera*, 9th ed. (Buenos Aires: Editorial Plus Ultra,1964), p127. His portrayal follows an Adam and Eve line, with spiritual man seduced by a materialistic woman.

9. John King, "Latin American Cinema," in *The Cambridge History of Latin America*, ed. Leslie Bethell, Vol. 10 (New York: Cambridge University Press), pp. 455–518.

10. See the chart in Jorge A. Schnitman, "Economic Protectionism and Mass Media Development: Film Industry in Argentina." in *Communication and Social Structure Studies in Mass Media Research, eds.* Emile G. McAnany, Jorge A. Schnitman, and Noreen Janus (New York: Praeger, 1981), p269. For useful details see D. de Nublia, *Historia del Cine Argentino.* 2 vols. Buenos Aires, 1959.

11. Quoted in Jason Wilson, *Buenos Aires: A Cultural and Literary Companion* (New York: Interlink Books, 2000), p. 203.

CONFRONTING THE OLIGARCHY

1. Alem dressed in black. His father, Leandro Alén, served in Rosas' Mazorca, only to be publicly hanged when Rosas' regime ended. At the time, his son was only 11 years old. Alem adopted the new name to distance himself from the disgrace. It seems probable that the family experience left a difficult psychological legacy.

2. In the early 1900s a pattern of oligarchal withdrawal appears in Latin America. The Mexican elite faced a revolution in 1910. The modified regime of Álvaro Obregón that followed laid the groundwork for a social compromise. In Peru, the *República Aristocrática* gave way in the election of 1912. Other examples suggest that a complex process across Latin America may have been in play as modernization took hold and created new interest groups that had to be accommodated.

3. Quoted in H.S. Fern, *Argentina* (New York: Praeger, 1969), p.262.

4. Raúl Prebisch, "The Argentine Economic Policies of the 1930s: Recollections," in *The Political Economy of Argentina, 1880–1946*, eds. Guido di Tella and D.C.M. Platt (New York: St. Martin's Press, 1986), pp. 133–153.

5. Imperial preferences had been discussed in the early 1900s with the notion that maturing colonies needed a solid economic reason to remain part of the empire.

6. Prebisch recalled that they deliberately soft-pedaled talk of industrialization in order not to alarm agricultural interests. Raúl Prebisch, "The Argentine Economic Policies of the 1930s: Recollections," *The Political Economy of Argentina, 1880–1946*, eds. Guido di Tella and D.C.M. Platt (New York: St. Martin's Press, 1986), p. 138.

7. Defense of traditional culture could be linked with anti-imperialism. Some Nationalists viewed feminism as an American invention used by the United States to weaken resistance to American imperialism. Salvador Ferla, *Doctrina del nacionalismo* (Buenos Aires: 1947), p. 49.

8. Quoted in Mariano Ben Plotkin, *Mañana es San Perón: A Cultural History of Perón's Argentina* (Wilmington: Scholarly Resources, 2003), p. 14.

9. Raúl Scalabrini Ortiz, *El Hombre Que Esta Solo y Espera,* 9th ed. (Buenos Aires: Editorial Plus Ultra), Lector, front matter.

10. As late as the 1970s a textbook during the military regime defined democracy as a separate concept independent of the structure of government. David Rock, *Authoritarian Argentina: The Nationalists Movement, Its History and Its Impact* (Berkeley: University of California Press, 1993), p. 230.

11. Argentina declared war on Germany and Japan on March 27, 1945—too late to make any political gains. Argentina was the very last Latin American country to do so.

THE AGE OF PERÓN

1. Quoted in David Rock, *Authoritarian Argentina: The Nationalist Movement, Its History and Its Impact* (Berkeley: University of California Press, 1993), p. 140.

2. Quoted in Juan José Sebreli, *Los Deseos Imaginarios del Peronismo* (Buenos Aires: Legasa, 1983), p. 63.

3. Gary Morris, "Queen Norma-Shearer," *Bright Lights Film Journal,* April 1996. He notes the insecurity that Norma masked, the impact of manic depression, and the mechanical aspect of her behavior that suggests some speculative comparisons with Evita.

4. Quoted in Spruille Braden, *Diplomats and Demagogues: The Memoirs of Spruille Braden* (New Rochelle: Arlington House, 1971), p. 323.

5. Quoted in Rock, *Authoritarian Argentina,* p. 154.

6. Quoted in Solingen, p. 37.

7. Quoted in Juan Carlos Torre and Liliana de Riz, "Argentina since 1946," in the *Cambridge History of Latin America,* Vol. VIII, p. 84.

8. Perón's first wife died from the same diagnosis. Barron H. Lerner, "The Illness and Death of Eva Perón: Cancer, Politics, and Society," *The Lancet,* June 3, 2000, pp. 1988–1991.

A DISTANT SHADOW

1. Novelist and journalist Tomás Eloy Martínez's fictionalized *La Novela de Perón* (Buenos Aires: Legasa, 1985) suggested that age had deprived the general of both energy and self direction to the extent that he depended on others to manage his activities. The novel depicts an old man forced to rally one more time in spite

of a personal desire to remain in Spanish exile. Based on interviews with Perón in Madrid, the novel captured the pathos of an individual acting beyond his time.

2. The name, borrowed from the guerrillas that fought for independence from Spain, provided an emotional connection with Argentina's heroic past.

3. The breakdown of authority encompassed a generational revolt. President Cámpora's two sons, who served as advisors, controlled access and wrote his speeches. They did so in the interests of the Montoneros, not their father. The favorite nephew of the elderly Rear Admiral Francisco Alemann and his wife, under the pretext of introducing his girl friend, let kidnappers into the apartment. Adriana, daughter of Marxist turned Peronista sociologist Rodolfo Puiggros, appointed rector by the radicals, manipulated her father in the interest of the guerrillas. Lack of respect, betrayal, and amoral cruelty became required acts of ideological loyalty necessary for peer approval. For other examples see Paul W. Lewis, *Guerrillas and Generals: The "Dirty War" in Argentina* (Westport, Conn.: Praeger, 2002), pp.63–68.

4. Jorge Correa, *Los Jerarcas Sindicales* (Buenos Aires: Editorial Obrador, 2nd. ed., 1974). Correa listed all the corrupt details. The first edition sold 10,000 copies in two months and served as a guide to the assets of union bosses.

5. Quoted in Paul W. Lewis, *Guerrillas and Generals*, p. 147.

6. Heriberto Muraro, "Dictatorship and Transition to Democracy: Argentina 1973–86," in *Media and Politics in Latin America: The Struggle for Democracy*, ed. Elizabeth Fox (Newbury Park, England: Sage Publications, 1988), p. 116.

THE PROCESO'S DARK SHADOW, MENEM, AND NEOLIBERALISM

1. Admiral Massera's impassioned defense caused an immediate hush: "I didn't come here to defend myself. No one has to defend himself for having won a just war, and the war against terrorism was a just war. Nevertheless, I am on trial because we won a just war. If we had lost it none of us—neither you nor we—would be here now. Because long before this, the high judges of this court would have been replaced by turbulent 'people's tribunals' and a ferocious, unrecognizable Argentina would have replaced the old fatherland. But, here we are—because we won the war of arms, and lost the war of psychology." Quoted in Lewis, *Guerrillas and Generals*, p. 219.

2. C. Menem and E. Duhalde, *La revolución productiva: de la Argentina especuladora a la Argentina del trabajo* (Buenos Aires: Energeia, 1989).

3. Horacio Verbitsky, *El Vuelo* (Buenos Aires: Planeta, 1995). Verbitsky was a former Montonero and star reporter for the newspaper *Página 12*. In 2004–2005 Scilingo became the first Argentine accused of criminal involvement in the Dirty War to be tried in Spain.

4. At one point Argentina had the highest number of telephone subscribers per capita in Latin America. Telephones, in wide use in Buenos Aires in the 1920s, with modern switching equipment installed in the 1930s, serviced urban areas while telegraph remained the most affordable means of long-distance communication. Nationalization led to a decline in service, a virtual freeze on new installations, and a under served population and economy.

5. Quoted in Mario Baizán, *Carlos Menem: The Man Who Has Changed His Country* (Buenos Aires: Fundación Intergración Americana, 1994), p. 39. A non-commercial edition published for overseas public relations purposes.

6. Quoted in Jorge Arias, *Menem: El Rescate de la Argentina Perdida* (Buenos Aires: Vergara, 1995), p. 88.

7. Domingo Cavallo, *El peso de la verdad:Un impulso a la transparencia en la Argentina de los 90* (Buenos Aires: Planeta, 1997).

8. Questionnaire interview with Carlos Saúl Menem by William Ratliff, 2003. Question 14. Hoover Institution Archive.

9. Quoted in Omar Lavieri, "The Media in Argentina: Struggling in the Absence of a Democratic Tradition," *Communication in Latin America: Journalism, Mass Media, and Society, ed.* Richard R. Cole (Wilmington: Scholarly Resources, 1996), p.184.

10. Questionnaire interview of Carlos Saúl Menem by William Ratliff, 2003. Questions 1 and 2. Hoover Institution Archive.

11. Menem conceded that Menemistas existed in support of his policies, but insisted that "I am not a Menemista, I am Peronista." Questionnaire interview of Carlos Saúl Menem by William Ratliff, 2003. Question 3. Hoover Institution Archive.

12. Vicente Palermo, "The Origins of Menemismo," in *Peronism and Argentina* ed. James P. Brennan (Wilmington: Scholarly Resources, 1998). Palermo defined Menemismo as a desire to escape the past, rather than faith in a better future, p.174.

13. Quoted in Paul Blustein, "Argentina Didn't Fall on Its Own: Wall Street Pushed Debt till the Last," *Washington Post,* Sunday, August 3, 2003, p. A01.

14. Joseph E. Stiglitz, "Argentina, Shortchanged: Why the Nation that Followed Rules Fell to Pieces," *Washington Post,* Sunday, May 12, 2002, p. B01.

15. Luis Fernando Calviño and Victor Eduardo Lapegna, *La Inevitable Vigencia del " Incorregible" Peronismo: Del "Menemismo Utópico" al "Menemismo Científico"* (Villa Ballester, Argentina: Energeia, 2002). An interesting attempt to codify Menem's pragmatic ideas. It consists of a series of previously published pieces."

16. He noted that circumstances did not permit the imposition of structural reforms that would have made for a sustainable fiscal policy. Questionnaire interview of Carlos Saúl Menem by William Ratliff, 2003. Question 5. Hoover Institution Archive.

17. A new edition kept the controversy alive. *El Otro. Eduardo Dulhade: una biografia política* (Buenos Aires: Grupo Editorial Norma, 2002).

18. Quoted in Plotkin, *Argentina on the Couch.* p. 216.

19. *The New York Times,* May 16, 2003, p. A10.

20. Judge Baltasar Garzón is one of six investigating judges of Spain's National Court. Under Spanish law as of 1998, crimes against humanity worldwide may be tried in Spanish courts.

21. An interesting sideshow involved a proposal made by a Peronist deputy, Mario O'Donnell, to rename part of Avenida Sarmiento in honor of Sarmiento's arch enemy Juan Manuel Rosas. The descendents on both sides became intensely engaged in the over-a-century-old feud.

22. Quoted in the *Economist,* July 5, 2003, p. 33.

23. Quoted in Larry Rohter, "Argentina's Economic Rally Defies Forecasts," *The New York Times*, December 26, 2004, p. A01.

CONCLUSION: WHO OR WHAT IS TO BLAME?

1. Martinez Estrada's life followed a dreary and bitter trajectory. After a post office job he taught at the National University in Mexico (1959–1962), then went on to Cuba to work on a study of José Martí. He became an outspoken admirer of Fidel Castro, although the two never met. An embittered Martínez Estrada died in Bahía Blanca, Argentina.

2. Naipaul subsequently excused his harsh comments with the explanation that his intensity sprang from being between novels. Nevertheless, he did not retract or soften his judgments. See the short note in front of the first Vintage edition of *The Return of Eva Perón* (New York: Vintage, 1981).

3. Quote from Tomás Eloy Martínez, "A Culture of Barbarism," in *Argentina in the Crisis Years, (1983–1990): From Alfonsin to Menem*, eds. Colin M. Lewis and Nissa Torrents (London; Institute of Latin American Studies,1993). Eloy Martínez left Argentina in 1975 after discovering a bomb in his office. He spent time in Venezuela and the United States as a professor of Latin American Literature.

4. Quoted in Lewis, *Argentina Capitalism*, p. 30.

5. Brennan noted that domestic as opposed to foreign influences are the most important "determinative variables" in Latin American labor history. James P. Brennan, *The Labor Wars in Córdoba, 1955–1976* (Cambridge: Harvard University Press, 1994), p. 344.

6. Gerardo della Poalera, María Alejandra Irigoin and Carlos G. Bózzoli, "Passing the buck: Monatary and fiscal policies," in *The New Economic History of Argentina*, eds. Gerardo della Poalera and Alan M. Taylor (Cambridge: Cambridge University Press, 2003).

7. Silvia Bleichmar, *Dolor Pais* (Buenos Aires: Libro de Zorzal, 2001).

8. Luis Fernando Calviño and Victor Eduardo Lapegna, *La Inevitable Vigencia*, p. 105.

9. The Urugayan representative charged that Brazil did not want commercial integration, but political integration, and if "that is the case then Mercosur is not worth it for Uruguay." Both quotes in *LATAM FLASH* (New York: Toyota Latin American Research, July 9, 2004).

10. In contrast, the United States went through its Jacksonian Revolution before the massive waves of immigration swept the country. In Porfirian Mexico (1876–1911) the refusal of the regime to allow the formation of political parties in 1892 led to the Francisco Madero's ineffectual accommodation in 1912. Revolutionary violence became unavoidable as a result. Argentina's accommodation managed to avoid a revolution, but failed to create stability.

11. See the discussion in Kay Lawson and Peter H. Merkl, *When Parties Fail: Emerging Alternative Organization* (Princeton: Princeton University Press,1988).

12. Putnam used the term as he explored the question of what makes democracy work, examining the modern Italian civic tradition and the instructive contrast between southern and northern Italy. Robert D. Putnam, *Making Democracy Work: Civic Tradition in Modern Italy* (Princeton: Princeton University Press, 1993).

13. Edward C. Banfield, *The Moral Basis of a Backward Society* (New York: Free Press, 1958), pp. 83–101.

14. Quote in the *Economist*, June 14, 2002, p. 34.

15. Quote in Plotkin, *Couch*, p. 213.

16. The Mexico City earthquake of 1985 provides an example. The failure of the state to respond effectively resulted in citizen action. Solidarity led to the formation of the Congress of Barrios and other grassroots organizations that assumed authority and established an alternative source of legitimacy. Significantly, the earthquake introduced the era of comic book super heroes, indicating the withdrawal of confidence from the government and politicians and weakening one-party rule. How much this factored in the loss of the PRI's grip on the country is impossible to determine.

17. Latinobarometro for the *Economist*, August 17, 2002, pp. 29–30.

18. For the complete lyrics in Spanish and English see Pablo Semán, Pablo Vila, and Cecilia Benedetti, "Neo-liberalism and Rock in the Popular Sectors of Contemporary Argentina," in *Rockin' Las Americas: The Global Politics of Rock in Latin/o America*, eds. Deborah Pacini et al. (Pittsburgh: University of Pittsburgh Press, 2004), p. 285. San Jauretche refers to writer Arturo Jauretche, who died in 1974 at 73 years of age. He began his political career as a conservative, became a prominent Nationalist intellectual, moved to the UCR, supported FORJA, and became a Perónist and a vocal critic of imperialism and dependency, advocating the "third way." He criticized the Nationalists for not drawing in the masses His terse sound bites such as " we have to adapt the hat to the head, not the head to the hat" are used to support anti- globalization and attack neo-liberalism. Partido Justicialista de Moreno, info@pjmoreno.org.ar.

Selected Bibliography
of Works in English

The following selected works in English offer a guide to secondary as well as the primary material used for the reconstruction of the past. All of these works have provided details and ideas and have formed my view of what happened and why, although they cannot be held responsible for my interpretation. Those interested in further study will find them useful to refine their understanding. As to be expected, interpretations differ on various points, but they all stimulate a reflective examination of the Argentine puzzle. The literature on Argentina is immense for obvious reasons, and not all important works are included in this bibliography. The interested reader, however, will not be lost in the wilderness. Works listed here collectively provide an in-depth guide to further study in English, Spanish, and French.

Concise essays on important aspects of the nation's history are in *The Encyclopedia of Latin American History,* edited by Barbara A. Tenenbaum, 5 vols. (New York: Scribners, 1996). *The Cambridge History of Latin America,* edited by Leslie Bethell, is a multi-volume, useful compilation by first-rate scholars. *The Handbook of Latin American Studies,* edited by the staff of the Library of Congress, reviews the current literature on a broad array of topics in English, Spanish, and other languages, online at lcweb2.loc.gov/hlos. Information on the aboriginal population can be found in *Cambridge History of the Native Peoples of the Americas,* vol. 3, ed. Stuart Schwartz (New York: Cambridge University Press, 2000). A recent contribution by Geraldo della Paolera and Alan M. Taylor, *The New Economic History of Argentina* (Cambridge: Cambridge University Press, 2003) includes a searchable compact disc with historical data on the country's economic history.

Modern histories of Argentina, each with a different emphasis, are Colin M. Lewis, *Argentina: A Short History* (Oxford: Oneworld Publications, 2002); Daniel K. Lewis, *The History of Argentina* (New York: Palgrave Macmillan, 2001); Leslie Bethell, ed, *Argentina since Independence* (Cambridge: Cambridge University Press, 1993); David Rock, *Argentina, 1516–1987: From Spanish Colonization to Alfonsín* (Berkeley: University of California Press, 1987). Dated but still useful is James R. Scobie, *Argentina: A City and a Nation* (Oxford: Oxford University Press, 1964). All have extensive bibliographies.

Adelman, Jeremy. *Republic of Capital: Buenos Aires and the Legal Transformation of the Atlantic World.* Stanford: Stanford University Press, 1999.

Alonso, Paula. *Between Revolution and the Ballot Box: The Origins of the Argentine Radical Party.* Cambridge: Cambridge University Press, 2000.

Amaral, Samuel E. *The Rise of Capitalism on the Pampa: The Estancias of Buenos Aires, 1785–1870.* Cambridge: Cambridge University Press, 1998.

Baily, Samuel L. and Eduardo José Míguez, eds. *Mass Migration to Modern Latin American.* Wilmington: Scholarly Resources, 2003.

Baily, Samuel L. *Immigrants in the Lands of Promise: Italians in Buenos Aires and New York City, 1870–1914.* Ithaca, N.Y.: Cornell University Press, 1999.

Baily, Samuel L. *Labor, Nationalism and the Politics.* New Brunswick, N.J.: Rutgers University Press, 1969.

Baizán, Mario. *Carlos Menem: The Man Who Has Changed His Country.* Buenos Aires: Fundación Intergración Americana, 1994.

Banfield, Edward C. *The Moral Basis of a Backward Society.* New York: Free Press, 1958.

Beezley, William H. and Linda A. Curcio-Nagy, eds. *Latin American Popular Culture: An Introduction.* Wilmington: Scholarly Resources, 2000.

Brennan, James P. *The Labor Wars in Córdoba, 1955–1976.* Cambridge: Harvard University Press, 1994.

Brennan, James P., ed. *Peronism and Argentina.* Wilmington: Scholarly Resources, 1998.

Brown, Jonathan C. *A Socioeconomic History of Argentina, 1776–1860.* Cambridge: Cambridge University Press, 1979.

Brunstein, Luis Fabrián. "A Case Study of the Relationship Between Agricultural Productivity and the Political and Social History of Argentina from 1960 to 2000." Unpub. Ph.D diss., University of California, Riverside, 2002.

Burdick, Michael. *For God and the Fatherland: Religion and Politics in Argentina.* Albany: State University of New York Press, 1995.

Carlson, Marifran. *Feminismo: The Women's Movement in Argentina from its Beginnings to Eva Perón.* Chicago: Academy, 1988.

Chasteen, John Charles, *National Rhythms, African Roots: The Deep History of Latin American Popular Dance.* Albuquerque: University of New Mexico Press, 2004.

Coatsworth, John H. and Alan M. Taylor, eds. *Latin America and the World Economy Since 1800.* Cambridge: Harvard University Press, 1999.

Cole, Richard, ed. *Communication in Latin America: Journalism, Mass, Media, and Society.* Wilmington: Scholarly Resources, 1996.

Collier, Simon. *The Life, Music, and Times of Carlos Gardel.* Pittsburgh: University of Pittsburgh Press, 1986.

Crowley, Frances Geyer, *Domingo Faustino Sarmiento*. New York: Twayne Publishers, 1972.

Deutsch, Sandra McGee. *Counter Revolution in Argentina, 1900–1932: The Argentine Patriotic League*. Lincoln: University of Nebraska Press, 1986.

Di Tella, Guido and D.C.M. Platt. *The Political Economy of Argentina, 1880–1946*. London: Macmillan,1986.

Di Tella, Guido and Donald Cameron Watts, eds. *Argentina between the Great Powers, 1939–1946*. London: Macmillan, 1989.

Edsall, Thomas More. "Elites, Oligarchs, and Aristocrats: The Jockey Club of Buenos Aires and the Argentine Upper Class, 1920–1940." Unpub. PhD diss., Tulane University, 1999.

Erro, David G. *Resolving the Argentine Pardox: Politics and Development, 1966–1992*. Boulder, Colo.: Lynne Rienner Publishers,1993.

Feitlowitz, Marguerite. *Lexicon of Terror*. Oxford: Oxford University Press,1999.

Ferns, H. S. *Britain and Argentina in the Nineteenth Century*. Oxford: Oxford University Press,1960.

Ferns, H. S. *Argentina*. New York: Praeger,1969.

Ford, A. G. *The Gold Standard, 1880–1914: Britain and Argentina*. Oxford: Oxford University Press, 1962.

Fox, Elizabeth, ed. *Media and Politics in Latin America: The Struggle for Democracy*. Newberry Park, England: Sage Publications, 1988.

Fuente, Ariel de la. *Children of Facundo: Caudillo and Gaucho Insurgency during the Argentine State Formation Process*. Durham, N.C.: Duke University Press, 2000.

Gill, Anthony. *Rendering unto Caesar: The Catholic Church and the State in Latin America*. Chicago: University of Chicago Press, 1998.

Gillespie, Richard. *Soldiers of Peron: Argentina's Montoneros*. New York: Oxford University Press, 1982.

Gravel, Roger. *The Anglo-Argentine Connection, 1900–1939*. Boulder, Colo.: Westview,1985.

Greenfield, Gerald M. *Latin American Urbanization: Historical Profiles of Major Cities*. Westport, Conn.: Greenwood, 1994.

Guy, Donna J. *Sex and Danger in Buenos Aires: Prostitution, Family, and Nation in Argentina*. Lincoln: University of Nebraska Press, 1995.

Guy, Donna. *Argentine Sugar Politics: Tucumán and the Generation of Eighty*. Tempe, Ariz.: Arizona State University Latin American Center, 1980.

Halperín Donghi, Tulio, Iván Jaksic, Gwen Kirkpatrick, and Francine Masiello, eds. *Sarmiento: Author of a Nation*. Berkeley: University of California Press, 1994.

Haring, Clarence H. *Argentina and the United States*. Boston: World Peace Foundation, 1941.

Haring, Clarence H. *South America Looks at the United States*. New York: Macmillan, 1928.

Hodges, Donald C. *Argentina, 1943–1976: The National Revolution and Resistance*. Albuquerque: New Mexico University Press, 1976.

Horowitz, Joel. *Argentine Unions, the State and the Rise of Perón, 1930–1945*. Berkeley: University of California Press, 1990.

Hower, Ralph M. *The History of an Advertising Agency: N. W. Ayers & Son at Work, 1869–1949*. Cambridge: Harvard University Press, 1949.

James, Daniel. *Resistence and Intergration: Peronism and the Argentine Working Class, 1946–1976.* New York: Cambridge University Press, 1988.

Johnson, John J. *Political Change in Latin America: The Emergence of the Middle Sectors.* Stanford: Stanford University Press,1958.

King, John. *Magical Reels: A History of Cinema in Latin America.* New York: Verso, 2000.

King, John. *Sur: A Study of the Argentine Literary Journal and Its Role in the Development of Culture, 1930—1970.* Cambridge: Cambridge University Press, 1986.

Komlos, J. and J. Bate, eds. *The Biological Standard of Living in Comparative Perspective.* Stuttgart: Franz Steiner, 1998.

Lawson, Kay and Peter H. Merkl. *When Parties Fail: Emerging Alternative Organizations.* Princeton: Princeton University Press,1988.

Lewis, Paul H. *The Crisis of Argentine Capitalism.* Chapel Hill: University of North Carolina Press, 1990.

Lewis, Paul H. *Guerrillas and Generals: The "Dirty War" in Argentina.* Westport, Conn.: Praeger, 2002.

Liss, Sheldon B., *Marxist Thought in Latin America.* Berkeley: University of California Press, 1984.

Londres, Albert. *The Road to Buenos Aires.* New York: Boni and Liveright, 1928.

Loveman, Brian and Thomas Davies, eds. *The Politics of Anti-politics: The Military in Latin America.* Wilmington: Scholarly Resources, 1997.

Lynch, John. *Argentina Caudillo: Juan Manuel de Rosas.* Wilmington: Scholarly Resources, 2001.

Lynch, John. *Argentine Dictator: Juan Manuel de Rosas, 1829–1852.* New York: Oxford University Press, 1981.

Lynch, John. *Massacre in the Pampas, 1872, Britain and Argentina in the Age of migration.* Norman: University of Oklahoma Press, 1998.

Marichal, Carlos. *A Century of Debt Crises in Latin America: From Independence to the Great Depression, 1820–1930.* Princeton: Princeton University Press, 1989.

Martinez, Albert B. and Maurice Lewandowski. *The Argentine in the Twentieth Century,* 3rd. ed. rev. London: T. Fisher Unwin, 1911.

McGann, Thomas F. *Argentina, the United States, and the Inter-American System, 1880–1924.* Cambridge: Harvard University Press, 1957.

McGuire, James. *Peronism without Perón: Unions, Parties, and Democracy in Argentina.* Stanford: Stanford University Press, 1997.

Meyer, Doris. *Victoria Ocampo: Against the Wind and the Tide.* Austin: University of Texas Press, 1990.

Mora, José. *Cousin and Strangers: Spanish Immigrants in Buenos Aires, 1850–1930.* Berkeley: University of California Press, 1998.

Page, Joseph A. *Perón: a Biography.* New York: Random House, 1983.

Paolera, Gerardo della and Alan M. Taylor, eds. *A New Economic History of Argentina.* Cambridge: Cambridge University Press, 2003.

Peloso, Vincent C., ed. *Work, Protest, and Identity in Twentieth-Century Latin America.* Wilmington: Scholarly Resources, 2003.

Perala-Ramos, Monica. *Political Economy of Argentina: Power and Class since 1930.* Boulder, Colo.: Westview, 1992.

Perren, Richard. *The Meat Trade in Britain, 1840–1914*. London: Routledge and Kegan Paul, 1978.

Pierce, Russell. *Gringo-Gaucho: An Advertising Odyssey*. Ashland, Ore.: Southern Cross Publishers, 1991.

Pion-Berlin, David. *Through Corridors of Power: Institutions and Civil-Military Relations in Argentina*. University Park: Pennsylvania State University Press, 1997.

Platt, D.C.M. and Guido di Tella. *Argentina, Australia & Canada*. London: Macmillan, 1985.

Plotkin, Mariano Ben. *Mañana es San Perón: A Cultural History of Perón's Argentina*. Wilmington: Scholarly Resources, 2003.

Plotkin, Mariano, ed. *Argentina on the Couch: Psychiatry, State,and Society, 1880 to the Present*. Albuquerque: University of New Mexico Press, 2003.

Plotkin, Mariano. *Freud in the Pampas: The Emergence and Development of a Psychoanalytic Culture in Argentina*. Stanford: Stanford University Press, 2001.

Potash, Robert A.*The Army and Politics in Argentina, 1928–1945: Yrigoyen to Perón*. Stanford: Stanford University Press, 1969.

Potash, Robert A. *The Army and Politics in Argentina, 1945–1962: Perón to Frondizi*. Stanford: Stanford University Press, 1969.

Potash, Robert A. *The Army and Politics in Argentina.1962–1973: Frondizi to Perón*. Stanford: Stanford University Press, 1992.

Putnam, Robert D. *Making Democracy Work: Civic Traditions in Modern Italy*. Princeton: Princeton University Press, 1993.

Quintero Ramos, Angel M. *A History of Money and Banking in Argentina*. Río Piedras: University of Puerto Rico, 1965.

Ratliff, William and Roger Fontaine. *Argentina's Capitalist Revolution Revisited: Confronting the Social Costs of Statist Mistakes*, Essays on Public Policy #41. Stanford: Hoover Institution, 1993.

Ratliff, William and Roger Fontaine. *Changing Course: The Capitalist Revolution in Argentina*, Essays on Public Policy #20. Stanford: Hoover Institution, 1990.

Redick, John R. *Nuclear Illusions: Argentina and Brazil*, Occasional Paper # 25. Washington, DC: Henry L. Stimson Center, 1995.

Richmond, Douglas. *Carlos Pellegrini and the Crisis of the Argentine Elites, 1880–1916*. Westport, Conn.: Greenwood, 1989.

Rock, David. *Authoritarian Argentina: The Nationalist Movement, Its History and Its Impact*. Berkeley: University of California Press, 1993.

Rodríguez, Jaime E. O., *The Independence of Spanish America*. Cambridge: Cambridge University Press,1998.

Romero, José Luis. *A History of Argentine Political Thought*. Stanford: Stanford University Press, 1963.

Romero, Luis Alberto. *A History of Argentina in the Twentieth Century*. University Park: Pennsylvania State University Press, 2002.

Savigliano, Marta E. *Tango: the Political Economy of Passion*. Boulder, Colo.: Westview, 1995.

Shumway, Nickolas. *The Invention of Argentina*. Berkeley: University of California Press, 1990.

Slatta, Richard. *Gauchos and the Vanishing Frontier*. Lincoln: University of Nebraska Press, 1983.

Smith, Peter H. *Argentina and the Failure of Democracy: Conflict among Political Elites 1902–1955*. Madison: University of Wisconsin Press, 1974.

Smith, Peter H. *Politics of Beef in Argentina: Patterns of Conflict and Changes*. New York: Columbia University Press, 1969.

Socolow, Susan Migden. *Merchants of Buenos Aires, 1778–1810: Family and Commerce*. New York: Cambridge University Press, 1978.

Solberg, Carl E. *Immigration and Nationalism, Argentina and Chile, 1890–1914*. Austin: University of Texas Press, 1970.

Solberg, Carl E. *Oil and Nationalism in Argentina*. Stanford: Stanford University Press, 1979.

Solingen, Etel. *Industrial Policy, Technology and International Bargaining: Designing Nuclear Industries in Argentina and Brazil*. Stanford: Stanford University Press, 1996.

Szuchman, Mark D. *Mobility and Integration in Urban Argentina: Córdoba in the Liberal Era*. Austin: University of Texas Press, 1980.

Toledano, Roulhac d'Arby. "The Rise and Fall of the Argentine Military Industrial Complex: Implications for Civil-Military Relations." Unpub. PhD diss., Tulane University, 2000.

Waisman, Carlos. *The Reversal of Development in Argentina*. Princeton: Princeton University Press, 1987.

Walter, Richard J. *The Socialist Party of Argentina 1890–1930*. Austin: University of Texas Press, 1977.

Whigham, Thomas. *The Politics of River Trade: Tradition and Development in the Upper Plata, 1780–1870*. Alburqueque: University of New Mexico Press, 1991.

Williams, John. *Argentine International Trade under Inconvertible Paper Money, 1880–1900*. Cambridge: Harvard University Press, 1920.

Wilson, Jason. *Buenos Aires: A Cultural and Literary Companion*. New York: Interlink, 2000.

Yool, Andrew Graham. *The Forgotten Colony: A History of the English Speaking Communities in Argentina*. London: Hutchinson, 1981.

Index

About the Author

COLIN M. MACLACHLAN is John Christie Barr Distinguished Professor of Latin American History at Tulane University. He is a member of the Executive Board of the Rocky Mountain Council of Latin American Studies, the Advisory Board of the Latin American Labor Institute, and a former member of the Board of Governors of the Pacific Coast Council of Latin American Studies. He is the author, co-author, or editor of a dozen books, including histories of Mexico, Brazil, and Latin America.